The Signs of Christianity

in the Work of

Walker Percy

Ann Mace Futrell

The Signs of Christianity

in the Work of

Walker Percy

Ann Mace Futrell

Catholic Scholars Press
San Francisco - London
1994

Library of Congress Cataloging-in-Publication Data

Futrell, Ann Mace.
   The signs of Christianity in the work of Walker Percy / Ann Mace
Futrell.
      p. cm.
   Includes bibliographical references and index.
   ISBN 1-883255-11-2 : $59.95. -- ISBN 1-883255-04-x (pbk.) : $39.95
      1. Percy, Walker, 1916- --Religion. 2. Christian fiction,
American--History and criticism. 3. Fiction--Religious aspects-
-Christianity. 4. Christianity and literature. I. Title.
PS3566.E6912Z685 1994
813'.54--dc20   93-23354
                                                              CIP

Copyright 1994 by Ann Mace Futrell

Editorial Inquiries:
International Scholars Publications
P.O.Box 2590
San Francisco, CA 94126

To order: (800) 99-AUSTIN

for Nancy, David, Robin
and Nancy W.

TABLE OF CONTENTS

PREFACE

I can imagine Walker Percy saying it to himself: Ann Futrell is onto something.

Like many admirers drawn to Percy's work by its almost uncanny conjurings of the faint scent of mystery in an odorless world of "everydayness," Futrell has set out to understand where at least some of the good doctor's multitudinous intellectual furnishings were acquired. More reason to praise Futrell, she has gone where most of her predecessors have been least inclined to tread. Earlier explorations of Dr. Percy's intellectual debts have tended to focus on the existential tradition--Heidegger, Camus, Sartre, Marcel, and particularly Kierkegaard--or upon the southern literary connection. Yet scholars have only begun to scratch the surface of Percy's equally important connection with a number of language theorists.

Considering the crucial importance of language to Percy, and his belief in its unique and mysterious character, the scantness of attention to this subject is somewhat surprising. Patricia Lewis Poteat's <u>Walker Percy and the Old Modern Age: Reflections on Language, Argument, and the Telling of Stories</u> was, until now, the only book-length treatment, and for all its virtues, as Futrell notes, it falls far short of an adequate consideration of the most important influence on Percy's thinking about language, Charles Sanders Peirce. This is a considerable lacuna. Percy in his last years was hardly being modest when he dubbed his theory of language the Peirce-Percy theory. In fact, he might have been claiming a little too much credit.

On the other hand, anybody who dares to enter the dense thickets of Peirce's thought deserves some credit. It is not easy going. Peirce is arguably America's preeminent philosopher. As well as launching the pragmatist tradition, he ranged so widely across so many areas of thought--from logic to metaphysics to semiotics (not to mention a number of practical disciplines such as cartography and engineering)--that he became virtually a modern Aristotle. Peirce was as deep as he was wide, and his prose was uncompromisingly rigorous. It did not make for easy reading, though he could write a fluent and accessible essay when so inclined. Then, too, his thoughts evolved, took on new shades of emphasis and meaning, even while (one could argue) he remained, at the core, a philosophical realist.

I believe it was Peirce's realist insistence on the essential character of the word--an insistence that he elaborated first through his tetradic and then through his triadic theory of language--that drew Percy to Peirce. That a thinker could make a science of language without reducing the phenomenon to a simple stimulus-response behavioral model was astounding and invaluable to Percy. His discovery of this thinker--most likely in the late 1940's, while he was living in the house of a New Orleans philosopher--launched Percy on one of his more important quests.

Beyond saying these general words about Percy's debt to Peirce, however, I would be hard-pressed to elaborate. Debts and borrowings are complicated matters in the world of the mind, for the borrower always remakes what he borrows, and one is always interested in how this is done and what the result is. One is also interested in the question of why someone is inclined to borrow from a particular thinker. What is it about the latter that disposes the former to him? These are crucial matters, requiring close and well-informed consideration.

And it is with such matters that Ann Futrell here wrestles, doing so with admirable clarity and a commendably strong point of view. I am not sure I always agree with her, but I always admire the boldness of her argument. When she emphasizes the Calvinist character of the Peirce-Percy theory, for example, I am tempted to point to the common Thomist ground of Peirce's and Percy's realism. But, after all, Calvinism is certainly not ignorant of Thomism, and Futrell's elaboration of Calvinism's understanding of the Beloved Community and the connection of this ideal with both men's notions of language is fascinating. Her emphasis also makes me reconsider how important Percy's early years in the Presbyterian church might have been--and in many ways more profound than I would earlier have thought.

For such illuminations and interpretations, of which there are many in this small book, we who are interested in Percy owe Ann Futrell a large debt.

--Jay Tolson

October 22, 1993

PREFACE

In The Signs of Christianity in the Work of Walker Percy Ann Mace Futrell offers the first extended consideration of Walker Percy's semiotic thought. The territory she explores has been, for the most part, previously uncharted, and she is to be commended as a pathfinder. Those who follow her--and it is to be hoped that she herself is among them--will find the land staked and ready for development.

The title itself speaks eloquently to the scope and complexity of the subject to be treated. At first glance the book is to consider "Signs," those speech events by which one person is able to convey a thought to another--a purely immanent study, it would be assumed. But on reflection the book is to consider "Signs of Christianity," those phenomena of the immanent world that offer the faithful an introduction to transcendent realities. In the fullness of time the author reveals that the two apparently discrete themes have never really been separate; on the contrary, the gift of the capacity for speech is the greatest Sign of the love of God for humans, who speechless could not be aware of his love. In John's formula, the Word inspires the word.

In her Introduction, the author offers a survey of previous scholarships on Walker Percy. She identifies three groups of critics: "the philosophical readers" (1), who have been mainly concerned with Percy's response to existentialism; the aesthetic readers (2), who have been mainly concerned with Percy's response to the south; and the language theorists (3). The last group she treats in some detail, for they are her predecessors in the study of Percy's theory of language. Perhaps to save space, the author treats some of these critics in the text and some in notes. In the process two, William H. Poteat and Weldon Thornton, seem to be ignored. Her assessment of the remainder is judicious, but necessarily brief. Chiefly, she questions each text for the presince of a consideration of the work of Charles Sanders Peirce as the primary influence for Walker Percy's language theory.

Such reductivism is understandable and legitimate, given that the thesis of her book is that Peirce's thought is seminal to Percy's identification of "the Delta Factor," the leap into speech by which the creature becomes human. Percy's thought she develops in Chapter 1, "The Christian Semiotic of Walker Percy," mainly by tracing, in chronological order, the essays that constitute The Message in the Bottle (1975). In this way she can draw from the text those "pre-Peirce" influences whom Percy cites, Susanne Langer, Ernst Cassirer (Mrs. Langer's mentor), Gabriel Marcel, among others. But Jacques Maritain also needs to be emphasized, especially his Ransoming the Time, for Maritain stimulated a "catholic language theory that Percy never abandoned, even as he--according to the author--began to be acquainted with a "Protestant" language theory that was conveyed to him through the work of Peirce. Maritain was important as a commentator not only on Thomas Aquinas but also on John Poinsott, whom Percy was studying when he was fatally stricken.

The next two Chapters, 2 and 3, "The Cosmic Semiotic of Charles Sanders Peirce" and "The Christian Semiotics of Charles Sanders Peirce," constitute the heart of the book, not only spatially but conceptually. The author uses her previous strategy of apparent duplexity, for the titles picture lines that for the secular reader will run parallel to infinity. But when the reader reflects, he realizes that the former is absolutely dependent on the latter. The passion and intensity inherent in these chapters argue that the author, like Peirce and Percy before her, scorns the Cartesian split and has dedicated herself to spreading the good news that subject and object may be reconciled through the Word/word.

The author then builds a continuity between Biblical times and the nineteenth century, so Chapter 4 is entitled "Christian Semiotic Tradition." In this part of her exploration, the author rides fast and does not tarry. Again, space seems to have been a consideration, for some of the most significant points have been relegated to the chapter notes.

In Chapter 5, "Walker Percy's Christian Semiotic at Work: 'The Message in the Bottle' as Gloss on The Moviegoer," the author makes the long-awaited application of Walker Percy's Peirce-influenced semiotic to his fictional technique. Since she cannot possibly at this point apply the full semiotic to the full range of Percy's fiction, the author very wisely restricts her consideration of the semiotic to that part found in the essay "The Message in the Bottle" and her subject matter under analysis to The Moviegoer, Percy's first published and most widely admired work. The results are so encouraging that the reader is left wishing for much, much more.

But, after all, the author has done enough for us by laying out the necessary tools. She has argued convincingly that the thought of Charles Sanders Peirce is an essential ingredient to an adequate reading of Walker Percy's non-fiction and fiction. Now it is up to us to use those tools to develop a new understanding of the "incarnational, historical, and predicamental" (MB 111) world view that Percy saw as the true territory of the Christian novelist.

Lewis A. Lawson

AUTHOR'S PREFACE

I happened upon Walker Percy's unusual language theory while reading his 1983 pop psychology book, Lost in the Cosmos. In it, a short chapter on his semiotic led me to his collection of semiotic essays, The Message in the Bottle. Those strange, dense essays further directed me into the even stranger and more abstruse writings of Charles Sanders Peirce, father of American pragmatism, a thinker who schooled such greats as John Dewey and William James, but who, in his own right, had fallen into relative obscurity. Although Walker Percy's philosophical essays are not simple reading, Peirce's call for a more-than-passing acquaintance with predecessors in theological semiotics, writers like Ralph Waldo Emerson, Jonathan Edwards, John Calvin, Augustine, and Thomas Aquinas.

The results of my initial interest in Walker Percy's triadic theory of language may be seen in the pages that follow. In Chapter 1, I trace the chronological development of Percy's semiotic, first (in 1954) the theory that man uses symbols (language) in a different manner from other animals and that this unique ability makes man, not merely a higher, adaptive animal, but a "transcendent," knowing being. In his final semiotic, unveiled in an essay published in 1972, "Toward a Triadic theory of Meaning," Percy acknowledges his debt to C.S. Peirce and names the adopted Peircean concept, human triadicity, as fundamental to his own thinking. The theory of human triadicity has two crucial effects on the philosophy of Walker Percy: first, it sets him at odds with behaviorists, in whose doctrines he was thoroughly schooled, and second, it argues, to his satisfaction, that man is capable of a higher destiny than that of other organisms.

In Chapter 2, I establish the connection between Percy and Peirce by examining Peirce's "cosmic" semiotic: his system of the categories of Firstness, Secondness, and Thirdness; his triadic theory of man as sign, as evolving self, and as social being; and his theory of evolution.

In Chapter 3, I focus more specifically on the theological implications of Peirce's semiotic--his Christian semiotic: theological implications of signs, the theological use of signs, and the doctrine of the "Divine Triad."

Chapter 4 traces the Christian semiotic tradition, beginning with Peirce's acknowledged precursor, John Duns Scotus, moving back via Augustine to the Apostle Paul, then forward through the American Calvinist tradition and the secularizing extension of James Marsh, Ralph Waldo Emerson, and, finally, to the pragmatism of Peirce and his followers.

In the last chapter, I demonstrate Walker Percy's Christian semiotic at work in The Moviegoer by letting his essay "The Message in the Bottle" operate as a gloss to his novel.

Ann Mace Futrell

Acknowledgments

I am particularly indebted to Professor Richard Rand, University of Alabama, for his patient reading of my manuscript-in-the-making. His assistance was invaluable.

I wish to acknowledge other readers and critics along the way: Bob Jungman and Terry McConathy, who assisted with translations, Dianne Douglas, Carole Tabor, Tom Lewis, Pat Garrett, Elizabeth Meese, Ralph Voss, and Don Noble.

I am grateful to Louisiana Tech University's Loan Librarian, Fred Hamilton, who searched out and procured obscure journal articles for me.

I wish to acknowledge Professor Fred Hobson for reviewing my Percy bibliography and for offering new listings.

Finally, I wish to express my gratitude to my family for suffering patiently through the emotional highs and lows during the long process of research and writing.

ABBREVIATIONS

Aids	Aids to Reflection
Conversations	Conversations With Walter Percy
CP	Collected Papers of Charles Sanders Peirce
Doctrine	On Christian Doctrine
Images	Images and Shadows of Divine Things
LR	Love in the Ruins
MB	The Message in the Bottle
Mg	The Moviegoer
Problem	The Problem of Christianity
Summa	Summa Theologica
Trinitate	De Trinitate
WP	Writings of Charles Sanders Peirce

1

INTRODUCTION

> Since true prophets, i.e., men called by God to communicate
> something urgent to other men, are currently in short supply,
> the novelist may perform a quasi-prophetic function.
>> ("Notes for a Novel About the End of the World")

> The entire enterprise of literature is like that of a physician,
> undertaken in hope. . . . This literary-diagnostic method is
> . . . appropriate to the fictional enterprise of the late
> twentieth century.
>> ("The Diagnostic Novel")

Trained as a pathologist, Walker Percy has assumed a diagnostician's role in society, not as a physician, however, but as a metaphysician, a quasi-prophet, he calls himself, concerned with "the strange spiritual malady of the modern age" ("The Diagnostic Novel" 40). For something is wrong with the world, with individual man, Percy maintains, and adds that it is the duty of the serious novelist "to render the unspeakable [malady] speakable" (40):

> For I take it as going without saying that the entire
> enterprise of literature is, like that of a physician, undertaken
> in hope (40).

It is clear, then, that Walker Percy's primary concern is the spiritual health of man. Critics generally agree on this fact, but this general agreement is qualified by certain biases and interests that divide his readers and critics into categories which I call philosophical, aesthetic, and linguistic.

In the first group of critics, those I call the philosophical readers, the existentialists are by far the most numerous, following the lead of Martin Luschei, who is credited with the definitive work on Percy's indebtedness to European existentialists, particularly to Soren Kierkegaard. Luschei first maps out Percy's reading of the Europeans, begun, he says, during a prolonged illness when Percy was in his early twenties: Kierkegaard, Marcel, Dostoevsky, Camus, and Sartre (5-6). Then Luschei traces the development of Percy's own career as a writer, citing credits and allusions to the existentialists and concluding that one must have a "working acquaintance" with the existentialists to understand Percy's "new vision of things" (19). Although Luschei admits that "such an acquaintance does not come easily" and that "it seems to go against the grain" with pragmatic American philosophy, he nevertheless argues that the secret to reading Walker Percy lies in the knowledge of Kierkegaard's Christian existentialism: the authentic-inauthentic choice; the stages or "spheres of existence," that is, the aesthetic, the ethical, and the religious modes; the leap into the absurd; and other existentialist theories. To understand what Walker Percy attempts in his novels and essays, Luschei argues, one must know Kierkegaard. And virtually every critic since Luschei cites the "seminal" achievement of his work The Sovereign Wayfarer and begins with the a priori fact of Percy's Kierkegaardian philosophy.[1]

There are other philosophical renderings of Percy's works, the most common after the existentialists being orthodox Christian interpretations. Included among these are the Catholic readings of Robert H. Brinkmeyer, Lawrence Cunningham, and Peter S. Hawkins, who give evidence of Percy's Catholic "sensibility," and "eschatologists" Paul L. Gaston, Eric L. Jones, and Thomas LeClair, who cite Biblical sources for Percy's apocalyptic vision.[2]

The philosophical critics give a way of reading Percy's fiction, but it is not a radical, all-inclusive reading, for it does not link the language theory with the fiction, does not account for the influence of Charles Sanders Peirce, nor for the integration of metaphysics with semiotics. It is interesting and often clever, but it is incomplete.

I call the second classification of Percy's critics aesthetic because these critics are more concerned with his art or with the source of his artistic devices.[3] The largest group of writers in this category deals with Percy's southern affiliation: Percy as southern writer. Louis D. Rubin, Jr., has posed a question for contemporary writers: "The question is not whether there will continue to be literature written in the South, but whether it will be <u>southern</u> literature" (27). And his answer, using Walker Percy as support, is that there will continue to be a southern literature, that Percy's fiction, as an example of it, "seems to be conducted very much along recognizably Southern literary lines": the sense of class or caste, the sense of "decline and fall," the need for community, the "weight of the past," the moral dilemma of black-white relations (27). These are qualities found in Percy's fiction, Rubin notes, and they make it "southern." Other southern critics concur: Cleanth Brooks, Lewis P. Simpson, David C. Dougherty, and William Rodney Allen cite evidence of Percy's use of regional materials.[4]

Like the philosophical writers, the aesthetic critics view Percy's work with narrow sights; they have nothing to say about the language system, do not even mention C. S. Peirce. There is, in other words, the same limited vision of Walker Percy as that of the philosophers; the ideas are interesting, but they tell only a small part of the story.

The final classification of critics is the group of writers concerned primarily with Percy's language theory. These are the critics I wish to examine rather closely because they offer the only interpretation given, thus far, of Percy's semiotic,[5] the subject of my own investigation.

These critics deal with the fundamental principle of triadicity in Percy's system, the idea that all knowledge comes in the form of signs, more specifically symbols and primarily language, and the idea that only humans ("symbol mongers," Percy names them) can "read" and interpret these symbols. The event is a mental coupling of a thing (or idea or experience) with a name, hence triadic behavior. This contrasts with the dyadic behavior of organisms which respond to stimuli, adapting to the environment according to biological needs. Percy begins with the symbol-reading mind, then follows the lead of

Charles Sanders Peirce, who explores the full implications of this transcendent capacity, that is, man's need to know all things, including, Percy argues, the origin and end of man himself.

In <u>Walker Percy and the Old Modern Age: Reflections on Language, Argument, and the Telling of Stories</u>, Patricia Lewis Poteat argues that Percy's interest in language is "broadly phenomenological and 'situational' rather than narrowly analytic and theoretical" (3) and that even Percy's illustration of a "coherent theory of man" (i.e., the Judeo-Christian tradition) is not a philosophical argument but a "story" of a "Child" (34). This inclination, she says, explains why his language theory is lost in a maze of abstractions: Percy "abstracts" the three components in the symbol triad so that "Helen [Keller, the person he uses in his illustration of the semiotic triad] is no longer a girl or a person" but an "element" and "shares this dubious distinction with a certain word and a certain liquid" (48). By this interpretation, then, Percy becomes, she says, not the opponent of Descartes, but a Cartesian theoretician. Further, Poteat argues, in the triadic scheme, Percy isolates Helen and places her "absolutely alone with her word and her water . . . ; not even Annie Sullivan has a place in this scheme" (48). Regarding Percy's language system described in "A Theory of Language," Poteat adds that his "attempt to suture Chomsky's black box onto the human inferior parietal lobule" confuses his theory even more and reinforces her argument that Percy does not escape the "mind-body dualism of Descartes" (171). Poteat's own bias is apparent in her conclusion that Percy is superb as a storyteller but wrongheaded as a theorist, for she has misread the Helen Keller illustration of triadic behavior, has missed the alternative position of the behaviorists, and has skipped over the Peircean connection altogether. Reading Percy with this literary bias and without researching the links that Percy has named, Poteat has failed to understand even the semiotic triad, the most basic principle in

Percy's philosophical system, a concept which I shall explain fully in subsequent pages.

In the first of two essays that straddle the fence between Walker Percy's linguistics and his metaphysics, "Logos and Epiphany: Walker Percy's Theology of Language," Charles P. Bigger writes provocatively that "The Message in the Bottle is a series of reflections on the birth of a human world through the mystery of language" and cites Charles Sanders Peirce as the "major hero" of Percy's essays--the first American scientist to become concerned with semiotics, i.e., "the way the world enters into the being of language through the mystery of naming" (198). Bigger explains how Percy "cuts through" Cartesian dualism by his "close attention to the act of naming" (200) and how he arrives at his "epiphany of the logos" by studying Helen Keller's breakthrough into language, the "mystery of the symbolic event" (200). In his second essay, "The Resonance of the Word," Bigger explains the task that Percy has set for himself in an effort to restore the "strangeness to the name and to ourselves, the users of names": the "mystery of being human" (44). It is the "resonance" or harmony between the word and the thing it represents that makes possible human knowing and human community, for it is through the resonance of the word that one "grasps identities" or essences of things (47). Finally, Bigger links Percy's semiotic with existentialist-phenomenologist Edmund Husserl, whom Percy actually rejects, instead of Charles Peirce, whom Percy names as his predecessor. Like Poteat, Charles Bigger has skipped over the scientific and metaphysical connections with Charles Sanders Peirce, and in doing so has examined Percy's semiotic with limited tools and, indeed, in the case of Husserl, has misread the intention.

I have reserved critic Paul Tellotte to conclude my examination of Percy's language theorists because only he has dealt with the Percy-Peirce connection at all. In two essays--"Walker Percy: A Pragmatic Approach" and

"Charles Peirce and Walker Percy: From Semiotic to Narrative"--Tellotte has explored the links between the two theorists. In the first, he applies Peirce's theory of pragmaticism to Percy's "existential quester": man can never know anything absolutely, can never "reach perfect certitude nor exactitude" (Tellotte quotes Peirce, 222). And again Tellotte cites Peirce's essay "The Fixation of Belief," the idea that the "irritation of doubt" prompts action and inquiry, an uneasiness which becomes the rule of life because a "calm and satisfactory state" of belief is transitory; thus Peirce "foreshadowed modern existential thought with its elevating the act of being over and above any fixed and timeless nature or essence" (222-223). From this it can be argued, as Tellotte does, that Percy's "existential leanings" may be attributed to Peirce as much as to Kierkegaard. The "incessant questioning activity" found throughout the writing of Percy may indeed come from Peirce rather than from the existentialists (224).

In the second essay, Tellotte explains the symbolic (meaning) triad, by which a thing is understood, and the communication tetrad, by which that meaning is shared, then links the two to the theory of Charles Peirce. But again the movement of the argument is toward the fictional use Percy makes of it. Fiction, like other symbols, is made to "mean" something, a triadic transaction, and here lies the strength of Percy's storytelling, Tellotte argues; "the vital importance of this naming process is Percy's fundamental truth, that upon which he grounds all his fictional constructs" (78). Tellotte concludes that "Percy has rummaged about in his philosophical heritage, resurrected a long-neglected approach to language, and applied it in holistic fashion to the modern human situation" (78). This critic has begun in the right place, with Charles Sanders Peirce, but he has not followed the leads, has not involved Peirce fully in all the theological implications of Percy's writing.

This exploration of the "full theological implications" of the Peircean-Percy connection is what I shall do in the following pages. The purpose of my study is to determine the underlying beliefs which control Walker Percy's writing and to demonstrate the essential unity of his work, the direct correspondence between his nonfiction and his fiction--to show how the latter is actually a working model of his philosophy, what I have called Protestant Christian orthodoxy. I shall argue that Walker Percy's work, from the first to the present, both fiction and nonfiction, is clearly Protestant from the lineage of American Calvinism. Whether he writes a discourse on civil rights, as he has done a number of times, or an essay on modern language theory, Percy's theological position remains the same: man is divided within himself, alienated from God, separated from other men--lost, isolated, alone. His only hope--and Percy holds out hope--lies in the Body of Christ, the Church or Beloved Community, which re-educates man, teaches him again the meaning of words that have been "used up" and displaced in postmodern technological society, words like "salvation," "baptism," "faith," teaches man again the holistic, curative power of love that is practiced in the spirit of Christ, who personifies it. Percy's theology is, in short, a neo-orthodox strand of Calvinism emerging from the nineteenth century semiotic system of Charles Sanders Peirce.

Each work of Percy's is, I contend, a Protestant homily concerned with the spiritual emptiness and contrariness of man and with the hope for wayward man within the Body of Christ. Each work is a statement of his theological position; whether essay or novel, each serves to diagnose the malady of postmodern society, "to give it a name, . . . to render the unspeakable speakable," as he says in "The Diagnostic Novel" (40).

When Walker Percy writes about the civil rights issue in "The Failure and the Hope," for example, he is concerned with the failure of the church to

8

lead the way to universal brotherhood; for such a failure is theological, not social, he says, because the church as the mystical body of Christ holds "that men can be reconciled here and now but that they can only be reconciled through the mediation of God and the love of man for God's sake" (17). The reluctance of the church to open its doors and its heart to blacks, Percy argues, repudiates the fundamental principle of brotherhood on which the church is founded. But the failure is not irrevocable, Percy maintains; there is hope if the church will overcome its complacency and "demonstrate the relevance of its theology to the single great burning social issue in American life" (21).

It is not only his social arguments that reflect Percy's fundamental Calvinist philosophy; when he writes about scientific subjects like psychiatry, his position is the same: man is lost to himself, to God, and to others and stands in critical need of redemption, which comes only through a recognition of that fact and a response to his need for God via the church. Further, in all his scientific essays, Percy calls into question the fundamental theory of behaviorists, that man is an organism, only quantitatively different from the amoeba and the cat and responds to stimuli just as lower organisms do, to satisfy certain biological needs. This position is absolutely false, Percy argues again and again; man is a transcendent being who possesses a "God-directedness" and who is "capable of higher perfections" than other animals ("The Coming Crisis in Psychiatry" 415). Tragically, postmodern man has been misled by science, Percy insists, and has been taught to distrust and to cast aside his innate inclination toward a higher destiny. This is the "coming crisis" that psychiatry must face, he argues, a recognition of man's spiritual self, and in doing so, science will be forced to recast, radically, its theory of man. Here again is the Protestant position regarding lost man, man in need of redemption; but here, as he often does, Percy expresses his theology in scientific terms, for science has always been, and continues to be, a bulwark in his life; scientific investigation, empirical data--these are positive and sure accounts of experience. And it is precisely here that Percy links his own Protestant beliefs with the "scientific" philosophy and secularized Calvinism of Charles Sanders Peirce.

To verify this link, one has only to examine a speech of Walker Percy, delivered in May, 1989, in Washington, D.C.: "The Fateful Rift: The San Andreas Fault in the Modern Mind," the eighteenth annual Jefferson Lecture in the Humanities. In the published adaptation of the speech ("The Divided Creature"), Percy explains again behaviorism's flawed theory of man as responding organism: in the sciences of man--sociology and cultural anthropology, for example--human beings are studied as groups of organisms, the first dealing with "such things as self, roles" and the latter with "such things as sorcery, rites" (79), but without a "linking" science to explain "how you get from organism to roles and rites" (79). In other words, there is, Percy maintains, no explanation given by scientists to account for what they themselves do with the data they accumulate: deduce formulas and patterns and trends, then write papers, present arguments, and project future developments. In short, Percy insists that man, the thinking animal, is "left over" when all scientific theories are in. This scientific schism, this gap between man the organism and man the thinking, reasoning creature, Percy calls the "fateful rift," an "incoherence" in the modern mind, and ascribes it to the "dualism" of Descartes (78):

> Descartes . . . divided all reality between the res cogitans, the mind, and the res extensa, matter. God alone, literally, knew what one had to do with the other. (78)

That is the flaw of modern science, in Percy's view, a theory which leaves man soulless and rootless, for until the "new modern age," he reminds us, it stood as a priori knowledge that man has (or is) a soul, that he was created in the image of God but now stands out of harmony and out of favor with God because of an aboriginal Fall, and that he may be restored to favor with God through the mediation of Jesus Christ.

To restore the rift in the modern mind, to restore man's soul in modern science, Percy turns to the philosophy of Charles Sanders Peirce, which defines man as a "triadic" being who, through the unique gift of language, thinks, reasons, understands, and knows. In the scientific community and, indeed, in all postmodern society, this theory is revolutionary and far reaching, Percy holds, just as revolutionary and far reaching as Emerson's theory of the infinitude of man and for much the same reason.

To illustrate his theory of man as transcendent being, Percy describes the interaction of the elements of the Peircean triad--object, name, and mind:

> The child points to a flower and says flower. One element of the event is the flower perceived by sight and registered by the brain. . . . Another is the spoken word flower, a gestalt of a peculiar little sequence of sounds of larynx vibrations, escape of air between lips and so on. But what is the entity of the apex of the triangle, that which links the other two? Peirce . . . called it by various names, interpretant, interpreter, judger. It . . . was also called . . . "mind" and even "soul." (86)

If, then, as Percy suggests, man can see, name, and thereby know the universe in which he lives; if, as Percy and Peirce and other realists before them say, the universe is made up of real, knowable things, objects that exist regardless of what man thinks or says about them; and if, as Percy and Peirce and other empiricists insist, knowledge comes from the universe of natural phenomena, then the consequences for man, the naming, knowing intelligence, are great indeed. For the universe becomes the textbook, the tacit language of itself and of its origin and Originator; and man, the interpreter of the universe of things, becomes a non-material agent in the triad of meaning.

As for naming the coupling agent in man, Percy suggests deferring that for the present, but as for recognizing the reality and the work of this third element, he becomes insistent, becomes a crusader, as I shall argue, to gain recognition and acceptance for it because this is the component which makes man the "nonmaterial cosmic agent" of interpretation. And although he does not name this element (of interpretation) in man, Percy does identify specific criteria by which it can be known:

> For one thing, it is there. It is located in time and space, but not as an organism. . . .
>
> For another, it is peculiarly and intimately involved with others of its kind so that, unlike the solitary biological organism, it is impossible to imagine its functioning without the other, another. . . . Peirce's triad is social by its very nature. As he put it, "Every assertion requires a speaker and a listener." The triadic creature is nothing is not social. Indeed he can be understood as a construct of his relations with others.
>
> [Third], . . . this strange new creature, not only has an environment, as do all creatures. It has a world. Its world is the totality of that which is named. . . . There are no gaps in the world of this new creature, because the gaps are called that, gaps, or the unknown or out there, or don't know.
>
> . . . [M]oreover, words, symbols and things symbolized are subject to norms, something new in the world. They can be fresh or grow stale. They can be dull and everyday, then sharp as a diamond in the poet's usage. (86-87)

Percy stops here in his scientific argument for his theory of human triadicity, but in the conclusion to the speech, he suggests metaphysical implications, likenesses which he finds in existentialist writers; and in his own metaphysical writings he proposes, in more specific terms, the Christian application of the idea.

Finally, as a modern day "prophet," a title Percy claims the right to as a novelist-humanist, he predicts that "the modern scientist of man will be obliged to take account of these fanciful notions, not by the existentialists but by their cold, hard-headed compatriot, Charles Peirce" (87).

The concern expressed by Walker Percy in the Jefferson Lecture of 1989 is the same problem he has explored ever since his first published philosophical essay thirty-five years ago, "Symbol As Need," in which he commends linguist Susanne Langer for "breaking away from the restrictive a prioris of pragmatism and psychologism" (MB 291) and for identifying and delineating "the universal symbolific function of the human mind" (MB 292). Then, as now, Percy contends that the symbol-using mind of man is "radically different" from the signal-responding behavior of beasts, that the symbol acts as a "vehicle of meaning," a "sensory form which is in itself the medium for organizing and re-presenting meaning" (293).

In the Jefferson speech, however, Dr. Percy has, for the first time, boldly stated his philosophical terms of agreement with Charles Peirce, a matter of crucial significance to my own argument, for until now Walker Percy has been called a Christian existentialist linked first with the European existentialists and then with his own converted faith, Roman Catholicism. For the first time, he has made it clear that his semiotic, which includes not only his science but his theology as well, rests squarely on the fundamental Peircean principle of human triadicity. And herein lies the significance of my own position.

Until now, Percy has treated his debt to Charles Peirce with reticence, showing an alliance primarily in linguistics. Until now he has not acknowledged the full metaphysical implications of Peircean semiotics, has not noted the radical nature of Peircean triadicity, more radical than existentialism with which he is associated, more radical, even, than Roman Christianity which he embraces. I shall demonstrate in subsequent pages what Percy has hinted before and spoken more plainly in his Jefferson Lecture, that

Charles Sanders Peirce is the source of his semiotic, a radical system beginning with the physical reality at the empirical level of language (sign) investigation but extending also to metaphysical "reality" (what must be true, based on evidence). I shall demonstrate that Percy's system does bridge the scientific split in an unexpected manner by bringing into play Peirce's whole pragmatic system; for Peirce's pragmatism is fundamentally an intellectual system, "a method of ascertaining the meanings of hard words and abstract concepts" (CP 5. 464),

> the experimental method by which all the successful sciences
> . . . have reached the degrees of certainty that are severally
> proper to them today; this experimental method being itself
> nothing but a particular application of an older logical rule,
> 'By their fruits ye shall know them.' (CP 5. 465)

In Peirce's system the experimental data convey not only concepts of existential facts to the human mind but concepts of existential "laws," not only what is but also what would be if certain conditions prevailed. In this way Peirce demonstrates that man, who reads the signs around him, can with scientific certainty, project, speculate, and act from an empirical understanding. All this rests on the theory of thirdness or triadicity, the key that Walker Percy borrows from Charles Sanders Peirce to create his own philosophical system and to bridge the gap left open by Cartesian dualism.

To demonstrate this, I shall trace the development of Percy's philosophy by a close examination of his essays in The Message in the Bottle, beginning with the earliest one, "Symbol As Need," written in 1954, and working through each one to the final, introductory essay for the collection, "The Delta Factor," written in 1975, at the time of publication. I shall establish Percy's dogma, couched as it is in scientific and philosophical terms; then I shall trace the source of his science and theology through Charles Sanders Peirce, whom Percy names as progenitor of his Christian semiotic. Finally, I shall review Charles Peirce's own philosophical lineage through his credits and citations: scholastic theologian Duns Scotus back to Paul the Apostle then forward through Augustine, the American Calvinists (primarily Jonathan Edwards), Ralph Waldo Emerson, James Marsh, and back to Peirce and his circle of pragmatist-behaviorists: William James, George Mead, Charles Morris, John Dewey, and Josiah Royce. The purpose of this historical search is to link Walker Percy with the American Protestant tradition that descends from Apostle Paul by way of John Calvin. In the final chapter of my paper, I shall examine The Moviegoer as an example of Percy's cognitive fiction and show how it does, indeed, support the Pauline doctrine which underlies all that Walker Percy has written.

NOTES

[1] Walker Percy himself has encouraged this link: in interviews, in essays, and in his fiction, he has frequently noted his philosophical ties to European existentialists.

It would be impossible to list all of Percy's critics who cite the Kierkegaardian connection; all do in various ways; the following, however, are the most significant ones. Although Martin Luschei is most often given credit for laying out Percy's Kierkegaardian philosophy, it was Lewis Lawson, most prolific of Percy's critics, who first marked the influence of Kierkegaard on Walker Percy. In an 1969 essay entitled "Walker Percy's Indirect Communications," Lawson points out the two key Kierkegaardian elements used by Percy to "translate the abstract ideas of his articles into the human action of his novels" (869): first, the "stages" or "spheres of existence"--the aesthetic, the ethical, and the religious modes--and second, an indirect way of speaking to the reader, i.e., phenomenologically, through fictional characters placed in a "predicament." Lawson also notes other connections to Kierkegaard in Percy's work: the problem of alienation and man's attempt to escape it by "repetition" and "rotation," the "rite of certification," and the search as relief from despair (878ff).

Anselm Atkins ("Walker Percy and Post-Christian Search,") finds the post-Christian search in The Moviegoer beginning from an "invincible apathy" and proceeding to an unknown object.

Eugene Chesnick ("Novel's Ending and World's End: The Fiction of Walker Percy") contends that writing about the apocalypse is Walker Percy's way of staving it off or of preventing it altogether, shocking his readers by what could happen if history continues as it is going. Chesnick writes about the apocalyptic vision in The Moviegoer, The Last Gentleman, and Love in the Ruins.

Barbara Filippidis ("Vision and the Journey to Selfhood in Walker Percy's The Moviegoer") examines Percy's peculiar use of alienation in The Moviegoer.

Janet Hobbs ("Binx Bolling and the Stages on Life's Way,") explores the Kierkegaardian stages in Binx's life.

Mark Johnson ("The Search for Place in Walker Percy's Novels") examines Percy's use of man's sense of alienation and homelessness in the novels, calling attention to Kierkegaard's "levels of existence" reflected in environments.

Phillip H. Rhein ("Walker Percy's European Connection") traces Percy's connections with Albert Camus.

Lewis J. Taylor, Jr. ("Walker Percy's Knights of the Hidden Inwardness") and ("Walker Percy and the Self") writes about Walker Percy's fictional application of Kierkegaardian terms and ideas, particularly the "lonely journey" toward selfhood by a "knight of the hidden inwardness."

John F. Zeugner ("Walker Percy and Gabriel Marcel: The Castaway and the Wayfarer") examines Percy's "obsession" with intersubjectivity--a concept he borrows from Gabriel Marcel and which "the corpus of Percy's work suggests is the ground of being, the basis of consciousness, the way out of alienation, and a path to salvation" (22).

Robert Coles, early biographer and friend of Walker Percy, finds the strength of Percy's work in the spiritual message it brings: "a contemporary existentialism" balanced with "the pragmatism and empiricism of an American physician" (Walker Percy: An American Search, xvii). In reading it and in writing about it, Coles finds, he says, "a way of learning what I believed--how I saw and comprehended the world" (That Red Wheelbarrow, 108).

[2] Robert H. Brinkmeyer, Jr., includes Percy in Three Catholic Writers of the South, though he does not point out a distinctly Catholic position or distinctly Catholic treatment of material. Lawrence Cunningham produces more evidence for Percy's Catholic affiliation in "Catholic Sensibility and Southern Writers," citing Percy's view of the world as "a locus of the Sacred" (8), and contrasting that view with a more secularized Protestant view of the world. In more general Christian terms, Peter S. Hawkins studies Percy's language in the fiction as a cause for the present "deafness to the gospel" (54).

Paul L. Gaston, Eric L. Jones, and Thomas LeClair apply the Biblical teachings on eschatology or apocalypse to various works of Walker Percy: Gaston cites the book of Revelation as his doctrinal source, Jones applies the Christian doctrine of the second coming of Christ to Percy's novel The Second Coming, and LeClair establishes the death theme from the existential awareness, though he treats the theme from a more orthodox view.

In writing "Walker Percy's Christian Vision" in Love in the Ruins, W. L. Godshalk demonstrates Percy's application of "man's Faustian pride, his fall from grace, his call for spiritual aid, and his final return to the common life of Christendom" (140). And Susan S. Kissel describes Walker Percy's use of "radical religious conversions," that is, discoveries which lead to "final reversals" in the lives of his protagonists: they "arrive at a new awareness of their human condition, of themselves as neither beasts nor angels or ghosts but men" (135). Finally, Ralph C. Wood presents an interesting argument for an ongoing tension in Walker Percy, the philosopher, the idea that Percy has not yet resolved his own internal conflict between Christian theory and humanistic practice. What Percy seeks to achieve in his life as well as in his fiction, Wood contends, is a "true humanism," which "can account for both the terrible perversion and the wondrous exaltation of human life as it exists before God" (1123), and which leads ultimately to a search for God in Percy's fiction. The problem, Wood argues, is that

> Percy's Christian humanism comes, at its worst, to value the pilgrimage more than the Shrine. What matters is less the Object of the pilgrim's journey than the subject's own endless peregrination. (1126)

Woods concludes that Percy's Christianity and his humanism "remain in conflict precisely because transcendent grace and the human quest for it" (1126) are unequally balanced.

There is one other group of philosophical critics that I should cite; they are the "southern conservatives," those critics who examine southern stoicism in Percy's fiction. Lewis A. Lawson gives the best treatment of this, using Walker Percy's foster father, William Alexander Percy's, autobiography, Lanterns on the Levee and Walker Percy's own essay "Stoicism in the South" as biographical sources. The origin of the tradition is Roman Marcus Aurelius, but the South adopted conservative humanitarian qualities into an agrarian society that

> enshrined the human aspects of living for rich and poor, black and white . . . , gave first place to a stable family life, sensitivity and good manners between men, chivalry toward women, an honor code, and individual integrity. (Quoted by Lawson from Percy's essay, 15)

Lawson finds this tradition reflected in Aunt Emily Cutrer in The Moviegoer and in Will Barrett's father in The Last Gentleman. One other writer deserves mention here: Michel T. Blouin considers the South in Walker Percy's fiction as more than a place, "at once maternalistic and paternalistic" (29), both a source of pride and a point of shame and guilt, "an ever-present memory and interior burden and barrier for the young idealistic Southerner of life and legend" (30).

[3] Harold Bloom, editor of the 1986 Chelsea collection of essays on Walker Percy, finds the moralism an interference, the pleasure of reading Percy's works "somewhat darkened by intimations . . . of the moral and religious obsessions" and concludes that in the "downward path to wisdom," the fiction suffers (1). In fact, Bloom notes a "curious progression," a kind of "metamorphosis from the language of story" in the first novel "to the urgencies

that transcend art" in the latest novels, a movement toward a "theocentric anxiety" that marks "the waste of Percy's authentic talents" (3).

[4] Cleanth Brooks finds in Percy's fiction "a little bouquet of descriptions of Southern women" (35), and David C. Dougherty describes Percy's southern gothic motifs that lead to "a critique of empty and decadent southern romanticism" (154). Lewis P. Simpson cites Percy's use of "Southern Aesthetic of Memory," that leads into "prophecy and apocalypse" (226).

In Walker Percy: A Southern Wayfarer, William Rodney Allen attempts to trace the autobiographical links in Percy's fiction, noting particularly the father-son theme, a "thematic obsession," he calls it, and supports his argument by Percy's frequent use of suicide among protagonists' fathers and a subsequent search by the protagonists for father figures.

Anneke Leenhouts also writes about Percy's preoccupation with southern traditions but adds that "by the time Percy began to publish, the emphasis had shifted away from the suggestion that viable alternatives to the traditional manner of living could not be found" (51), that in the New South there are other means of coping:

> love, concern, readiness to assume responsibilities, mature acceptance of human frailties will make, not a Southern gentleman . . . but the contemporary equivalent of all that is good in the tradition. (51)

Other critics in the southern tradition should be cited:

William Winslow ("Modernity and the Novel: Twain, Faulkner, and Percy") acknowledges that Percy "resists attempts to place him under the rubric of Southern literature," but, nevertheless, finds "traces of a unique and precious vibrance" of southern tradition there and contends that to understand Percy, one must recognize these.

David L. Vanderwerken ("The Americanness of The Moviegoer") writes less of the southern tradition than a composite of American stereotypes.

A. Lawson ("'English Romanticism . . . and 1930 Science' in The Moviegoer") describes the visionary elder Jack Bolling, who, like Byron, took off to the war in Greece with a copy of romantic poetry in his pocket and never returned.

Jac Tharpe (Walker Percy) analyzes Percy's art, linking him to Emerson and Whitman, to Emerson's "original uses of language" and to Whitman's concept of poet as priest (8). He also has a chapter placing Percy into the southern tradition of literature, a chapter on "Techniques," a chapter on Percy's Christian creed, and a chapter on each novel, except the last one.

Simone Vauthier ("Title as Microtext: The Example of The Moviegoer") analyzes Percy's use of a title, "Moviegoer," to suggest a way of providing "a symbolic language which can unite narrator and narratee, author and reader" (224).

⁵ J. Gerald Kennedy has written about Percy's semiotic as applied to The Second Coming, that is, Percy's use of signs and symbols to support the plot in his "most densely semiotic narrative" (105). Especially significant, Kennedy argues, is the manner in which the novelist uses signs and symbols "to explore the code of images inscribed in human memory and recalled through both deliberate and involuntary recollection" (105). Kennedy's primary interest in the analysis is the images which Percy uses to create in Will Barrett's mind memories from his past that ultimately prompt his search for God.

Linguist Frank Parker does a thorough analysis of Percy's syntactics but is put off by his semantic triad and the Delta Phenomenon, interpreting the latter variously as the same thing as the object itself, as the idea or mental image of the object, and as a stimulus which elicits a response. [See explanation in Chapter 5.] Parker argues that "the only conclusion a linguist can reach after reading The Message in the Bottle is that "either Percy has not read the literature on the subject or that he has simply not comprehended it" (163). As a technician of language formations, Parker has looked at one small portion of Percy's much larger scheme of language theory. That he does not recognize the intention of Percy's semiotic is understandable because he has not read the works of Charles Sanders Peirce out of which Percy's semiotic emerges.

CHAPTER 1

THE CHRISTIAN SEMIOTIC OF WALKER PERCY

Preliminary System

Ever since 1954, when Walker Percy read and reviewed Susanne Langer's Philosophy in a New Key and Feeling and Form (in "Symbol As Need"), he has been, as he testifies, "mildly obsessed" with language and with its implications regarding man, the "languaged" animal. In that initial work of Percy's career as a writer-philosopher, one can find taking shape a "human semiotic," that is, a systematic theory of man's use of language. It was in Langer's works, apparently, that Percy first discovered the element which became the key to his own philosophy, to his theory of human behavior, to his religion: the "universal symbolific function of the human mind" (MB 292). The idea is critical to Percy's entire philosophic system, not only because it rejects the traditional scientific concept of man as an organism adapting to an environment, differing only quantitatively from the amoeba, but also because it establishes at this early period in his career the most important principle of his system: the "transformational character of the symbol function" (293). In positivist-behavioral terms, man responds in all situations, whether speech acts or physiological behavior, in adaptive manner--in measurable, predictable causal responses. To Langer and to Percy, however, this interpretation of the human act of understanding and of communication omits the denotative value (meaning) of words and ignores the symbol-reading process of man, for a symbol, in contrast to a sign (or signal) that announces its object as thunder announces rain, is the vehicle for meaning and somehow carries within it the idea of the thing it names:

> The transformation of experience into concepts, not the elaboration of signals and symptoms, is the motive of language. Speech is through and through symbolic. (Philosophy in a New Key 126)

The value of language for the human mind, according to Langer and to Percy, then, is that it names (denotes) a thing, ascribes a meaning so that the mind might store it for continual use; by a name and only by a name can one know a thing. Denotation Langer defines as the "essence of language" because it frees the symbol from the object or situation that gave it birth, thereby allowing the mind to use it independently of the object or situation:

> A denotative word is related at once to a conception, which may be ever so vague, and to a thing (or event, quality, person, etc.) which is realistic and public; so it weans the conception away from the purely momentary and personal experience and fastens it on a permanent element which may enter into all sorts of situations. (Philosophy 134)

With this innovative concept, then, Percy began to formulate other possibilities that he later incorporated into his philosophical-religious system:

> Is it not possible that this startling semantic insight, that by the word I have the thing, fix it, and rescue it from the flux of Becoming around me, might not confirm and illuminate the Thomist notion of the interior word, of knowing something by becoming something? that the "basic need of symbolization" is nothing more or less than the first ascent in the hierarchy of knowledge, the eminently "natural" and so all the more astonishing instrument by which I transform the sensory content and appropriate it for the stuff of my ideas, and that therefore the activity of knowing [can] be evaluated . . . by nothing short of Truth itself? (MB 197)

It appears that Susanne Langer's theory of symbolization in language served as a catalyst to the young Percy, prompting him to become both a rebel and a crusader. His adulthood conversion to Catholicism (in 1946 at age thirty), together with his childhood upbringing in the southern Protestant tradition, led Percy to redefine science, to view it as dehumanizing, and to reject behaviorism, which defines man as an organism adapting to his environment according to specific, mainly physiological, needs. Thoroughgoing scientist that he was, however, Percy could not desert the field entirely and cast aside, as he says, twenty-five years of study; instead he began at that point to develop a system whereby he might satisfy his love and respect for the scientific method and, at the same time, to remain loyal to his religious predilection. To do this, he found the link he needed in language.

In his conclusion to the 1954 review of Langer's work (see quotation above), Percy gives a number of clues to his expectations for language: first, there is the "Thomist notion of the interior word," explained by Aquinas as the concept in the mind that is generated by the exterior word, that is, the union of a vocal sound and the "signification of the sound" (I, Q. 34, Art. 1). This is a tripartite relationship of three different "words," explained by Aquinas this way:

> First and chiefly, the interior concept of the mind is called a word; secondarily, the vocal sound itself, signifying the interior concept, is so called; and thirdly, the imagination of the vocal sound is called a word. (I, Q. 34, Art. 1)

Even more to Percy's spiritual purpose, Aquinas links man's language and the knowledge which he gains via language to the Word of God as "begotten knowledge" (I, Q. 34, Art. 1, reply 2), for God is truth itself, "the supreme and first truth" (I, Q. 16, Art. 5). This is what Percy alludes to as the "hierarchy of knowledge," which, according to Aquinas, always begins at the sensory level, undergoes a synthesis (of word, image, and idea) in the mind, becomes an abstraction (removed by the mind from particular objects and made universal form), and finally becomes, by logical extension, a spiritual truth. F. C. Copleston explains Aquinas' theory of this movement:

> Aquinas held that the mind is dependent on the image, not only in the formation of its ideas but also in their employment, in the sense that there is no thinking without the use of images or symbols. Since the mind is active and possesses the power of active reflection, it is not confined to the knowledge of material things; but at the same time it can know immaterial things only in so far as material things are related to them and reveal them . . . . We cannot conceive immaterial things, even when their existence is known by revelation, except in an analogy with visible things, though we attempt to purify our ideas of them. (183)

Thus, the "first ascent in the hierarchy of knowledge," suggested by Percy as the "basic need of symbolization," is the synthesizing action of the mind, linking the word-sound with the word-object into a word-concept, the "stuff of . . . ideas."

The final clue to Percy's philosophy coming out of the 1954 essay is his suggestion of the ultimate purpose of language--"nothing short of Truth itself." The capitalization of the term reinforces the theological import and the link with Aquinas, who places truth in the intellect and defines it as a "squaring of thought and thing":

> A house is said to be true that expresses the likeness of the form in the architect's mind, and words are said to be true so far as they are the signs of truth in the intellect. In the same way natural things are said to be true in so far as they express the likeness of the species that are in the divine mind . . . . Thus, then, truth is principally in the intellect and secondarily in things according as they are related to the intellect as their principle. (Q. 16, Art. 1)

Such a conformity between thought and thing is initiated by the senses but cannot be known by the senses; it is a matter of judgment of the mind: "This it does by composing and dividing, for in every proposition it either applies to or removes from the thing signified by the subject, some form signified by the predicate" (I, Q. 16, Art. 2). The mind, in other words, interprets the image-word it receives by its knowledge of the form and purpose of the thing and judges the veracity of the image given by sense perception. Thus, it follows that truth is contingent upon knowledge of the nature of the thing:

> The truth of our intellect is according to its conformity with its principle, that is to say, to the things from which it receives knowledge. The truth also of things is according to their conformity with their principle, namely, the divine intellect. (I, Q. 16, Art. 5, rep. 2)

Indeed, according to Aquinas' theology, it is the purpose of natural phenomena to direct the mind toward the Supreme Truth by way of "causal connections and critical acuity" (Eco 141). There is, in Aquinas' theology, a certain suspicion of poetic language because its figures often mislead, but he does recognize Biblical allegory:

> It is befitting Holy Writ to put forward divine and spiritual truths under the likeness of material things. For God provides for everything according to the capacity of its nature. Now it is natural to man to attain to intellectual truth through sensible things, because our knowledge originates from sense. (I, Q. 1, Art. 9)

When the mind receives images in corporeal form, it can more easily follow the meaning "to the threshold of the truth" (Eco 150).

In summary, Percy's 1954 essay, "Symbol As Need," establishes his position on certain critical concepts about man and language. The first major concept found in this early essay has to do with the science of language per se: as a medium for meaning, language properly acts as the beginning of all science, for by it all knowledge is formulated, organized, and shared. The second concept is the symbolizing ability of man: man is inherently capable of naming and thereby "creating" and conceiving the world he inhabits. By language man is conscious, for, according to Percy, the mind is never "merely" conscious, but is always conscious of something which is imaged and denoted by language. Thus, according to Percy's theory, the mind itself engages in a constant essential act of language; that is what makes man a transcending being. In support of this theory, Percy makes clear in this first essay the theological implications of language. By the word-symbol, man has a way to know God, to ascend through "hierarchies" of knowledge to the Source of being and of knowledge. His use of Aquinas reveals, at this early period in his writing, Percy's hope for language and for man. Finally, Percy's early language theory makes it clear that the "community" of man is possible only by language; he calls it (after Martin Buber and Gabriel Marcel) the "metaphysics of we are" because language "validates" common existence by facilitating shared experience.

I have called Walker Percy a rebel, an outspoken opponent of American empiricism and its canons of reductive experimentation. In his second published essay, "Symbol As Hermeneutic in Existentialism" (1956), he resumes his campaign with more vigor, naming four "notorious difficulties" with empiricism in its study of man: (1) the various disciplines of science cannot agree on the ultimate reducible for its subject, man, i.e., "cultural unit, libido, social monad, generic trait"; (2) the list of human "needs" given by biologists includes "cultural" need, which because of its abstract nature, transcends the scientific definition of man as an organism; (3) behavioral psychologists "smuggle" in "existential activities" whereby man is required to make choices so that he may be "diagnosed," in the very act of "overcoming resistances"--all of which contradict the deterministic view of man as responding organism; (4) the empirical scientist transcends his own objective position toward man; that is, he views man as an organism responding to stimuli according to specified biological needs, while the scientist himself observes, records, analyzes, speculates, and seeks to understand; in other words, the scientist studies man as homo sapiens, while he performs as homo symbolificus. Again, as in the first essay, Percy is unwilling to reject the whole system of empirical science; its limits may be overcome, he insists, if "the doctrinal precondition" of the science of man can be overthrown, i.e., the deterministic view of man as a "fixed social unit" with "quantifiable needs" (MB 278-79). In short, Percy is campaigning here, as in the first essay, for a new view of man, not as a responding organism adapting to an environment, but as a thinking being, naming (by symbol) and thereby knowing a world:

> The need of the empirical sciences of man is an insight, a proper empirical finding, that will introduce an order of reality, a reality of existential traits, which latter, if they cannot be reduced to supposedly prime elements or verified by measurement, can at least be validated experientially and hierarchically grounded in a genuinely empirical framework. (MB 279)

It is not science per se that Percy would dismiss but the deterministic view of man that he wishes to subvert.

In the second essay, he adds a new opponent; Percy views as his foe, not only American empiricism, but European existentialism as well. Existentialism held (and still holds) attractions for Walker Percy for a number of reasons.[1] Specifically, there is in Sartre the recognition of man as an independent consciousness, a theory that appeals to Percy's concept of transcendent man. In Marcel there is the recognition of a collective consciousness, a mutuality in knowing--an intersubjectivity created by the I and the Thou participation (introduced first by Martin Buber). This community of knowers becomes paramount in the language theory that Percy later develops. But the most dramatic appeal of all the existentialists for Percy is Kierkegaard's Christianity, which he writes about in his essays and speaks of in interviews and uses as themes in novels, the idea of despairing, alienated man in search of God.[2]

Experiencing a prolonged, debilitating illness and suffering from grief over his foster father's death, Percy found comfort in Kierkegaardian Christianity. There, he found a suffering man (not mankind) in despair and alienation, plotting ways to satisfy an innate longing but incapable of doing so until he "comes to himself" in the realization that he is lost and in desperate need of God. At that point, the man chooses his course of action and makes a blind leap of faith into belief in the "absurd" claims of Jesus Christ and Christianity. These were the attractions of the European existentialists for the young Walker Percy in the 1940s and 1950s.[3]

But I have identified existentialism as a flawed system in Percy's view, one that he could not then (nor later) accept as his philosophy. And the reasons are not difficult to find, for he names them throughout his essays and interviews. First, the Sartrean philosophy of man, which does recognize an individual human entity, does not recognize a link between the independent mind and the things that mind knows; "prereflective cognito," Sartre calls the "transphenomenal consciousness," a "being-for-itself," and the "transphenomenal object" a "being-in-itself": "The prime reality of human consciousness is . . . but a pure impersonal awareness" (Percy quotes Sartre, MB 282). The fallacy here, Percy points out, is that there can be no consciousness apart from human consciousness; therefore, Sartre's "There is consciousness of this chair" does not designate a particular object, does not recognize a symbolic denotation, and cannot be communicated between minds. The correction of this flawed concept, Percy states as "This is a chair for you and me" (MB 282). The all-important symbol is missing in Sartrean philosophy; thus a dualism of mind and object is established that cannot be overcome by existentialist philosophy:

> The symbolic corrective is that both the empiricists and the existentialists (excepting Marcel) are wrong in positing an autonomous consciousness, whether a series of conscious "states" or a solitary subjective existent. (MB 282-83)

In Marcel's idea of intersubjectivity, a concept so vital to Percy, there is, to be sure, a mutuality established between the speaker and another subject, but there is not the vital link by the word or other symbol; hence, there cannot be, in Percy's system anyway, a "meeting of the minds." Marcel concedes that "there can be no message of any kind without emission, transmission, and reception" (The Existential Background of Human Dignity 41); but instead of grounding human intersubjectivity in "real," named objects, he turns to what he calls parapsychological links between minds. In regard to the world of existents, he has this to say:

> [I]f I limit myself to regarding the world as represented . . . I become incapable of taking into account its aspect of existing; then the troubling question of the existence of an external world inevitably arises and in such a way as to be unanswerable . . . . [T]he world called "external" is on the same footing as to its mode of existence with my body, from

which I can only abstract myself by tedious mental effort.
(47)

Thus, the deficiencies of Marcel to the incipient philosophy of Walker Percy are obvious. There is not the crucial symbolization of the world of existents by the independent mind in collusion with another mind (or community of minds).

Kierkegaard, the existentialist with whom critics link Percy most frequently and fully and indeed the philosopher whom Percy himself credits most often as influencing his religious philosophy, may, all credits notwithstanding, be viewed as a venerable opponent to the systematic philosophy of Walker Percy. In Percy's 1956 essay, Kierkegaard's philosophy is mentioned only once as "psychological," but in later writings, Percy makes it clear that Kierkegaard's scheme of philosophy is unacceptable to his own beliefs. Although Kierkegaard verbalized for young Percy the doubt he himself had been feeling regarding the limitation of science and introduced the possibilities of religion,[4] Percy found serious flaws in the Kierkegaardian concept of Christianity that rendered it useless in the overall scheme of his own religious semiotic. First, there are the subjectivity and the dualism already mentioned in relation to Sartre. In this case, it is the duality of human and heavenly "worlds"; the two never meet in Kierkegaardian theology: man becomes convinced by his own feeling of despair and alienation that there is a God and then makes an existential choice and a "leap of faith" despite doubts, to embrace an "Absolute Paradox" and "absurd" claim of Christ. For Percy the absolute paradox holds true, but the leap by blind faith, he cannot accept because there are many verifiable facts regarding Christ and the Christian religion: there is a nation (the Jews) with recorded history and prophecy from which came a man, Jesus Christ, who lived and taught of mysteries, the most astounding of which was his own Incarnation. And there followed a universal movement, a body of believers (the church), which to this day gives credence to the claims of Christianity. And so the claim of Kierkegaard that Christianity cannot be arrived at by knowledge, that

> one simply gets clear on what the Christian life entails, then if that is his choice, makes a 'leap of faith,' elects to believe despite the ineradicable doubt, opts to believe not in virtue of evidence but by virtue of the absurd (Bradley Dewey 119-20),

is untenable to Percy's belief in Christ and His church. Percy calls Kierkegaard's Christianity "contentless," that is, without a ground for belief but simply "something of inwardness" (120).

Equally as important to Percy is the second flaw he finds in Kierkegaardian philosophy, and that is the absence of a link between human beings and between the human mind and the natural universe. Again I refer to the symbol (language), which allows man to name and know the world about him and to communicate that knowledge with other human beings. This is, of course, the central ingredient in Percy's whole system, central not only to his theory of language, but to his theory of man and of religion as well; Percy's semiotic is a unified system which integrates everything he has written, from linguistics to theology.

To summarize Percy's attraction to and rejection of existentialism, he found the individual consciousness he sought in Sartre, but it was disconnected to the world it inhabited. He found in Marcel the community of minds (intersubjectivity) he sought, but without symbolic mediation. In Kierkegaard, who most appealed to Percy's religious inclination, he found the Christianity he sought, but it was disconnected from facts, from history, from reality. In short, Percy liked the Christian sentiment in Kierkegaard, the phenomenology of Sartre (and Camus), the intersubjectivity of Marcel, but in the final analysis rejected the system out of which these came because of a lack of unifying principle which he saw in symbolization--that is, a "human semiotic."

In the 1956 essay, "Symbol As Hermeneutic for Existentialism," Percy is still in search of a system to suit his dedication to science as well as his devotion to religion. By the following year, 1957, in an essay entitled "Semiotic and a Theory of Knowledge," he begins to focus more explicitly on language, particularly the "mysterious naming act" as a link between the two:

> It is my hope to show that a true "semiotic," far from being the coup de grace of metaphysics, may prove of immense value, inasmuch as it validates and illumines a classical metaphysical relation--and this at an empirical level [Percy's emphasis]. (MB 245)

The "classical metaphysical relation" refers to the scholastic concept of the word about which Percy writes in the 1954 essay in connection with Aquinas' interior/exterior word and to which he returns in the 1957 essay. Here, he explains the scholastic theory of naming, the mysterious transformation of the word-into-thing by which a name is paired with an object ("two real entities," separate, distinct, unrelated) then immediately loses its own identity in the object, "disappears" before the thing, and becomes the vehicle of meaning--the only way the object may be known or communicated: "In Scholastic language, the symbol has the peculiar property of containing within itself in alio esse, in another mode of existence, that which is symbolized" (MB 261). In a footnote Percy adds a statement by John of St. Thomas:

> What may be that element of the signified which is joined to the sign and present in it as distinct from the sign itself? I answer: No other element than the very signified itself in another mode of existence. (MB 261n)

In two subsequent essays--"The Act of Naming" and "Metaphor As Mistake"--Percy explores more closely the mystery of language transformation. He repeats his point of protest: Man is not simply a "higher animal" but a unique creature who "stands apart" from the universe, names all the things he apprehends, and by that naming "creates" his world and knows it through the names or symbols he has assigned. Semanticists and other scientists call this a "cosmic blunder," Percy notes, because "A [name] is clearly not B [thing]" (MB 157), but it is, in fact, this "cosmic blunder" that makes man human and not beast: "Unless [man] says A is B, he will never know A or B; he will only respond to them" (MB 157).

Again taking the position of the scholastics in relating man's nature to his naming ability, Percy sees the consequences of this concept as metaphysical:

> The Scholastics, who incidentally had a far more adequate theory of symbolic meaning in some aspects than modern semioticists, used to say that man does not have a direct knowledge of essences as the angels but only an indirect knowledge, a knowledge mediated by symbols. (MB 156)

In brief, the modern "minimal concept" of man must be changed, in Percy's view, because symbolization, the transforming naming act "[reveals that] the ordinary secular concept of man held in the West [is] not merely inadequate but quite simply mistaken" (MB 158):

> Man is not merely a higher organism responding to and controlling his environment. He is [paraphrasing Heidegger] that being in the world whose calling it is to find a name for Being, to give testimony to it, and to provide for it a clearing. (MB 158)

The religious intent of Percy becomes clearer and the protest more intense. Scientists' view of man is wrong in Percy's eyes, and he is intent on finding a systematic way to prove it.

In his 1958 essay, "Metaphor As Mistake," Percy draws a tighter focus on the metaphysics of language and explores the problem of intentionality and purpose in naming. It is a remarkable combination of Kantian, mythical, and empirical concepts, in which he gives to the name an "ontological status" equivalent to the thing it names; as an "inscape" of the thing it names (Percy borrows Hopkins' term), the name "validates" the existence of the object. To begin, Percy asserts that "metaphor is the true maker of language," subsequently ascribing to the term "metaphor" both discursive naming and poetic analogy; the two, he demonstrates, have the same origin. First, he speculates on the primitive beginnings of names--the intentionality and the purpose; then he considers the implication of these concepts for his own philosophical purpose.

According to Percy and to Ernst Cassirer, whom he cites, there is in the mind of man a "need to know," a desire that calls for the satisfaction of doubt or uncertainty or simple curiosity when faced with a distinctive object or experience. This, Cassirer (after Unser and Spieth) calls the "mythico-religious Urphenomenon," the origin of language itself--when a primitive person faces something he does not understand, a thing "both entirely new to him and strikingly distinctive, so distinctive that it might be said to have a presence" (MB 69). There follows a "sense of unformulated presence of the thing" and a subsequent "emotional cry of the beholder" that becomes the word (and vehicle) by which the thing is then conceived:

> In the vocables of speech and in primitive mythic configurations, the same inner process finds its consummation: they are both resolutions of an inner tension, the representation of subjective impulses and excitations in definite object forms and figures. (Unidentified quotation by Percy, MB 69)

The thing (object or experience) is thereby given "existence" and is "validated" as having existence: it is and it is something. Thus, the name receives the power of identity and renders the object knowable and communicable. In no other manner can a thing be either conceived or shared. This method of making language, of naming names, is a matter of debate, Percy concedes, but the fact that "all peoples of our family from the Ganges to the Atlantic designate the notion of standing by the phonetic group sta-; in all of them the notion of flowing is linked with the group plu" (MB 79n) supports the mythic theory of origins to his satisfaction. There must be, he concludes, "some mysterious connection which the mind fastens upon, a connection which, since it is not a kind of univocal likeness, must be a kind of analogy" (MB 79n). To illustrate his naming theory, Percy cites a childhood experience during a hunt in south Alabama, when "at the edge of the woods we saw a beautiful bird. He flew as swift and straight as an arrow, then all of a sudden folded his wings and dropped like a stone into the woods" (MB 64). When the young Percy asked about the bird, the guide gave him the name from regional folklore, "blue dollar hawk." Later, the boy's father corrected the guide's name; it was correctly named "blue darter hawk." The point Percy makes is that the first name fitted better for the child, rendered a more appropriate ontological identity for the "dazzling speed and the effect of alternation of its wings, as if it were flying in a kind of oaring motion" (MB 64). Looking back on this childhood experience, the philosopher Percy concludes that the name is more than semantic convention, that the disappointment felt by the boy upon hearing the "correct" name was caused by the descriptive application of what the bird "did" (dart) as opposed to what the bird "was":

> Blue darter tells us something about the bird, what it does, what its color is; blue-dollar tells, or the boy hopes it will tell, what the bird is. For this ontological pairing . . . of identification of word and thing, is the only possible way in which the apprehended nature of the bird, its inscape, can be validated as being what it is. This inscape is, after all, otherwise ineffable. (MB 71-72) [Percy's emphasis]

The usefulness of Percy's conclusions regarding naming becomes clearer as his own semiotic is more fully developed, but he suggests the most important conclusion at the end of "Metaphor As Mistake": man does not know intuitively "as the angels know, directly and without mediation" or as beasts, in response to overt stimuli, but "as men, who must know one thing through the mirror of another" (MB 82). He means, of course, that cognition comes by the symbol, the only way human beings know anything at all.

Besides the mysterious naming act, there is in Percy's 1957 essay "Semiotic and a Theory of Knowledge" a new emphasis on mutuality in language (intersubjectivity) as a fundamental and irreducible element of symbolization. Just as there cannot be symbolization without a namer and a name, so there cannot be symbolization without a hearer (or receiver) of a name: "Without the presence of another [human mind] symbolization cannot conceivably occur" (MB 257):

> The irreducible condition of every act of symbolization is the rendering intelligible; that is to say, the formulation of experience for a real or an implied someone else. The presence of the two organisms is not merely a genetic requirement, a sine qua non of symbolization; it is rather its enduring condition, its indispensable climate. Every act of symboliza-tion, a naming, forming an hypothesis, creating a line of poetry, perhaps even thinking, implies another as a co-conceiver, a co-celebrant of the thing which is symbolized. Symbolization is an exercise in intersubjectivity. (MB 257)

In Percy's "human" semiotic, there exists, then, a "new and noncausal bond" between human beings, a bond of language that is the source of all human knowledge, of all human communication, and ultimately even of human identity. This is what he calls a "symbol tetrad" in his early system, because it calls for two minds, an object, and a symbol (i.e., name). Thus, in this preliminary stage of his philosophy, Percy holds that symbolic behavior is "irreducibly tetradic in structure" (MB 200).

This 1957 essay moves Percy's semiotic closer to an empirical bond between symbol and object and closer to a metaphysical (immaterial) bond between man and symbol, "between knower and the thing known" (MB 263). Percy states his hope for his system this way:

> The symbol meaning relation may be defined as not merely an intentional but as a cointentional relation of identity. The thing is intended through its symbol which you say and I can repeat, and it is only through this quasi identification that it can be conceived at all. Thus it is, I believe, that an empirical and semiotical approach to meaning illumines and confirms in an unexpected manner the realist doctrine of the

> union of the knower and the thing known. The metaphysical implications of semiotic are clear enough. Knowing is not a causal sequence but an immaterial union. It is a union, however, which is mediated through material entities, the symbol and its object. (MB 263)

Through 1958 Percy continues to write on his theme of dissent against modern science and on his theme of hope for a more radical science using semiotic, a human semiotic that will take account of the whole spectrum of human assertions--language, art, religion. In "Culture: The Antinomy of the Scientific Method"[5] and "The Loss of the Creature,"[6] Percy is particularly critical of scientists, especially semioticists, who "find themselves in a position of protesting as objective scientists against the very subject matter of their science" (MB 229). Once again he explains the "stumbling block" of science as the symbolizing behavior of man and concludes the first essay this way:

> [I]t is high time for ethnologists and other social scientists to forgo the luxury of a bisected reality, a world split between observers and data, those who know and those who behave and are "encultured." Scientists of man must accept as their "datum" that strange creature who, like themselves, is given to making assertions about the world and, like themselves, now drawing near, now falling short of the truth. It is high time for social scientists in general to take seriously the chief article of faith upon which their method is based: that there is a metascientific, metacultural reality, an order of being apart from the scientific cultural symbols with which it is grasped and expressed. The need for a more radically scientific method derives not merely from metaphysical and religious argument but also from the antinomy into which a nonradical science falls in dealing with man. (MB 242)

Percy is clearly calling for a new scientific view of man, one that will allow a higher mental dimension to incorporate cognition, intentional naming and meaning, and, not incidentally, the possibility of knowing God, the most radical of all epistemologies. In "The Loss of the Creature," published the same year, Percy scolds both the scientists who claim as their right all realms of knowledge and the laymen who relinquish without question their right to "sovereignty," the "seduction of the layman by science" (MB 63), Percy calls it. And so Percy repeats his protests against modern scientific theory and method and points out, once again, the fallacies in viewing man as a responding animal, calling instead for a new look at language, the thing man does that makes him unique among all creatures.

As Percy rails against science, he also continues his crusade for Christianity. The seriousness of his intention becomes clear in 1959 in a short allegory entitled "The Message in the Bottle."[7] The story brings together his two "themes"--man, the symbolizer, and language, the symbolizing process--in a metaphysical mission. With this piece, Percy begins in earnest his attempt to propagate his Thomist theory of language as the instrument of cognition and of faith. He opens with two contradictory quotations, one from Aquinas ("The act of faith consists essentially in knowledge") and the other from Kierkegaard ("Faith is not a form of knowledge") and concludes by taking the side of Aquinas:

> It is well known that Kierkegaard, unlike Saint Thomas, denies a cognitive content to faith--faith is not a form of knowledge. His extreme position is at least in part attributable to his anxiety to rescue Christianity from the embrace of the Hegelians. (MB 145)

> The fact is that Kierkegaard, despite his passionate dialectic, laid himself open to his enemies. For his categories of faith, inwardness, subjectivity, and Absolute Paradox seem to the objective-minded man to confirm the worst of what he had thought all along of the Christian news. (MB 145)

> [T]he message in the bottle is not enough--if the message conveys news and not knowledge sub specie aeternitatis. There must be, as Kierkegaard himself saw later, someone who delivers the news and who speaks with authority. (MB 148)

The allegory tells of a man shipwrecked on an island, a castaway who has lost his memory and so does not know anything about his past; he does not know who he is or where he comes from, and although he makes the best of life on the island--"gets a job, builds a house, takes a wife, raises a family, goes to night school, and enjoys the local arts of cinema, music and literature" (MB 119)--the castaway knows that he does not belong there, and soon begins to search the beach for bottles containing messages, hoping to learn about himself and about his rightful home. The trouble is not that he finds no messages; rather the reverse is true: he finds thousands of bottles, "tightly corked," each one containing a message, "a single piece of paper with a single sentence written on it" (MB 120). The astute castaway systematically sorts through the messages to determine which ones make scientific statements capable of being verified and which ones make "news" statements concerning life itself and the needs of the islander. Thus, the castaway who is in a "predicament" of lostness seeks news that is relevant to him, that will give him knowledge he desires about his condition. There is a second "canon of acceptance of news" that concerns the castaway, and that is the "credentials of the newsbearer" (MB 135):

> If the newsbearer is my brother or friend and if I know that he knows my predicament and if he approaches me with every outward sign of sobriety and good faith, and if the news is of a momentous nature, then I have reason to heed the news. If the newsbearer is known to me as a knave or a fool, I have reason to ignore his news. (MB 135)

And, in a footnote to clarify his meaning, Percy adds,

> If one thinks of the Christian gospel primarily as a communication between a newsbearer and a hearer of news, one realizes that the news is often not heeded because it is not delivered soberly. Instead of being delivered with sobriety with which other important news would be delivered--even by a preacher--it is spoken either in a sonorous pulpit voice or at a pitch calculated to stimulate the emotions. (MB 135n)

The message in "The Message in the Bottle" is a metaphysical appeal to postmodern man who has lost touch with the Christian concepts of sin and salvation, of God and the Incarnate Christ, and of his own spiritual identity

and purpose. It is about modern man's spiritual sickness, his "homesickness,"
because, Percy contends,

> in [man's] heart of hearts he can never forget who he is:
> that he is a stranger, a castaway, who despite a lifetime of
> striving to be at home on the island is as homeless now as
> he was the first day he found himself cast up on the beach.
> (MB 143)

Remaining true to his semiotic, Percy concludes that faith in God must
come via communication, by assertions, by symbolization. It is a "divine"
word, delivered by an "apostle" from the "sphere of transcendence":

> How then may we recognize the divine authority of the
> apostle? What, in other words, are the credentials of the
> newsbearer? The credential of the apostle is simply the
> gravity of his message: "I am called by God; do with me
> what you will, scourge me, persecute me, but my last words
> are my first; I am called by God and I make you eternally
> responsible for what you do against me." (MB 147)

In this manner, then, Percy begins delivering his message to his readers, a
"crusade," I have called it, whereby he himself might act as a quasi-apostle
sending messages in novels to castaways caught up in the modern predicament
created by atheistic science.[8]

Final Semiotic System

For eleven years, between 1961 and 1972, Walker Percy published no
new work on language, though he was active in fiction, in criticism, and in
philosophy. There is good reason for the interruption, I believe, for in the
next three essays, the last three to be written for the 1975 collection (The
Message in the Bottle)--"Toward a Triadic Theory of Meaning,"[9] "A Theory
of Language," and "Delta Factor"--he reaffirms certain enduring principles,
shifts others slightly, and adds three new components to his semiotic for which
he credits Charles Sanders Peirce, the nineteenth century American scientist-
philosopher who developed American pragmatism and originated modern
semiotics. The constants are those elements in his system which have existed

from his earliest writings in the fifties: his Christian world view, his unswerving belief in the Judeo-Christian concept of God; his devotion to science and to his search for a system which will link the empirical consequences with their metaphysical causes; and finally his theory of man as a transcending being and of language as the manifestation of man's transcendence and therefore the scientific key for unlocking, not only the complexities and contradictions in man, but some of the mysteries of God as well. In other words, from first to last, Percy is intent on merging his science with his religion for himself as well as for his readers--to inform, to warn, and, if possible, to persuade his audience about the "predicament" and the destiny of postmodern man.

The shifts in the final system are subtle, to be sure, but they should be noted. The symbol and the naming of a symbol remain paramount in Percy's final system, but an earlier concept of "pairing" becomes, in the later system, a matter of "coupling." The shift is one of focus, earlier on the symbol or word, later on the mental act of symbol-making, from ontological pairing to epistemological coupling. Closely related to this symbolization process in the mind is the shift from the earlier symbolization tetrad, comprised of two minds plus word (symbol) and object, to the ontological triad, comprised of one mind (interpretant) plus word (symbol) and object. The tetrad in his final system, he identifies as "molecular," that is, reducible as opposed to the "atomic" triad, and as the communication formula that requires intersubjectivity or mutuality rather than a symbolization formula that does not involve, directly, another person.

There are three new components in Percy's final system. The most important of these is his "Delta Factor" (Peirce's Thirdness), a way of explaining man as transcending being and thereby ascribing to him the capacity not only for empirical knowledge and understanding, but for metaphysical knowledge and understanding as well. Another new element in Percy's final semiotic is his science of language, explained in "Toward a Triadic Theory of Meaning" and "A Theory of Language." In these essays Percy treats all human speech, whether word or groups of words, as sentences (assertions), either a naming sentence, which links an object or an event with a particular sound (word) or a declarative (conventional syntactical) sentence (NP+VP). The third addition to Percy's final system is the theory of abduction (another borrowing from Peirce), a method of reaching an hypothesis and an explanatory working model for a concept. This is the way a mind works successfully, he says, because it is attuned to nature from which it came.

As I have demonstrated, Percy's early and final semiotic systems are consistent in his major philosophical positions toward religion and science; the changes occur in the scientific methods of linking the two.

I have named Charles Sanders Peirce as the mentor credited by Walker Percy for his final, "human" semiotic, for both his system of linguistics and the religious integration of that system.[10] To analyze Percy's semiotic and its connections with Charles Peirce's system, I shall generally follow the order of Percy's own arrangement of his completed (Peircean) semiotic, that is, the last three essays written for the 1975 collection: "The Delta Factor," "Toward a Triadic Theory of Meaning," and "A Language Theory."[11] I choose this arrangement because it follows a progression from elemental to complex structures: the Delta factor represents the human intellect itself; the "triadic theory" represents the process of human knowing and understanding; and the "Language Theory" represents the complex process of human communication, a sharing of knowledge in a community of "knowers." Following my examination of Percy's theories, I shall examine his sources and finally find parallels and discrepancies between the two.

I have made the point already that Percy has some inconsistencies in his essays, considered as a whole, and that these may be explained by the evolution of his semiotic in twenty years of study. I have further concluded that his system may be divided into a preliminary stage, which comes primarily from the work of Susanne Langer and Ernst Cassirer, and a final semiotic which comes primarily from the work of C. S. Peirce. Studied in the order of chronological development, the incongruities may be explained as shifts, which I have pointed out, and as a few new components from Peirce. I should repeat, however, that there are certain important constants in Percy's twenty-year development (e.g., his naming theory) and that I shall refer to those permanent elements and to preliminary essays in the course of my examination of Percy's Peircean semiotic.[12]

Percy places "The Delta Factor" at the beginning of his collection of essays for good reason; it describes the most critical component in his system, for by "Delta" he can, at last, after twenty years of trial and error, bring together his science and his religion. He can prove, to his satisfaction anyway, that because of the Delta phenomenon, man is a transcending being, and he can demonstrate by the use of Delta how language gives man this stature, not just qualitatively different from beasts, but quantitatively above them.

In a Biblical reference from Revelation at the beginning of the essay (Christ's statement "I am the Alpha and the Omega, the beginning and the end . . ."), Percy identifies Delta with man himself:

> In the beginning was the Alpha and the end is Omega, but somewhere between occurred Delta, which is nothing less than the arrival of man himself and his breakthrough into the daylight of language and consciousness and knowing, of happiness and sadness, of being with and being alone, of being right and being wrong, of being himself and being not himself, of being at home and being a stranger. (MB 3)

This epigraph suggests the theories Percy develops about the Delta phenomenon: first, it is associated with the "creation" of man; second, it gives man the ability of language and by language, consciousness and knowing; and finally, it has something to do with man's complex, paradoxical, and moral nature.

To illustrate the functions of Delta, Percy quotes Helen Keller's account of her own breakthrough into language at age eight, delayed because of blindness and deafness--a sudden, spontaneous event occurring at the well as Helen's teacher, Ann Sullivan, poured water over one hand and spelled the word in the other:

> Someone was drawing water and my teacher placed my hand under the spout. As the cool stream gushed over one hand, she spelled into the other the word water, first slowly then rapidly. I stood still, my whole attention fixed upon the motion of her fingers. Suddenly I felt a misty consciousness as of something forgotten--a thrill of returning thought; and somehow the mystery of language was revealed to me. I knew then that "w-a-t-e-r" meant the wonderful cool something that was flowing over my hand. That living word awakened my soul, gave it light, hope, joy, set it free! There were barriers still, it is true, but barriers that could in time be swept away.
>
> I left the well-house eager to learn. Everything had a name, and each name gave birth to a new thought. As we returned to the house every object which I touched seemed to quiver with life. That was because I saw everything with the strange, new sight that had come to me. On entering the door I remembered the doll I had broken. [She had earlier destroyed the doll in a fit of temper.] I felt my way to the hearth and picked up the pieces. I tried vainly to put them together. Then my eyes filled with tears; for I realized what I had done, and for the first time I felt repentance and sorrow. (MB 34-35)

The first association suggested for Delta is a clue to the creation of man, a sudden leap from a lower, unintelligent being to a higher, intelligent being. Using a scientific frame, Percy speculates that this leap must have occurred rather recently, relative to the earth's age and life itself, and that Helen's breakthrough "must bear some relation to the breakthrough of the species . . ." (MB 38):

> Life has existed on earth for perhaps three billion years, yet Delta could not be more than a million years old, no older certainly than Homo erectus and perhaps a great deal more recent, as late as the time of Homo neanderthalensis, when man underwent an astonishing evolutionary explosion which in the scale of earth time was a sudden as the biblical creation. Was not in fact the sudden 54 percent increase in brain size not the cause but the consequence of the true urphenomenon, the jumped circuit by which Delta first appeared? The spark jumped, language was born, the brain flowered with words, and man became man. (MB 42)

And again,

> Man became man by breaking into the daylight of language-- whether by good fortune or bad fortune, whether by pure change, the spark jumping the gap because the gap was narrow enough, or by the touch of God, it is not for me to say here. (MB 45)

Obviously, Percy is suggesting that the genesis of man may have been, like the Genesis account, supernatural (the "spark jumped") and, like the biologists' account, natural (the brain of the beast suddenly increased in size and became capable of thought). It is one way, at least, of reconciling a religious predilection with a scientific education.

The second theory regarding Delta--that it is associated with "the daylight of language and consciousness and knowing"--is also demonstrated in Helen Keller's experience. For the first time she was conscious of "things" (as I have pointed out elsewhere, Percy believes that the mind is not conscious unless it is conscious of something), and knew that everything had a "meaning" and, further, that meaning of things was "held" in language. It was a transforming experience for Helen; she became, for the first time, a transcending being rather than the responding child she had been, signaling and answering to signals. And her first impulse as a "languaged" being was to learn: "Everything had a name and each name gave birth to a new thought.

. . . [E]very object which I touched seemed to quiver with life" (<u>MB</u> 35). In her new awareness of language, she realized that there was a "world" and that everything in the world had a name that gave it existence. And in the ensuing hours, words made the world "blossom" for her "'like Aaron's rod with flowers'": "a strange, new sight . . . had come to me" (<u>MB</u> 35). The word "sight" is figurative, of course, but an important figure of speech for blind Helen Keller, for the understanding that had just been opened in her mind was obviously like sight to her.

The last function of Percy's Delta has to do with man's nature: the complexities, the contradictions, the paradoxes of man. At the beginning of "The Delta Factor," there are six pages of questions about man's odd behavior, questions like

> Why does man feel so sad in the twentieth century? [and]
> Why is it that if [a commuter] suffers a heart attack and,
> taken off the train at New Rochelle, regains consciousness
> and finds himself in a strange place, he then comes to
> himself for the first time in years, perhaps in his life, and
> begins to gaze at his own hand with a sense of wonder and
> delight? (<u>MB</u> 4)

The writer asks fifty-five such rhetorical questions which serve to focus the reader's attention on the "upside-down" nature of man, for, Percy asserts, organisms (the scientific classification of man) by nature adapt to their environment and, given the satisfaction of all biological needs, are "contented." But such is not the case with twentieth century man. Again, Percy demonstrates his theory with Helen Keller, who underwent, not only an intellectual transformation, but a moral one as well. She tells of making her way to the hearth where she had broken her doll in a fit of temper and, picking up the pieces, tried vainly to mend the toy: "Then my eyes filled with tears; for I realized what I had done and <u>for the first time</u> [my emphasis] I felt repentance and sorrow" (<u>MB</u> 35). The implication is clear: Helen recognizes, for the first time, that there exists a moral law in the universe and that she has violated it. Following that realization, she feels remorse, "repentance and sorrow." Whatever the connection between language and moral awareness, Helen does not speculate, nor does Percy, directly, but the implication is there, and the relevance is critical in Percy's philosophy of language.

Percy compares his own breakthrough into the Delta theory to Helen Keller's breakthrough into the use of Delta, "on the day I was thinking about Helen Keller . . . [and] making a breakthrough like Helen's, the difference being that her breakthrough was a sudden understanding of what she did" (MB 30).

What he discovers is that Helen did not behave as behaviorists had taught him she should--like "an organism responding to a learned signal" (MB 31), but like a

> name-giving and sentence-uttering creature who begins by naming shoes and ships and sealing wax, and later tells jokes, curses, reads the paper . . . or becomes a Hegel and composes an entire system of philosophy. (MB 35)

Helen demonstrates a symbol-reading mind by coupling a name with a thing and producing a triangle of subjects: mind, word, thing:

> My breakthrough was the sudden inkling that the triangle was absolutely irreducible. Here indeed was nothing less, I suspected, than the ultimate and elemental unit not only of language but of the very condition of the awakening of human intelligence and consciousness.
>
> What to call it? "Triad"? "Triangle"? "Thirdness"? Perhaps "Delta phenomenon," the Greek letter, signifying irreducibility. (MB 40)

This "meaning triangle" or triad Percy refers to is the second Peircean concept he adopts for his own system, a theory he describes in his 1972 essay "Toward a Triadic Theory of Meaning" (MB 159), his first Peircean essay. He introduces his essay with credits to Charles S. Peirce but allows himself freedom in his adaptations from the earlier system:

> What follows is adapted freely from Peirce, with all credit to Peirce, and space will not be taken to set down what was originally Peirce and what are adaptations . . . . Peirce was unlucky, in that his views on language were put forward as part of a metaphysic . . . and in a language uncongenial to modern behavioral attitudes. . . . The problem is to disentangle from the metaphysic those insights which are germane to a view of language as behavior. (MB 160-61)

Percy's attempt to disentangle language behavior from the fundamental metaphysical philosophy is impossible, as Percy well knows, but for "scientific appeal," perhaps, or for reader appeal, Percy does avoid the "heavy metaphysic" which supports the whole Peircean system.

Percy introduces Peirce's triadic theory of signs by contrasting it with the theories of his old antagonist, behaviorism. From Charles Peirce he discovers that when an action (or stimulus) produces a reaction (or response), it manifests a "dyadic" relation, and here he quotes Peirce:

> All dynamical action, or action of brute force, physical or psychical, either takes place between two subjects . . . or at any rate is a resultant of such action between pairs . . . . (MB 161)

This is true of every non-intelligent interaction in the universe--an action and counteraction in inanimate nature or a stimulus and response in non-human animate life--a performance of pairs. Every natural phenomenon except thought may be termed dyadic, a relation or an interaction between two things. Human mental activity, however, is different, as Percy has demonstrated in Helen Keller's experience with language and meaning; this is a triadic activity and is generated, not by a "signal," in Percy's system, but by a symbol. For this distinction, Percy again quotes Charles Peirce:

> [B]y "semiosis" I mean . . . an action, or influence, which is, or involves, a cooperation of three subjects, such as a sign, its object, and its interpretant, this tri-relative influence not being resolvable into actions between pairs. (MB 161)

In other words, a triadic relationship involves "meaning" and is accomplished, in Percy's semiotic, only by a symbol which carries the meaning of an object or an experience to a symbol-reading mind.

To demonstrate Percy's theory of a meaning-producing activity, i.e., naming, which is the meaning triad in its simplest form, I shall refer to one earlier essay and to the final two essays written for The Message in the Bottle. In his first linguistic essay, "Symbol As Need," he explains the relationship between word and object (between name and thing), a scholastic theory that he finds repeated in Susanne Langer's work and that remains intact throughout his own linguistic development, the idea that the word "contains" the thing it names in "another mode of existence" and that the word (or name) disappears before the thing, loses its own identity and "becomes" the thing it represents. It forms a receptacle, and it becomes a vehicle to transfer meaning to the symbol-reading mind and between symbol-reading minds. In "The Delta Factor," the introductory essay for the collection and the last one to be written, Percy adds the third element in the symbol triad by demonstrating Helen Keller's triadic experience. Helen feels the word "water" formed in one hand and feels the cool liquid flowing over the other hand and mentally puts together (couples) the word with the object and "knows" that the word "means" the thing. It is, Percy emphasizes, an irreducible triad of elements: the mind, the symbol, and the object.

The term "coupling" (by the mind) is original with Percy, though the idea itself is Peircean. In the last essay in The Message in the Bottle--"A Theory of Language"--Percy explains the concept; it is his way of assigning to the human mind a unique natural ability that allows man to transcend his physical environment and to gain knowledge via language rather than by senses only. He compares his theory to Noam Chomsky's LAD (language acquisition device), an innate, unexplainable component of the mind that gives the human, by age two or three, the ability to use language and to understand language with only "minimal input," a transforming ability of the mind to couple sound (word or symbol) with the thing it represents. "Coupling" is Percy's explanatory hypothesis of the work of the human mind, a theory he compares with Malpighi's working hypothesis of the kidneys as a filter and with Harvey's theory of the heart as a unidirectional pump. The logic for his hypothesis is simple: If two ontological entities are coupled (as in the case of language), there must be a coupler. What the coupler does, then, he knows by the evidence, but what it is remains in question: "The apex of the triangle, the coupler, is a complete mystery. What it is, an 'I,' a 'self,' or some neurophysiological correlate thereof I could not begin to say" (MB 327). The "meaning" triad, in Percy's system, like Peirce's symbolic triad, is the fundamental structure of language, an irreducible unit.

Following the progression from elemental to complex language behavior in Percy's system, from the Delta phenomenon of language consciousness on the first level to the triad of meaning on the second level, I shall examine the communication process, what Percy calls his "tentative account of sentence utterance" (MB 166). For this too he credits Charles Sanders Peirce as its progenitor and gives "a loose set of postulates and definitions which I take to be suitable for a behavioral schema of symbol use and which might be adapted from Peirce's theory of triads" (MB 165).

The most important component of Percy's behavioral theory of language is his concept of sentence utterance. It is the "basic unit" of language behavior, and there are two types: the "naming" sentence and the declarative sentence. All triadic utterance should be understood as sentence utterance, for words conveying meaning in a symbol triad never stand alone, independent of context and intention. Because of intention and word content, whether single word utterances or syntactically composed sentences, "meaning" triads should be construed as sentences. The simplest is the naming sentence that may be comprised of only the pointing finger of a father toward a ball and the utterance of a single word "ball." If the child makes the connection and understands that the word "ball" is the object ball, a naming sentence has been accomplished:

> A word has no meaning except as part of a sentence. Single-word utterances are either understood as sentences or else they are not understood at all. . . . If I say "pickle" to you, you must either understand the utterance as a sentence- -this is a pickle, this is a picture of a pickle, pass the pickles, tastes like a pickle--or you will ask me what I mean or perhaps say, "What about pickles?" (MB 166)

Percy describes the process of the language facility of children as beginning with the naming stage, called "open construction," near the age of two when the child begins to learn names (and meanings) of things. He demonstrates the sentence formula this way:

> $S = (I) (E_c) (is) S_c$
> where $\underline{I}$, the index, is in this case an item of behavior (e.g., a pointing at or looking at), $\underline{E}_c$ is the thing or quality or action experienced by the child and indicated as one of a class of such experiences, (is) is the copula dispensed with until the final adult form, $\underline{S}_c$ is the contentive word, usually a sound--e.g., noun $\underline{ball}$, adjective $\underline{yellow}$, verb $\underline{hop}$--uttered as a member of a class of such words. (MB 313)

The second stage he calls the "pivot-open" constructions (Percy cites Brown, Bellugi, and Ervin) when a child uses two-word phrases--"$\underline{my\ sock}$, $\underline{my}$ $\underline{boat}$, $\underline{my\ plane}$"--that often serve as "functors" to designate specific objects or, as in the case of "my," ownership. Language use thus advances in coherent stages toward "adult" syntax.

The other basic class of linguistic sentences is the declarative sentence, the NP-VP sentence. This too is first acquired around the age of two but without the full syntactical form. Following the naming state (single contentive words), the declarative sentence simply adds another contentive word, e.g., baby highchair, which may mean "The baby is in the highchair" or "The baby wants his highchair," etc. Percy speculates on the development of the two basic sentences this way: The naming sentence is learned when the child learns to couple a semiological component (something seen or experienced) with a phonological component (uttered word) into, what Percy calls a "semophone" to build "an inventory, or lexicon, of semantically contentive words through which the world of experience is segmented, perceived, abstracted from, and named" (MB 316):

> The semological and phonological components of the semophone are thoroughly interpenetrated. The resulting configuration is a much more stable and enduring entity than can be expressed by association psychology. Thus it is not so much the case that words like yellow, wet, hop, Elmer, quick "call up" such and such an association or have such and such a "connotation." Rather is it the case that these sounds are interpenetrated and transformed by the classes of experience to which they refer. The contentive word in a sense contains the thing. "Yellow" becomes yellow. (MB 317)

At the second stage, the declarative sentence is then formed by coupling semophones. By the age of three or so, a child has the ability to form a "practically unlimited number of new sentences . . . following the input of limited and fragmentary data" (MB 317). Using his hypothesis of the mind as a coupler, Percy accounts for the phenomenal growth of language ability this way: If the number of semophones in a child's vocabulary is 100 by age three, that number (minus itself) may be squared ($N^2 - N$) and render a possible 9,900 open-open sentence combinations; e.g., "car wet, car Daddy, Daddy wet, Daddy sock," etc. (MB 317). To increase that number even more, a single pair of coupled semophones may be understood by its context to carry a number of different intentions:

> [C]ar Daddy can be reliably understood by the mother [to mean] "Daddy is getting in the car," "Daddy is washing the car," "Daddy is kicking the car," depending on whether in fact

"Daddy is getting in the car, washing the car, kicking the car.
(MB 317)

In the language theory of Walker Percy, as for C. S. Peirce, there is, by the very nature of language as a cultural component, an interpretative community. This is what Percy refers to in his preliminary essays as intersubjectivity; there can be no naming on the first level of development unless, as he explains, "you tell me that this thing is a chair and I understand that contentive word as being the object I sit in"; thus, we agree on the coupling and the content: "This is a chair for you and me" (MB 282). By the interpretative community, language is created and shared, Percy maintains; we are born into language; by it we are conscious, not only of ourselves, but of the world in which we live.

Language is also "received and uttered in a world" (MB 173). Everything man experiences must have a name; the world "must be totally accounted for"; this is part of human nature, Percy implies:

> A chicken will respond to the sight of a hawk but not to the sight of a tree. But a child wishes to know what a tree "is."
>
> A chicken does not know whether the earth is flat or round or a bowl, but a man, primitive or technological, will account for the earth one way or another. (MB 173)

There may, of course, be imaginary worlds, past worlds, future worlds, but language can facilitate all worlds and all contexts that are possible in the mind of man.

The last criterion of language utterance is the "normative" dimension, a "fundamental property of the coupling of the elements of the sentence" (MB 176). That is, the proposition of the statement may be good or bad, the fact of a sentence may be true or false; meaning may be measured by some standard to which it applies:

> "Clouds are fleece" is false as a literal statement, true in a
> sense as a metaphor, bad in the sense of being a trite
> metaphor.
>
> "This is a sparrow" may be a true assertion of a class
> relationship but it may also be perfunctory, a bored
> assignment of a commonplace object (English sparrow) to a
> commonplace class. (MB 177)

Thus, there can be mistakes in language behavior, mistakes in logic, data, intention, context, interpretation. And this creates problems for all "symbol-mongers," but especially, Percy suggests, for the "trader" in words, i.e., the novelist. So when words lose their original interpretive content, as theological terms have done (e.g., "baptism," "salvation," "sin"), the writer of Christian fiction must say what he wants to say in other words, must use all the "cunning and guile" and often shock in order to inform and to warn, as well as to entertain his readers.

The borrowings of Walker Percy from Charles S. Peirce are not always clear, for Percy has not documented them all, nor are they consistent because he has, as he says, adapted certain features and omitted others. To discover the indebtedness of Percy to his mentor Charles Sanders Peirce, I shall examine the fundamental features of Peirce's semiotic, using where I need to, some clarifying developments made by Josiah Royce, student and popularizer of Peirce.

NOTES

[1] Martin Luschei wrote the first definitive study linking Percy with Kierkegaard and tenuously with other European existentialists, a link that, Luschei says, resulted from Percy's reading of Kierkegaard, Dostoevsky, Camus, Sartre, and Marcel during a prolonged illness in 1942-45. It is true, Luschei admits, that there are difficulties in fitting Percy into the existentialist mold; it "seems to go against the grain," but he adds that "I have found in every case that the difficulty was inherent in the subject, the question only the extent to which I understood it" (20n).

[2] Percy has encouraged this critical interpretation of his writing by citing attractions to existentialism. In a 1961 interview with Judith Serebnick, Percy verifies his interest in the existentialist movement "that led directly to the writing of a novel, The Moviegoer" (597). And in a 1962 interview with Harriet Doar, he adds that his aim was "to Americanize the [European existentialist] movement" (Conversations 5). Repeatedly in interviews, Percy speaks of Kierkegaard's modes of existence found in his own novels, beginning with The Moviegoer, of his own application of existentialist phenomenology, that is, starting with "a man in a concrete situation, exploring reality in a way which cannot be one any other way" (Cremeens 27), of authentic-inauthentic existence, of rotation and repetition, of Kierkegaard's "root of all evil"-- everydayness. It is easy to see why critics continue to identify Percy with existentialism and to interpret his novels in those terms.

[3] In an interview with Bradley Dewey, Percy credits Kierkegaard with exposing Hegel's impersonal philosophy, saying "that Hegel knew everything and said everything, except what it is to be born and to live and to die" (Conversations 109). In other words, Kierkegaard expressed for the young Percy what the young man felt about "the whole scientific synthesis" and offered him a new way of viewing religion:

> So what was important about Kierkegaard to me
> was that he was a man who was trying to open up
> a whole new area of knowledge to me in the
> most serious way, the most precise way--and quite
> as serious as any science--or more serious. And,
> of course, it was religious too. This was a far cry
> from the other alternative that I had always read
> about, that the alternative to science is art, play,
> emotion. I saw for the first time through

> Kierkegaard how to take the alternative system
> seriously, how to treat it as a serious thinker, as
> a serious writer. Before that I would have simply
> seen it as just religion or emotion. (110)

[4] See Bradley interview, 1954, rpt. in <u>Conversations With Walker Percy</u>, 111.

[5] First published in <u>New Scholasticism</u> 32 (Oct. 1958): 443-75. Rpt. in <u>MB</u>: 215-42.

[6] First published in <u>Forum</u> 2 (Fall 1958): 6-14. Rpt. in <u>MB</u>: 46-63.

[7] First published in <u>Thought</u> 34 (1959): 405-33. Rpt. in <u>MB</u>: 119-49.

[8] In 1961 Percy published his first novel, <u>The Moviegoer</u>, which, like his later novels, may be read as an allegory illustrating his Christian concept of the lost man's search for God. He explains his purpose in an interview that same year for the <u>Library Journal</u>: "My novel is an attempt to portray the rebellion of two young people against the shallowness and tastelessness of modern life. . . . In Binx it is a 'metaphysical' rebellion--a search for meaning . . ." (<u>Conversations</u> 3) and again in a 1966 interview: "I use the fiction form as a vehicle for incarnating my ideas" (<u>Conversations</u> 9). In a later interview with Carlton Cremeens, he speaks of the seriousness of his purpose:

> Now, in changing . . . to creative writing, I am
> equally convinced of the absolute seriousness of
> that. . . . I think that serious novel writing . . . is
> just as important, and just as cognitive; it
> concerns areas of knowing, of discovering and
> knowing, just as much as any science. In fact, in
> art, particularly in the modern novel, you are
> dealing with areas of life which cannot be
> reached in any other way. (<u>Conversations</u> 27)

About his theological intention, he adds,

> [A]lienation, after all, is nothing more or less
> than a very ancient, orthodox Christian doctrine.
> Man is alienated by the nature of his being here.
> He is here as a stranger and as a pilgrim, which
> is the way alienation is conceived in my books.

> It's the orthodox sort of alienation, but expressed,
> I hope, in an unorthodox or fresh language.
> (<u>Conversations</u> 29)

By the mid-sixties Percy's purpose for his fiction writing is clearly established; he has a message for modern America (Christianity) and the mode of presenting it (the philosophical novel).

The second novel, <u>The Last Gentleman</u>, was published in 1966, and like <u>The Moviegoer</u>, it depicts a young man on a quest. Not only is Williston Barrett lost spiritually, he is also lost geographically, and so he sets out on a twofold mission: a search for an earthly father and a search for a heavenly Father. Compared with Binx, Barrett, Percy says, is "a good deal sicker":

> In the conventional view of things he is very sick.
> His symptoms of epilepsy, <u>deja vu</u>, and so
> on . . . . Both of them are alienated, but Binx
> enjoys his alienation. . . . Barrett, on the other
> hand, has a passionate pilgrimage that he must
> follow . . . . (<u>Conversations</u> 13)

In 1967, while working on his third novel, Percy wrote an essay--"Notes for a Novel About the End of the World"--in which he presents more fully his ideas about his own mission as a writer. First, he identifies himself as a writer who "is concerned with the radical question of man's identity and his relation to God or to God's absence" (<u>MB</u> 108). It is not a plot per se that interests him nor a large cast of characters, he says, but rather the movement of a single man, "a stranger in a strange land where the signposts are enigmatic but which he sets out to explore nevertheless" (<u>MB</u> 102). Further, as a writer with a message to present, Percy views his role as a "quasi-prophetic function" that "should shock and thereby warn his readers of last things. . . (<u>MB</u> 104). For example, the sort of protagonists he creates is the businessman or the professional who is reasonably well off financially, whose biological and cultural needs are met, but who is lost to himself and who, often, contemplates suicide: he is miserable with his existence and, subsequently, after experiencing some ordeal, "comes to himself," realizes his predicament of lostness, and initiates a search for some meaning to his existence and a quest for God. Again about his purpose, Percy adds,

> As it happens, I speak in a Christian context.
> This is to say, I do not conceive it my vocation to
> preach the Christian faith in a novel, but as it
> happens, my world view is informed by a certain

> belief about man's nature and destiny which
> cannot fail to be central to any novel I write.
> (<u>MB</u> 111)

Finally, Percy sees his mission as a task beset by major obstacles. For one thing, he has, he says, cast his lot with outmoded, "discredited Christendom"; it is no longer intellectually acceptable to believe in the claims of Christianity, for science has explained away the old-fashioned "myths" of the Church. Therefore, the vocabulary of Christianity is "defunct"; one cannot use terms like "sin," "salvation," "baptism"; they no longer apply to reality as postmodern man views it. So Percy concludes that as a Christian writer, he must "[call] on every ounce of cunning, craft, and guile he can muster from the darker regions of his soul. The fictional use of violence, shock, comedy, insult, the bizarre are the everyday tools of his trade" (<u>MB</u> 118).

The eschatological novel about which Percy writes in the 1967 essay was published in 1971--<u>Love in the Ruins: The Adventures of a Bad Catholic</u>. Among the first three novels, it is by far the most blatantly allegorical. The name of the protagonist, Thomas More, establishes a link with an earlier period in Church history and with a man who had great influence in that history, a martyr for his religious principles. The twentieth century American Thomas More, a distant descendant of the sixteenth century British prelate, reflects a post-Christian, scientific view of moral matters. Instead of preaching and teaching moral reform, Tom More, a medical doctor, designs an instrument, called a "Qualitative Quantitative Ontological Lapsometer," to test the condition of man's soul. Like his predecessor, More is a Roman Catholic, "Albeit a bad one," who believes in "the Holy Catholic Apostolic and Roman Church, in God the Father, in the election of the Jews, in Jesus Christ His Son our Lord, who founded the Church on Peter his first vicar, which will last until the end of the world" (<u>LR</u> 6). But he does not attend mass, has "fallen into a disorderly life," and ranks his priorities this way: "I love women best, music and science next, whiskey next, God fourth, and my fellowman hardly at all" (<u>LR</u> 6). Tom admits to professional pride in his new instrument, which "can probe the very secrets of the soul, diagnose the maladies that poison the wellsprings of man's hope" (<u>LR</u> 7) and secretly imagines himself being honored as "the latterday Archimedes who found the place to insert his lever and turn the world not upside down but right side up!" (<u>LR</u> 7). Of Sir Thomas More, the latter More offers praise for the man's good temper and strong faith and excuses for his own "longings for women, for the Nobel Prize, for the hot bosky bit of bourbon whiskey, and other great heart-wrenching longings that have no name"; then he adds, "Sir Thomas was right, of course, and I am wrong. But on the other hand these are peculiar times" (<u>LR</u> 23).

Specifically, the "peculiar times" represent, in Percy's novel, post-Christian, postmodern, atheistic, science-ruled America, where man is, like man in every age, lost and alienated, but where man, unlike man in Christian eras, has no inkling about his condition.

⁹ Psychiatry 35 (Feb. 1972): 1-19.

¹⁰ In C. S. Peirce's system, one finds the same dedication to Christianity that Percy demonstrates, and an even greater (and more complex) effort to systematize his religion by history and by investigative science. Early in his career Peirce developed his Christian world view based on history. In an address given in 1863--"The Place of Our Age in the History of Civilization"--he explains the theory, from which his logic is derived, by tracing the development of science and philosophy from ancient Greece to the present age. The entire history of metaphysics, the mother of science, may be divided into two systems: the Greek and the Jewish. The Greeks gave the world the idea of God; the Jews gave the world the substance of religion, the tangible evidence of God working in human history and ultimately entering history as a Human Being. Thus, in Peirce's view, all of history becomes a cosmic language expressing God's existence and purpose. The Jews, offering the earliest manifestation of God in history, understood the plan of God and the laws of God working through their race; they understood what the miraculous course of their history could convey, and they knew "that they were to be taken care of and saved as a nation" (WP 1. 107). Likewise, after the advent of the Messiah, when "the promise was extended to the Gentiles," sacred history incorporated a wider field, so that Christians, like the Jews,

> believe that Christ is now directing the course of history and presiding over the destinies of kings, and that there is no branch of the public weal which does not come within the bounds of his realm. And civilization is nothing but Christianity on a grand scale. (WP 1. 107-08)

In other words, Peirce views the whole history of man as a cosmic holy drama communicating to man the existence of God, the First Cause and the Eternal I AM.

Peirce adds, further, that in the course of history God has used three methods of revealing himself to man: [1] "by an inward self-development, . . . [2] by seeing [revelation] about us, and [3] by a personal communication from the Most High" (WP 1. 109). The first, "inward self-development," comes via nature which excites the mind with its beauty and sublimity "until the idea [of God] becomes rooted in [the] heart" (<u>WP</u> 1. 109). In the second, "seeing [revelation] about us," events of life itself as well as work of the Christian community manifest God daily: "we no sooner get to recognize religion, than we learn from people of higher attainment, as out of a book" (<u>WP</u> 1. 109). The third method, "personal communication" or immediate (subjective) revelation, is only a hope for the future, but as men now are, they "receive only sufficient grace to understand a portion of prophecy" (<u>WP</u> 1. 109). Christianity remains "objectively impressed" on the human consciousness in "its full manifestation of [Christ] and in lesser lights of the Church" (<u>WP</u> 1. 109).

Finally, drawing his system of historical religion closer to logic and objective science, Peirce recognizes again the two scientific views regarding reality--one (idealism), the theory of reality in ideas or abstractions and, the second (materialism), the theory of reality in things--then places himself between the two, naming his own philosophy Objective Idealism, by which he means that science (and religion) can begin only on what is known via the senses, the laws of nature. But, he adds, materialism will ultimately prove itself incomplete--by its own logical deduction of causes--and first, through poets, the prophets of the modern age, then through science, the seeker of causes,

> man will see God's wisdom and mercy, not only in the event of his own life, but in that of the gorilla, the lion, the fish, the polyp, the tree, the crystal, the grain of dust, the atom, for which God loves it, and that He has given to it a nature of endless perfectibility. (<u>WP</u> 1. 114)

Although this work came early in Peirce's career, the ideas it expresses were not temporary or isolated; throughout his life he pursued his goal of linking science and religion. Thirty years after the "History of Civilization" speech, he wrote an essay entitled "The Marriage of Religion and Science" in which he defines science as "a living and growing body of truth," a spirit "which is determined not to rest satisfied with existing opinions, but to press on to the real truth of nature" (<u>CP</u> 6. 429). Religion he defines as

> a deep recognition of a something in the circumambient All, which, if [man] strives to express it, will clothe itself in forms more or less extravagant, more or less accidental, but ever acknowledging the first and last, the [Alpha] and [Omega], as well as a relation to that Absolute of

the individual's self, as a relative being. (CP 6. 429)

In its development, science moved "unswervingly its own gait," letting itself "be guided by nature's strong hand," and religion, "compelled to define her position" and "inevitably [to commit] herself to sundry positions . . . [was] first questioned, then assailed, and finally overthrown by advancing science" (CP 6. 430), and since then the two have been forced into different camps, holding hostile attitudes toward each other. But Peirce concludes that a permanent separation is not inevitable; the two will eventually be linked by truth:

> The day has come . . . when the man whom religious experience most devoutly moves can recognize the state of the case. While adhering to the essence of religion, and so far as possible to the church, which is all but essential, . . . he will cast aside religious timidity that is forever prompting the church to recoil from the paths into which the Governor of history is leading the minds of men . . . and will gladly go forward, sure that truth is not split into warring doctrines, and that any change that knowledge can work in his faith can only affect its expression, but not the deep mystery expressed.

> Such a state of mind may properly be called a religion of science, . . . a religion so true to itself that it becomes animated by the scientific spirit, confident that all conquests of science will be triumphs of its own. . . . (CP 6. 434)

It is clear that C. S. Peirce, like his follower Walker Percy, was driven by the desire to bring together his two lifetime pursuits--science and Christianity. Because of this affinity, then, Percy was naturally drawn to Peirce's science of signs as the proper way to link the two.

[11] Jay Paul Tellotte has reviewed Walker Percy's debt to Charles Peirce and notes that whereas "Percy's existential leanings are common knowledge . . . what has to be established . . . is that Percy's work draws heavily on American intellectual tradition such as that represented by Peirce" ("Walker Percy: A Pragmatic Approach" 224) and then summarizes the particular points of indebtedness: the triadic theory of man, the abductive principle, pragmaticism, and methods of inquiry and "self-creation." In that essay and

less thoroughly in three others--"Walker Percy's Language of Creation," "A Symbolic Structure for Walker Percy's Fiction," and "Charles Peirce and Walker Percy: From Semiotic to Narrative"--he discusses the influence of Peirce on Percy's narrative form.

[12] Peirce uses the word "sign" as a generic term to mean any representational device and "symbol" to refer to a representational device that transfers meaning to a scientific (intelligent) mind; e.g., language, art, ritual. For Percy, the word "symbol" carries the same meaning as for Peirce, but for non-intelligent, responding creatures, he prefers the word "signal" rather than "sign."

CHAPTER 2

THE COSMIC SEMIOTIC OF CHARLES SANDERS PEIRCE

Introduction

In his semiotic, Charles Peirce uses the term "language" or "logos" in the broadest sense, of "cosmic" speech, that is, any sign in the universe from which man derives meaning and intention. By this view, language is not speech only and certainly not a single linguistic system, but all things that come into man's consciousness as identifiable entities. It quickly becomes apparent that "intentional" meaning given in natural phenomena in the universe must, like the intentional language of man, have a Speaker who intends meaning and who directs it to minds that perceive such "speech." What this means, of course, is that in Peirce's universal semiotic, there is a Creator God who established His own "semiotic" at creation to reveal to man, not only His existence, but His nature as well. This is the foundation of Peirce's semiotic theory; the particulars emanate from this theological center.

The particulars to which I refer are a complex of scientific and theological concepts so closely interrelated that they cannot be reasonably isolated for independent analysis; to do so would destroy the unity that is critical to the system. To ascribe a certain order of presentation, therefore, I shall arrange the analysis in an "ascending" order, a progression from the most scientific to the most metaphysical theories. This, I take to be Peirce's own intention because he, like Walker Percy following him, wanted to join the two worlds, the physical with the metaphysical, and to do so in an intellectual, systematic, and convincing manner; that means beginning with verifiable actuality and moving in logical steps toward an unverifiable probability. Following the design I have set for the presentation, then, I shall examine Peirce's semiotic from three perspectives: his system of categories (Firstness,

Secondness, Thirdness) and triadicity, his theory of man, and his theory of agapasm or evolutionary love.

<u>Peirce's Theory of Categories</u>

To understand Peirce's cosmic semiotic and its relation to theology, one must first understand his theory of universal categories, which is his explanation of the logic of the universe itself and the basic formula of thought by which anything is known. The Aristotelian system of philosophy acknowledges two universal categories or modes of being: there is, first, matter, which crowds out a place for itself and which, in the course of evolution, assumes a second form, in a universal mode of existence. Peirce retains these two fundamental categories of classical philosophy, which he names "Secondness" for the tangible existents and "Firstness" for the intangible, universal mode; then he adds a third category ("Thirdness"), equal to the other two and serving as a link between them. Thus did Peirce adapt his triadic scheme from the ancient binary scheme as a way of looking at and speaking of the universe. The immediate world, the "manifold of sense," exists "out there," as "Seconds" independent of and separate from human thoughts about it, but is made actual only by relation to a universal quality that does not exist materially ("Firstness"). It is the role of Thirdness to bring the two together by language or language surrogate (e.g., art and ritual).

As early as 1861, when Charles Peirce was only twenty-two years old, he had already devised his triadic theory of categories, representing three distinct "worlds" of being, which he identified, at that time, with the personal pronouns: I, IT, and THOU.[1] But it was not until 1894, apparently, that Peirce arrived at his final system of categories, based on his earlier principles, only more refined. Firstness, by definition abstract and unformulated, is a mere possibility, a feeling, or a quality. It may be thought of as a "monad," that is a "suchness <u>sui generis</u>" which comes to mind as "a vague, unobjectified, unsubjectified" sensation--a "sense of redness, or of salt taste, or of an ache, or of grief or joy, or of a prolonged musical note" (CP 1. 303). Firstness is what it is regardless of anything else and distinct from all else.

Edward Moore has drawn distinctions among three aspects of Firstness: possibility, quality, or feeling (406). As a possibility, Firstness exists only in and of itself, but in such manner that it "may perhaps come into relation with others" (406). It lies "between a mere nothing and an existing thing" (406): it cannot be said to be nothing because "nothing," as defined by Peirce, is self-contradictory, and a First as possibility cannot be said to negate itself, since it has the potential to become existent events. As a possibility, Firstness is also general or universal in the classical sense, that which belongs to the many. In an assertion or proposition, for example, the predicate is a First, a general quality, something that is said about an individual subject or any number of individuals.

As a quality, Firstness is identified as "sensible" elements of phenomena, "that in which we attend to each part as it appears in itself," e.g., red, sour, toothache as "sui generis and indescribable" (CP 1. 424). It is the overall impression of a thing without identification or signification:

> We naturally attribute Firstness to outward objects, that is
> we suppose they have capacities in themselves which may or
> may not be already actualized, which may or may not ever
> be actualized. . . . (CP 1. 25)

A "quality" of Firstness is manifested as a "disturbance of consciousness," a feeling "distinct from objective perception, will, and thought" (CP 1. 302). By "feeling," Peirce intends a kind of awareness that "involves no analysis, comparison, or any process whatsoever . . . that sort of element of consciousness which is all that it is positively, in itself, regardless of anything else" (CP 1. 306). Not to be confused with an event or an object, a feeling may be thought of as a "state," so that "whatever is in the mind in any mode of consciousness . . . [produces] an immediate consciousness and consequently a feeling" (CP 1. 310). Paradoxically, the feeling of Firstness cannot be analyzed or known by introspection because it is immediate consciousness, the "eyebeam of the eye":

> All that is immediately present to a man is what is in his mind in the present instant. His whole life is in the present. But when he asks what is the content of the present instant, his question comes too late. The present has gone by, and what remains of it is greatly metamorphosed. (CP 1. 310)

To be conscious is to feel ("Pure priman") (CP 1. 318), and a feeling is "nothing but a quality, and a quality is not conscious; it is mere possibility" (CP 1. 310).

Finally, it is important to note Peirce's theory of communicability of feelings of Firstness, the idea that red is the same hue for every human mind, that human beings can enter into one another's feelings, and that even men and animals can communicate on certain levels of emotion:

> You would never persuade me that my horse and I do not sympathize, or that the canary bird that takes such delight in joking with me does not feel with me and I with him. . . . (CP 1. 314)
>
> . . . Every scientific explanation of a natural phenomenon is a hypothesis that there is something in nature to which the human reason is analogous; and that it really is so all the successes of science in its application to human convenience are witness. . . . In the light of the successes of science to my mind there is a degree of baseness in denying our birthright as children of God and in shamefacedly slinking away from anthropomorphic conceptions of the universe. (CP 1. 316)

In other words, there exists an overarching unity or harmony in the cosmos, in Peirce's view of things, so that man may sense or feel, if not prove, what may finally be linked with God as Creator and Harmonizer of all things. Charles Hartshorne has noted the similarity between Peirce's absolutely non-relative First and the idea of "some primordial and eternal essence, or realm of essences, the pure possibility of existence in general" (460): "Theologically this must somehow coincide with the 'primordial nature' of God, or with his primordial creativity or power" (460). And in "A Guess at the Riddle," dated 1890, Peirce himself names the Absolute First as "the starting point of the universe, God the Creator" (CP 1. 362).

In Peirce's system the external, physical universe and all experience related to it make up his Secondness. This category may best be explained by its properties: individuality, duality, and actuality. In the idea of individuality, Peirce stands Secondness in relation to Firstness to distinguish the singular manifestations of Seconds, existents that are "governed by those characteristics which really dominate the phenomenal world" (CP 1. 427). By individual, Peirce also intends the concrete, determinate thing "to which the law of excluded middle applies in every respect" (407): this means it may be determined whether an object possesses any property that may be cited; a table, for example, has weight, but not locomotion; it has shape and color, but not flexibility (407). Further, the individuality of Secondness suggests a "definite place in the world," a "hereness and nowness," or "thisness"--Peirce refers to Duns Scotus' term for it, "haecceity": "Haecceity is the ultima ratio, the brutal fact that will not be questioned" (CP 1. 405).

Another property of Secondness is duality, which denotes relationship. It suggests otherness, an awareness in consciousness of an other existent outside the mind and not controlled by the mind. This means resistance and change, constraint and compulsion, experience and event--all activities having to do with "sudden changes of perception" and "shock" to the consciousness (CP 1. 335). Secondness is, in relation to the perceiving mind, then, an "onslaught" of reality "forcing its way to recognition":

> I instance putting your shoulder against a door and trying to force it open against an unseen, silent, and unknown resistance. We have a two-sided consciousness of effort and resistance, which seems to me to come tolerably near to a

> pure sense of actuality. . . . I call that Secondness. (CP 1. 24)

Duality in Secondness not only implies relationship between the ego and the non-ego, between mind and experience, but dyadic relationship in the external world, as well, "mutual action between two things, regardless of any sort of third or medium" (CP 1. 322); observable fact of cause-effect with another produces a reality of existents outside the mind's creation. It is important to note that this dyadic action is unintelligible, a simple dynamical reaction that Peirce defines as "the element of struggle" (CP 1. 45).

The third property of Secondness, actuality, is implied in the other two properties--individuality and duality--but more can be said about the brute fact of reality. It is, first of all, binary: the idea of force is reaction, which is "pure binarity" (CP 2. 84) and presupposes two tendencies acting in contrariety, each on the other, to effect a change. The idea of bruteness indicates "the absence of any reason, regularity, or rule" (CP 1. 84), which is a third or mediating element. The result of brute force upon the consciousness is doubt, which, Peirce contends, propels man to seek for "truth" (CP 2. 84); it is this doubt that directs the course of action in human behavior, and it is Secondness that forces into the mind the fact of reality, of actuality, of individuality, of duality, of all forces outside the mind itself.

In a logical progression of complexity in his categories, Peirce moves from monadic Firstness, the non-relative, independent mode of being (universals), to dynamic Secondness, the dual relative mode manifested in "brute" actuality (individuals), to triadic Thirdness, the mediating, tri-relative signs of meaning in the universe. Thirdness may best be explained by its various roles, not independent of one another, but nevertheless performing distinct functions of mediation, representation, and continuity.

In its first function, Thirdness acts as a mediator between absolute First (universals) and absolute Second (individuals), a role of Thirdness that suggests the possibility of a universal law of behavior within every event. Of the three primary modes of being, Thirdness is essential to account for man's intelligent perception for what he experiences and for the communication of that knowledge. Thus, Peirce proposes a system of signs, his "Thirds," to act as intermediary, linking devices between universals and individuals, to designate meaning and purpose in the reality of things: "By the third I mean the medium of connecting bond between the absolute first and last. The beginning is first, the end second, the means third" (CP 1. 337). Thus, Thirdness is meaning; it designates event; it is the means of an actualized experience: ". . . He who wills has a purpose; and that idea of purpose makes the act appear as a means to an end. Now the word means is almost an exact synonym to the word third" (CP 1. 532). In its mediating capacity as link between quality and object, there is interpretation, the desired end, and a means to that end. It suggests a molding of an idea "[into] conformity to the form to which the man's mind is itself molded" (CP 1. 343). Thus, the first role of thirdness may be called its synthetic function, creating links, posing possibilities, modifying the consciousness.

Another function of category the Third partakes more directly in the realm of the actual; it is "thought playing the role of Secondness, or event . . . of the general nature of experience or information" (CP 1. 537). This is the embodiment or the representation of the experience of Secondness, the only way a mind can know reality. The world of actuality cannot be known in its "raw" state; it can only be sensed and acknowledged; man can experience brute reality around him, but he cannot understand it unless it is given meaning, and that must be done indirectly through signs constituting Peirce's Third category. Therefore, a sign "stands for" an object or event or experience "to" a "scientific intelligence," that is, to a reasoning mind. The whole cosmos is a system of signs; the universe itself is a sign made up of signs--all embodying meaning, either natural or imposed, for the observing mind to "read." In an unidentified fragment of a work dated 1897, Peirce describes the sign's representative function this way:

> A sign, or representamen is something which stands to somebody for something in some respect or capacity. It addresses somebody, that is, creates in the mind of that person an equivalent sign. . . . That sign which it creates I call the interpretant of the first sign. The sign stands for something, its object. It stands for that object, not in all respects, but in reference to a sort of idea, which I have sometimes called the ground of the representamen. "Idea" is here to be understood in a sort of Platonic sense. . . . (CP 1. 228)

It is clear from this description of the sign's operation that Peirce observes a form of logic (which he does in fact equate with semiotic) in this manifestation of signs. A sign names or points out the object, either tacitly or verbally, in the form of an assertion so that the sign "becomes" the thing it represents, "in some respect or capacity," embodies and denotes an idea or set of ideas associated with the thing. The mind holds the representamen for its use, separate from the existent thing, and the "ground" or idea that is embodied in the object becomes likewise lodged in the sign and creates an equivalent idea or image in the mind. The existence of the idea does not depend on the mind at all; this point is critical in Peirce's system: reality and meaning lie outside man's control and in the reality of things. In a work entitled "Minute Logic," written in 1902, Peirce clarifies his position regarding meaning:

> [T]he idea does not belong to the soul; it is the soul that belongs to the idea. The soul does for the idea just what the cellulose does for the beauty of the rose; that is to say, it affords it opportunity. (CP 1. 216)

However, an idea cannot be said to have complete being until it enters some mind. In the same work, Peirce adds this qualification:

> If you ask what mode of being is supposed to belong to an idea that is in no mind, the reply will come that undoubtedly the idea must be embodied (or ensouled--it is all one) in order to attain complete being, and that if, at any moment, it would happen that an idea . . . was quite unconceived by any living being, then its mode of being . . . would consist in this, namely, that it was about to receive embodiment . . . and to work in the world. This would be a mere potential being. . . . (CP 1. 218)

In such a situation, the object of the idea is different from "dead" matter or "utter nothingness," which has no possibility of existence. In this case, it waits its turn to exist, that is the moment when an idea becomes associated with it via a sign, thereby conferring upon it "the power of working out results in this world" (CP 1. 220). The representative function of Thirdness "brings information into the mind, . . . determines the idea, gives it body" (CP 1. 537).

The most sophisticated function of Thirdness is as habit or law, the process of growth and continuity and the regulative principle of the universe. In this role Thirdness is the critical element in any scientific investigation because the law demonstrates not only what has occurred in cause-effect sequence, but also what will (or would) occur under specific circumstances. This law of continuity Peirce names "synechism," the Law of laws which maintains that all things are the result of some cause, and that although they swim in "a continuum of uncertainty and of indeterminacy" (CP 1. 172) (we can never know infallibly), all elements of the universe evolve regularly and consistently, taking habits with greater and greater predictability:

> [For] every conceivable real object, there is a greater probability of acting as on a former like occasion than otherwise. This tendency itself constitutes a regularity, and is continually on the increase. . . . [I]t causes actions in the future to follow some generalization of past actions; and this tendency is itself something capable of similar generalization; and it is self-generative. (CP 1. 409)

70

Thus, what the "scientific intelligence" observes in the world of existents is connected directly to some existent fact immediately preceding it, and that former one to its immediate predecessor, and so on to the origin of existents, which Peirce identifies with God. The observer of existing phenomena has access, theoretically, at least, via universal signs (laws), to the Universal Mind, God the Creator. Moving forward in the same logical, synechistic manner, predicting the future activity of existing phenomena, man reasons, judges, and acts from observations and conclusions. This is the essence of Peirce's pragmaticism; it means that a thinking person will be directed by logic (his contemplation of universal signs) to the ultimate good, which is God.[2]

Peirce has more to say about the significance of future-controlled thought in individual belief and behavior, a concept that is crucial to his philosophy because it lends credence to his argument for the reality of God as Creator and as Universal Mind:

> This reference to the future is an essential element of personality. Were the ends of a person already explicit, there would be no room for development, for growth, for life; and consequently there would be no personality. This remark has an application to the philosophy of religion. It is that a genuine evolutionary philosophy, that is, one that makes the principle of growth a primordial element of the universe, is so far from being antagonistic to the idea of a personal creator that it is really inseparable from that idea. ... But a pseudo-evolutionism which enthrones mechanical law above the principle of growth is at once scientifically unsatisfac-tory, as giving no possible hint of how the universe has come about, and hostile to all hopes of personal relations with God. (CP 6. 157)

It is clear that Peirce's entire scientific/philosophical system rests squarely on the work of Thirdness; it is an existential condition in Peirce's cosmology, a fundamental semiosis that Peirce attempts to "prove" by deduction from the evidence of things seen:[3]

> We have seen that the conception of the absolute first eludes every attempt to grasp it; and so in another sense does that of the absolute second; but there is no absolute third, for the

> third is of its own nature relative, and this is what we are
> always thinking, even when we aim at the first or second.
> The starting point of the universe, God the Creator, is the
> Absolute First; the terminus of the universe, God completely
> revealed, is the Absolute Second; every state of the universe
> at a measurable point of time is the Third. (CP 1. 362)

I have shown that Thirdness in Peirce's semiotic is the universal category of connection, representation, and continuity, the intelligent "realm" of existence that renders things and feelings understandable. I have shown that Thirdness works at every level of cosmic activity, that where effect follows cause, a law which all phenomena must obey, the change or growth is directly attributable to Thirdness. I have emphasized the role of God as Progenitor of Thirdness, the God who, Peirce believes, demonstrates to the human mind, not only the nature and the make-up of the universe, but the orderliness, the power, the very nature and mind of God.[4]

Charles S. Peirce establishes his whole scientific-philosophical system on the theory of Thirdness, a cosmic system, he calls it, because it incorporates, he says, all the sciences and likewise brings together science, philosophy, and religion.

Peirce's Theory of Man

In viewing Peirce's semiotic from the perspective of the human being, it is important to note first the connection between his semiotic at the human level and his semiotic on the cosmic level. Peirce holds that the universe itself is Divine Mind and that all matter is simply "effete mind": "inveterate habits becoming physical laws" (CP 6. 25):

> [A]ll mind is directly or indirectly connected with all matter,
> and acts in a more or less regular way; so that all mind more
> or less partakes of the nature of matter. Hence, it would be
> a mistake to conceive of the psychical and physical aspects
> of matter as two aspects absolutely distinct. Viewing a thing

> when we remember that mechanical laws are nothing but
> acquired habits, like all regularities of mind, including the
> tendency to take habits, itself. . . . (CP 6. 268)

Thus, the concept of mind serves as an analogue for the structure and operation of nature and as a scheme to demonstrate the correlation between man's mental activity and the universal mind (ultimately God).

In an essay entitled "Some Consequences of Four Incapacities" (published 1868), Charles Peirce refutes the Cartesian position that "the ultimate test of certainty is to be found in individual consciousness" and lists four "laws" of consciousness which state his own position:

1. We have no power of Introspection, but all knowledge of the internal world is derived by hypothetical reasoning from our knowledge of external facts.

2. We have no power of Intuition, but every cognition is determined logically by previous cognitions.

3. We have no power of thinking without signs.

4. We have no conception of the absolutely incognizable (CP 5. 265).

In explaining the first two statements above, I have made the point with considerable emphasis that, in Peirce's view, man knows all things by signs and only by signs--they are the mediating category of Thirdness, which conveys meaning to reasoning minds--and that signs themselves originate in the material world; hence, all knowledge comes from outside the mind. The mind does, however, possess a unique capacity for using signs; so crucial, in fact, are signs to the function of the mind in Peirce's system that he identifies the mind (and man himself) as a sign.

In examining Peirce's semiotic from the perspective of man, the human sign, I shall begin with the reasoning behavior of the mind: "Man makes the word, and the word means nothing which the man has not made it mean" (CP 5. 313). Next, I shall examine Peirce's theory of man's evolving personality:

word, and the word means nothing which the man has not made it mean" (CP 5. 313). Next, I shall examine Peirce's theory of man's evolving personality: "[The] personality, like any general idea, is not a thing to be apprehended in an instant. It has to be lived in time; nor can any finite time embrace it in all its fullness" (CP 6. 155). Finally, I shall examine Peirce's theory of man as a social being: "Man is not whole as long as he is single . . . ; he is essentially a possible member of society" (CP 5. 402n). In some points of Peirce's semiotic, I shall draw from theologian Josiah Royce, a member of the Peircean school and popularizer of certain theories of Peirce.

A. Man as Sign

In Peirce's philosophy, to say that a man is a sign is simply to affirm that man is a triadic being, that he can connect ideas logically, can recall facts from the past to apply to new data, can thus draw inferences from new experience, make judgments, and take action based on mental behavior. In a lecture of 1865, Peirce states it this way:

> We have already seen that every state of consciousness [is] an inference; so that life is but a sequence of inferences or a train of thought. At any instant then man is a thought, and as thought is a species of symbol, the general answer to the question What is man? is that he is a symbol. (CP 7. 583)

In the following description of Peirce's semiotic, I shall be concerned with the triadic nature of man, that is, the function of the mind. Like every other symbol in the universe, the mind functions as a mediating Third, bringing together the passive consciousness (unformulated feeling) and an external fact or "sensation of reaction" to form a thought, a cognition, a "learning." The Third element of the mind not only links the First (feeling) and the Second (sensation), it also "[brings] along other ideas with it" (CP 6. 135). In this way an idea spreads, becomes more generalized, less distinct, but, according to Peirce, never loses its "intrinsic quality"; it continues to affect others, though less so as time passes:

> The insistency of a past idea with reference to the present is a quantity which is less the further back that past idea is, and rises to infinity as the past idea is brought up into coincidence with the present. . . . (CP 6. 140)

> In fact, this is habit, by virtue of which an idea is brought up into present consciousness by a bond that has already been established between it and other idea while it was still in futuro. (CP 6. 141)

In this manner Peirce demonstrates that the mind coordinates ideas in an individual to establish a consistent personality and to form a centralized philosophy of life, so that behavior itself is consistent and logical, and conducted according to the logic performed by the mind:

> [T]he word coordination implies somewhat more . . . ; it implies a teleological harmony in ideas, and in the case of personality this teleology is more than a mere purposive pursuit of a predeterminate end; it is a developmental teleology. This is personal character. A general idea, living and conscious now, it is already determinative of acts in the future to an extent to which it is not now conscious. (CP 6. 156)

Murray Murphey has noted the relationship between Peirce's pragmatism and his semiotic: Peirce insists that "the significance of all thought ultimately lies in its effect upon our actions" (178), and this will be, Peirce insists, rational and harmonious and consistent, and relevant to "the highest existing authority in regard to the dispositions of heart which a man ought to have" (CP 2. 655). In this way, Peirce introduces the normative and, ultimately, the religious, nature of his theory of man; it means that man, if he follows his instinctive affinity with nature (and with God the Creator of nature), will seek his highest good, which directs his action toward the good of the human community because, logically, he prospers when the community prospers.

Peirce gives the operation of the mind a number of different terms,[5] the most prominent of which are "judgment" and "perceptual judgment," meaning that the function of the mind is "to press home, upon the self of the immediate future and of the general future, some truth" (CP 5. 546). The pragmatic duty of the mind is reinforced again and again in Peirce's system; the judgment is not only the "sole vehicle in which a concept can be conveyed to a person's cognizance or acquaintance . . . but involves an act, an exertion of energy, and is liable to real consequences or effects" (CP 5. 547).

Finally, regarding man's use of language, Peirce makes the point that the reasoning mind works only with language; by language, and only by language, it knows and is known. It creates words and learns new things from prior use of language, but there is an important qualification here:

> Man makes the word, and the word means nothing which
> the man has not made it mean, . . . [b]ut since man can
> think only by means of words or other external symbols,
> these might turn round and say: 'You mean nothing which
> we have not taught you . . . .' (CP 5. 313)

The relationship between man and word, therefore, is reciprocal by this theory; they act as co-educators: "each increase of a man's information involves and is involved by, a corresponding increase of a word's information" (CP 5. 313). In the most dramatic appeal to the triadicity of man, Peirce asserts that,

> there is no element whatever of man's consciousness [here
> I would suppose he means "mind" since the consciousness is
> defined as unformulated, unfocused feeling--a First] which
> has not something corresponding to it in the word; and the
> reason is obvious. It is that the word or sign which man
> uses is the man himself: For, as the fact that every thought
> is a sign, taken in conjunction with the fact that life is a train
> of thought, proves that man is a sign so, that every thought
> is an external sign, proves that man is an external sign. That
> is to say, the man and the external sign are identical, in the
> same sense in which the words homo and man are identical.
> Thus my language is the sum total of myself; for man is the
> thought. (CP 5. 314)

B. Man as Evolving Self

Not only does Peirce view man as a triadic being--a sign--he also interprets the individual as an "evolving" personality. I have already described Peirce's theory of mental operations as linear and continuous: ideas flow from past to future in contiguous and associative sequence, each thought generating the next, so that "the present is connected with the past by a series of real infinitesimal steps" (CP 6. 109). The function of the mind in the thought process is "equivalent" to the syllogistic process, Peirce asserts: since there is no "absolutely first cognition of any object" (all signs are developed from previous cognitions), the mind proceeds from premise, A, to conclusion, B, "only if, as a matter of fact, such a proposition as B is always or usually true when such a proposition A is true" (CP 5. 267):

> It is a matter of constant experience, that if a man is made to believe in the premisses, in the sense that he will act from them and will say that they are true, under favorable conditions he will also be ready to act from the conclusion and to say that that is true. (CP 5. 268)

> At any moment we are in possession of information, of cognitions, which have been derived by induction and hypothesis from previous cognitions which are less general, less distinct and of which we have a less lively consciousness. These in turn have been derived from other still less general, less distinct . . . so on back to ideal first which is quite singular and out of consciousness. (CP 5. 311)

Further proof of continuity of consciousness, Peirce says, is the fact that all experience moves through time, which is itself continuous and which involves learning (CP 7. 536).   This process requires reasoning (conscious interpretation) that calls for further reasoning extending without end:

> Every reasoning connects something that has just been learned with knowledge already acquired so that we thereby learn what has been unknown. It is thus that the present is so welded to what is just past as to render what is just coming about inevitable. The consciousness of the present, as the boundary between past and future, involves them both. (CP 7. 536)

Further, Peirce asserts that the "infinitesimal" intervals in movement of thought follow a temporal sequence of "beginning, middle, and end . . . in the way of immediate feeling" (CP 6. 111), so that the beginning of an interval of thought "is the middle of the former, and whose middle is the end of the former" (CP 6. 111) and so on without end. Thus, the present moment of thought exists both in the past and in the future. The natural flow of thought makes time itself to flow in linear fashion, from past to future, and hence makes "the present affectible by the past but not by the future" (CP 6. 128).

Directly associated with this synechistic view of sign interpretation is Peirce's theory of the evolving self. The developing self, as continuous thought, is ever-changing, growing in complexity as thought toward the future hypothetical self which the past self and the present self create. Peirce expresses the concept in "The Law of Mind":[6]

> This reference to the future is an essential element of personality. Were the ends of a person already explicit, there would be no room for development, for growth, for life; and consequently there would be no personality. (CP 6. 157)

For a fuller account of Peirce's evolving self, I go to Josiah Royce, Peircean advocate and popularizer, who develops Peirce's logic in theological terms in The Problem of Christianity. Explaining the developing self, Royce defines the present self as "this creature of the moment," a product of its own history plus time:

> Each one of us knows that he just now, at this instant, cannot find more than a mere fragment of himself present. The self comes down to us from its own past. It is a . . . history. (244)

Moreover, there is the continual application of the past, via memory, to the new self:

> Each of us can see that his own idea of himself as this person is inseparably bound up with his view of his own former life, of the plans he formed, of the fortunes that

78

> fashioned him, and of the accomplishments which in turn he
> has fashioned for himself. A self is, by its very essence, a
> being with a past. One must look lengthwise backwards in
> the stream of time in order to see the self, or its shadow, .
> . . strenuously straining onwards in pursuit of its chosen
> good. (244)

At any moment, therefore, the self is "hardly a self at all," but only "a flash of consciousness,--the mere gesticulation of a self" (244); it is memory that gives consistency, that links present to past self and ascribes a unity and a wholeness to life. And like a good Peircean pragmaticist, Royce emphasizes the individual choice by logical reasoning in producing a future self:

> What I yesterday intended to pursue, that I am today still
> pursuing.... My present carries farther the plan of my past
> ... [then applying a Wordsworthian Platonic concept, Royce
> quotes] 'The child is father to the man.' ... My days are
> 'bound each to each by mutual piety.' (245)

Finally, Royce describes the present self as an interpretation of the past. Here the basic triadic function of sign operation is demonstrated as it works in the man-sign; the present self interprets the past self (selves) to the future self: "[M]y idea of myself is an interpretation of my past--linked also with an interpretation of my hopes and intentions as to my future" (245):

> These facts about our individual self-consciousness are indeed well known.
> But they remind us that our idea of individual self is no mere present datum,
> or collection of data, but is based upon an interpretation of the sense, of the
> tendency, of the coherence, and of the value of a life to which belongs the
> memory of its own past. (245)

In summary, Peirce and Royce see man as a functioning sign, not mediating external information for the sake of knowledge itself, but for the sake of the interpreting self, that is the person he wants to be. Obviously, then, the personality is never completed, but constantly shifts as it reinterprets experience and its own past behavior.

C. Man as Social Being

The self, however, is nothing alone, as Peirce notes; man is by nature and by identity a social being. This is the most critical aspect of Peirce's human semiotic because this concept affords the link he desires between science and religion. In Peirce's theory, man is more than "mere animal"; he is a transcending being, an "outreaching self" that, in its highest achievement, reaches perfect harmony and full sympathy with another being or beings:

> When I communicate my thought and my sentiments to a friend with whom I am in full sympathy, so that my feelings pass into him and I am conscious of what he feels, do I not live in his brain as well as in my own. . . ? True, my animal life is not there but my soul, my feeling, thought, attention are. (CP 7. 591)

And again,

> Each man has an identity which far transcends the mere animal;--an essence, a meaning subtle as it may be. . . . [T]hat he has this outreaching identity . . . is the true and exact expression of the fact of sympathy, fellow feeling-- together with all unselfish interests. . . . (CP 7. 591)

The transcending self is, in effect, transferring a part of himself to the other person when it enters as thought into the other:

> I may write upon paper and thus impress part of my being there; that part of my being may involve what I have in common with all men, and then I would have carried the soul of the race. . . . Thus every man's soul is a special determination of the generic soul of the family, the clan, the nation, the race to which he belongs. (CP 7. 592)

This, according to Peirce, is the desirable state; in fact, individual man's existence "is manifested only by ignorance and error[;] so far as he is anything apart from his fellows, and from what he and they are to be, is only a negation" (CP 5. 317).[7] Thus, the community acts for Peirce as an enlarged self, an alter-mind that represents not so much a local body of men as a universal "holy community of dedicated men who by their dedication enter a

80

kind of communion with God" (Murphey 176). Man's need to attach himself
to it is logically sound, Peirce argues, "for he who recognizes the logical
necessity of complete self-identification of one's own interests will perceive
that only the inferences of that man who has it are logical . . . (CP 5. 356).

The idea of community does not end here, however; it applies to all
aspects of life--man's identity is "rooted in the social principle (CP 2. 654):
"No mind can take a step without other minds" (CP 2. 220). All interpretation
of signs relies on a social matrix; there can be no language, no thought, no
communication without an "other." In Peircean theory this other mind may
simply be the other self (internalized conversation), but the other "voice" must
be present before interpretation can take place, an other to represent the
universalized ego, i.e., the community:

> [M]an is not whole as long as he is single, . . . he is
> essentially a possible member of society. Especially, man's
> experience is nothing, if it stands alone. If he sees what
> others cannot, we call it hallucination. It is not "my"
> experience, but "our" experience that has to be thought of;
> and this "us" has indefinite possibilities. (CP 5. 402n)

To examine these "indefinite possibilities" of community, I shall go again to
theologian Josiah Royce, who develops the religious intent of Peircean theory
of community.

When ideas are communicated by one mind to another, a certain "unity
of ego" is established, and a community or "supra-mind" comes into being, an
aggregate personality made up of individual minds that both supply ideas to
and derive ideas from the "cognitive community." This is the way Royce
describes it:

> I, the interpreter, regard you, my neighbor, as a realm of
> ideas, of "leadings," of meanings, of pursuits, of purposes.
> This realm is not wholly strange and incomprehensible to
> me. For at any moment, in my life as interpreter, I am
> dependent upon the results of countless previous efforts to
> interpret. The whole past history of civilization has resulted
> in that form and degree of interpretation of you and of my

> fellowmen which I already possess, at any instant when I
> begin afresh the task of interpreting your life or your ideas.
> You are to me, then, a realm of ideas which lie outside of
> the centre which my will can momentarily illumine. . . .
> (314)

The community as a "repository of ideas" is the foundation of all cognitive activity, supplying language and other cultural phenomena for the development of individual minds. Man comes to self-consciousness as a moral being through what Royce calls "spiritual warfare of mutual observation, of mutual criticism, of rivalry" (111):

> And . . . [men] are inwardly enemies of the collective social
> will . . . because in a highly cultivated social order the social
> will is oppressively vast, and the individual is trained to self-
> consciousness by a process which shows him the contrast
> between his own and this, which . . . seems like a vast
> impersonal will. He may obey . . . [b]ut he will naturally
> revolt inwardly; and that is his inevitable form of spiritual
> self-assertion. (113)

Trained by a society such as this, man is taught independence and self-reliance, is taught to value his individual will, Royce explains: "My will, not thine be done" (115). But concomitant to this teaching of independence, there is an awareness of an inner despair, a divided self, a self detached from the community and living by its own natural law. This is "fallen" man, by Royce's definition:

> What Paul's psychology, translated into more modern terms,
> teaches, is that the moral self-consciousness of every one of
> us gets its cultivation from one social order through a
> process which begins by craftily awakening us, as the serpent
> did Eve, through critical observa-tions, and which then
> fascinates our divided will by giving us the serpent's counsels.
> "Ye shall be as gods." This is the lore of individualism, and
> the vice of all our worldly social ambitions. (118)

Fallen man is, then, in Peirce's and in Royce's theology, an independent "free spirit," directed by self-will, and alienated from his social community and his fellow man because of this sin.

82

But this is not the end for fallen man; there is hope, and this also has to do with a social unit, only this one has a spiritual source--the "Beloved Community," Royce calls it. It is the body of Christ (the universal Church), and it requires of its members utmost loyalty and devotion:

> Loyalty involves an essentially new type of self-consciousness,--the consciousness of one who loves a community as a person. Not social training, but the miracle of this love, creates the new type of self-consciousness.

> Only (as Paul holds) you must find the universal community to which to be loyal; and you must learn to know its Lord, whose body it is, and whose spirit is its life. (119)

This is not the end for the individual man, however; by grace man is impelled into the Beloved Community, but by choice he remains loyal to it or betrays it. In the latter case, the individual becomes a "traitor," in Royce's terms, a rebel who knowingly and voluntarily defies his enlightenment and transgresses his own moral code:

> The realm of the spirit has been graciously opened to him. He has chosen to serve. And then he has closed his eyes; and by his own free choice, a darkness far worse than that of man's primal savagery has come upon him. (Problem 161)

In his own eyes, the traitor stands condemned by his own "unpardonable sin," a deed so terrible that it consigns him to his own "hell of the irrevocable" (161) because

> . . . there was a moment when he freely did whatever he could to wreck the cause that he had sworn to serve. The traitor can henceforth do nothing that will give to himself . . . any character which is essentially different from the one determined by his treason. (162)

In the view of the traitor, he has wrecked the cause which he once loyally embraced, has cast off love, which "has inspired heroes, martyrs, prophets," and thereafter, according to Royce's theology, suffers remorse in the "irrevocable condemnation" of his deed. It is a sin against his concept of all

that is holy, and nothing he can do--not good deeds, not prayers, not penance-
-can restore his soul. He has had a cause, a purpose for living, and he has
betrayed it and destroyed the community "in whose brotherhood, in whose life,
in whose spirit, he had found his guide and his ideal" (175).

The result of the traitor's actions thereafter is self-condemnation,
Royce maintains; no longer can the traitor value himself as loyal servant to
his ruling cause or view his life as coherent in its meaning. No god has the
power to shut him away in hell; it is the traitor's own self-made hell of the
irrevocable, where none are allowed forgiveness, either by self or by others.
And so he stands alone, his crime ever present, unreconciled, unreconcilable
in endless punishment.

The significance of Royce's interpretation of the traitor is that he
represents enlightened modern man, who has rejected an "irrational" God
with, as man says, arbitrary laws and punishment. Nor does modern man
believe in hell or accept second-hand moral standards. Rather, he constructs
his own rational moral code and religious dogmas.

Further, the problem of the traitor is not only a personal betrayal but
a betrayal of human relations as well, Royce emphasizes--severed ties, broken
vows, destroyed harmony and unity:

> What human ties the traitor broke, we leave to him to
> discover for himself. Why they were to his mind holy, we
> also need not now inquire . . . he had found his ties; they
> were precious and human and real; and he believed them
> holy and he broke them. (174)

But herein lies the possibility for atonement, "a condition of the highest good
that the human world contains" (177), a creative act by a faithful and suffering
servant, who uses the treasonous act to bring about great good by his own
sacrifice and who makes the world a better place than it would have been
without the treasonous deed. Such an act transfigures the loss into gain,
according to Royce, raises new life out of a destructive act, and "re-wins" the

value of the traitor's own life by reconciling him to the community he has betrayed:

> All of us know of great public benefactors whose lives and good works have been rendered possible through the fact that some great personal sorrow, some crushing blow of private grief first descended, and seemed to wreck their lives. Such heroic souls have then been able, in these well known types of cases, not only to bear their own grief . . . they have been able also to use their grief as the very source of the new acts. . . . (182)

According to Royce's Christian doctrine, man and God are joined in a Beloved Community, which is the manifestation of the Holy (heavenly) Kingdom. The church, as man experiences it, is eminently fallible, comprised, as it is, of fallible human beings, but it represents an ideal body:

> We have to do . . . not so much with apostasy as with evolution. To be sure, at the very outset, the ideal of the Church was seen afar off through a glass, darkly. The well-known apocalyptic vision revealed the true Church as the New Jerusalem that was yet to come down from heaven. The expression of the idea was left, by the early Church, as a task for the ages. (79)

The Beloved Community, like the secular community, is, in its essence, a living organism, a "body" with a "mind," and, in Royce's theology, a "precious and worthy being," the "bride" of Christ, to which the Christian devotes himself:

> In Christ's love for the Church Paul finds the proof that both the community, and the individual member, are the objects of an infinite concern, which glorifies them both, and thereby unites them. The member finds his salvation only in union with the Church. . . . (95)

Yet, Royce notes, there remains an obstacle of being "completely absorbed by this ideal": the enemy is what Paul calls "the flesh" and is the result of man's social nature which is cultivated (by secular society) toward self-will and is "the basis of [man's] natural enmity both towards the law, and towards the spirit" (207). Still, the hope of man lies only in the Beloved Community; his natural proclivity, his fallen state, can be overcome only "by means of those unifying social influences which Paul regarded as due to grace" (207): Genius, and only genius--the genius which, in the extreme cases,

> founds new religions, which, . . . creates great social movements of a genuinely saving value, can create the communities which arouse love, which join the faithful into one, and which transform the old man into the new. When once we have come under the spell of such creative genius, and of the communities of which some genius appears to be the spirit, only then can we too die to the old life, and be renewed in the spirit. . . . To be won over to the level of such a community is, just in so far, to be saved. (207)

Such is the atoning work in the Christian community, "creative love," Royce calls it, self-sacrifice that creates a bond of brotherhood and generates loyalty and devotion to the Beloved Community on the part of Christians. It means, in other words, that the Church or Beloved Community, by these acts of love, becomes an interpretation of God's Self, so that the individual Christian compares his self with the corporate one and is inspired to devotion and loyalty to the Higher Self. In this way, the Beloved Community acts as mediating Third linking man and God, hence the only hope for redemption for modern alienated, self-willed man.

Peirce's Theory of Evolution

The final perspective by which I shall examine Peirce's semiotic system is his theory of evolution. To this scientific concept, which Peirce could not reasonably reject, he adapted his own overarching principle of love, Agapasm, he calls it, and thereby links scientific evolution to his metaphysical principle.

In his theory of scientific evolution, Peirce finds three modes of evolution to account for the change or growth that takes place in the universe: on the first level there is fortuitous development (pure chance), representing Darwin's natural selection, which Peirce calls tychasm; on the next level, there is mechanical necessity, representing a greater ordering, which Peirce calls anancasm; and, finally, there is, on the highest level, a growth toward unity in the universe, which Peirce calls agapasm.

According to the theory of agapasm, Love, which is the ultimate controlling force in evolution, is circular in its impulse, embracing all creation, good and evil, individuals and universals, "Projecting creations into independence and drawing them into harmony" (CP 6. 288). Thus, God, who is identified with this movement toward harmony, this agapastic energy in the universe, is not counterposed by any other force; there is no existing opposite evil force, for that would be admitting a duality in the Supreme Being, an equality of Satan with God, and, in Pierce's thinking, that is impossible. Further, God, who is identified as Love, cannot be self-love, for self-love is not love at all, but sinful egotism; therefore, God must love that which is "defect of love . . . just as a luminary can light up only that which otherwise would be dark" (CP 6. 287):

> It is a love which embraces hatred as an imperfect stage of
> it . . . even needs hatred and hatefulness as its object. (CP
> 6. 287)

Moreover, both tychasm and anancasm possess qualities of agapasm and thus, in Peirce's scheme, are "degenerate" forms of the overarching agapasm. Just as agapasm develops by reproduction, preserving the forms "that use the spontaneity conferred upon them after the Christian scheme," so also does tychasm, except that in the latter, "progress is solely owing to the distribution of the napkin-hidden talent of the rejected servant among those not rejected . . ." (CP 6. 304). In tychasm, growth results from destruction of the weak, whereas in genuine agapasm, growth results from "a positive sympathy among the created springing from continuity of mind" (CP 6. 304). And just as agapasm develops toward a conformity and a unity, so does anancasm, except that the latter responds "quite blindly by mere force of circumstances," whereas agapasm is moved "by the power of sympathy" (CP 6. 307): "The gospel of Christ says that progress comes from every individual merging his individuality in sympathy with his neighbors" (CP 6. 294). In Peirce's philosophy, individualism is viewed as an evil, contrary to the good of the individual and of society and, hence, of the universe itself. Since the harmonizing force is love, that means, not selfhood for the individual, but brotherhood and community. It is true that lower levels of this evolutionary force regenerate out of self-love; that is what Pierce observes in tychasm, the urge to reproduce one's likeness. In anancasm, too, there is the drive to adapt to circumstances for the well being of the individual, but the final tendency of evolution is toward harmony and unity in voluntary action. Throughout the spectrum of the evolutionary scale, then, agapé or creative love is at work. Murray Murphey calls it "the aim, end, and raison d'être of [Peirce's theory of] evolution" (352).

But there remains an unanswered question regarding the motive of an individual for renouncing his individuality in favor of the universal good: why would a person give up selfhood? The answer from Peirce is not immediately forthcoming, but is suggested in his late writing on pragmaticism. It is the "strength of an idea" that forces its way into the mind via reason and logic; Peirce calls it the "Neglected Argument," and it may be explained by his concept of developing mind. In an essay entitled "Evolutionary Love" (dated 1893), Peirce states it in theological terms:

> Everybody can see that the statement of St. John ("God is Love") is the formula of an evolutionary philosophy, which teaches that growth comes only from love, from I will not say self-sacrifice, but from the ardent impulse to fulfill another's highest impulse. Suppose, for example, that I have an idea that interests me. It is my creation. It is my creature; for as I have shown . . . , it is a little person. I love it; and I will sink myself in perfecting it. It is not by dealing out cold justice to the circle of my ideas that I can make them grow, but by cherishing and tending them as I would the flowers in my garden. The philosophy we draw from John's gospel is that this is the way mind develops; and as

> for the cosmos, only so far as it yet is mind, and so has life,
> is it capable of further evolution. Love, recognizing germs
> of loveliness in the hateful, gradually warms it into life, and
> makes it lovely. That is the sort of evolution which every
> careful student of my essay "The Law of Mind" must see that
> synechism calls for. (CP 6. 289)

An individual mind is drawn toward an idea, adopts it, and gives it life in his own life; i.e., it becomes the governing principle of his life. In fact, Peirce calls the human personality a developing "teleological harmony" of ideas, a living out of dominating ideas, and taken as an entity, the human mind is a general idea made up of the coordination of parts of that idea (CP 6. 155-56). Further, the general idea determines future behavior "to the extent to which [the mind] is not now conscious" (CP 6. 156):

> This reference to the future is an essential element of
> personality. Were the ends of a person already explicit,
> there would be no room for development, for growth, for
> life; and consequently there would be no personality. (CP 6.
> 157)

By the law of synechism, ideas flow in linear fashion, so that connected thoughts produce "an immediate community of feeling between parts of the mind infinitesimally near together" (CP 6. 134). This does not mean that individual ideas "surrender their peculiar arbitrariness and caprice" entirely, but "that there is a living idea, a conscious continuum of feeling which pervades them, and to which they are docile" (CP 6. 152). When ideas are communicated by one mind to another, a certain "unity of ego" is established, and a community or "supra-mind" comes into being, an aggregate personality made up of individual minds that both supply ideas to and derive ideas from the cognitive community. Thus, the interpretive community as a repository of ideas is the foundation of cognitive activity, supplying the language and other cultural phenomena for the development of individual minds. And, according to Peirce and to theologian Royce, this corporate mind directs individual minds toward a harmony and a spiritual unity in a "Beloved Community." Royce explains it this way:

> The mere form of interpretation may be indeed momentarily misused for whatever purpose of passing human folly you will. But if the ideal of interpretation is first grasped; and if then the Community of Interpretation is conceived as inclusive of all individuals; and as unified by the common hope of the far-off event of complete mutual understanding; and, finally, if love for this community is awakened,--then indeed this love is able to grasp, in ideal, the meaning of the Church Universal, of the Communion of Saints, and of God the Interpreter. (319)

This leads finally to the motive of individual minds for giving up personal gain for communal goals and for universal ends, and that is Peirce's argument for the personhood of God and for a personal relation with Him.[8] In his "Neglected Argument," Peirce applies three logical theories to support his belief in God and in the attraction of the human personality to Him. The first, called the Humble Argument, calls for "musement" or "free speculation" on the natural universe, an activity which, Peirce believes, will stir man's heart "by the beauty of the idea and by its august practicality, even to the point of earnestly loving and adoring his hypothetical God" (CP 6. 467). This comes from a common sense or "quasi-instinctive" belief out of a judgment from the "sensible heart" (CP 6. 493). Ultimately, however, as Murphey suggests, it is the "ravishment" by the "beauty and adorability of the Idea," its appeal to reason and logic in accounting for the origin of things and for the aspiration toward "an Ideal of conduct" (CP 6. 465). This is the crux of Peirce's semiotic, for the whole universe acts as a symbol (or symbols) of God's very nature--the power, the beauty, the orderliness, the goodness--"a great symbol of God's purpose, working out its conclusions in living realities" (CP 5. 119).

Tracing the Percy-Peirce Connection

In assessing the Percy-Peirce connections, I shall discount, not only Percy's claim to Christian existentialism, which I have already addressed, but also his claim to Catholic-based Christianity. I shall demonstrate his fundamentally Protestant position, emanating, as it does, from the system of Charles Sanders Peirce, founder of American pragmatism, a tradition that can be traced back without interruption to colonial American Calvinism and before that to the source of Calvinism in the Apostle Paul by way of Augustine and later scholastic writers like Thomas Aquinas and John Duns Scotus. To set up the historical connections that I have proposed, I shall first examine C. S. Peirce's avowed debt to Duns Scotus, thirteenth century scholastic, then trace the course of Scotus' theology from its interpretation of Apostle Paul and Augustine forward to the American Calvinists through the secularizing process of Emersonian Transcendentalism and finally back to the Peircean school of pragmatism.[9]

My purpose in beginning this historical trek with Duns Scotus instead of the immediate forebears of C. S. Peirce is that the influence of this scholastic writer on Peirce serves to focus my study on theological-semiotic concepts which were adopted by Reformers as crucial to their Protestant view of man and God, and, more important, which offered the Reformers a logical means of bringing the two together.

The appeal of Scotus to the nineteenth century American pragmatists like C. S. Peirce, William James, John Dewey, and George Mead is best expressed in James' essay "The Will to Believe": "We want to have truth; we want to believe that our experiments and studies and discussions must put us in a continually better and better position towards it" (10). James speaks not for absolutists, who believe one cannot only attain truth but can know when he attains it, but for empiricists, who believe that one can arrive at truth but that he "cannot infallibly know when" (12). Historically, James notes, it has been the scientists who have held the latter view, whereas philosophers and theologians have clung to the more restrictive view. But because scientists have mostly given only lip service to a nondogmatic end in the matter of religion and have in fact held a hostile position against it, James calls for a nonjudgmental reevaluation of the scholastic's "objective evidence" approach to theology:

> But please observe, now, that when as empiricists we give up the doctrine of objective certitude, we do not give up the quest or hope of truth itself. We still pin our faith on its existence, and still believe that we gain an ever better position towards it by systematically continuing to roll up experiences and think. . . . [F]or us the strength is in the outcome, the upshot, the terminus ad quem. . . . It matters not to an empiricist from what quarter an hypothesis may come to him: he may have acquired it by fair means or by foul; passion may have whispered or accident suggested it; but if the total drift of thinking continues to confirm it, that is what he means by its being true. (17)

There are, however, questions that cannot be settled by objective criteria alone, moral questions "whose solution cannot wait for sensible proof. . . . Science can tell us what exists; but to compare the worths, both of what exists and of what does not exist, we must consult not science, but what Pascal calls our heart" (22). And in the ultimate issue of God and the origin, meaning, and purpose of life, James contends that the stakes are too high to avoid the confrontation and the choice in the matter. For one thing, religion tells us that "the best things are the more eternal things, the overlapping things, the things in the universe that . . . say the final word" (25) and that we are better off with a faith in God and eternal verities than without such a faith. The skeptic who refuses to believe until all the facts are in, for fear of being duped or of falling into error, says by his choice, "Better risk loss of truth than chance of error," thereby "playing his stake as much as the believer" (26). Thus, for scientists

> to preach skepticism to us as a duty until 'sufficient evidence' for religion be found, is tantamount to telling us, when in the presence of religious hypothesis, that to yield to our fear of its being error is wiser and better than to yield to our hope that it may be true. (27)

92

Asserting the hypothesis, then, that religion may in fact be true, James concludes his argument by citing three "reasonable" appeals to faith. First, the "more perfect and more eternal aspect of the universe" presents to us a "personal form," and "[the] universe is no longer a mere IT to us, but a THOU" (27) if we see it as a creation and a reflection of an Infinite Mind. Second, the appeal of faith is so strong in our "heart of hearts" that the desire propels us to meet it halfway, to act on our belief and not to "shut [ourselves] up in snarling logicality and try to make the gods extort [our] recognition willy-nilly, or not get it at all" (28), thereby relinquishing altogether our only opportunity of making God's acquaintance:

> This feeling, forced on us we know not whence, that by
> obstinately believing [that there is a God] we are doing the
> universe the deepest service we can, seems part of the living
> essence of the religious hypothesis. (28)

Finally, true to his pragmatic form, James adds in a note that "The whole defence of religious faith hinges upon action" (29) and that one cannot "put a stopper on [his] heart, instincts and courage, and wait . . . till doomsday, or until such time as our intellect and senses working together may have raked in evidence enough. . . (29-30).

This sounds like an argument Peirce himself might make, or Walker Percy, for that matter, both empiricists, rigorously trained in the science of verifiable method but nurtured in a faith with even stronger appeal. The dilemma is the same as with William James, and so the attraction to scholastic writer John Duns Scotus is a logical one, since the movement to faith begins with verifiable things, real things "out there" that exist independently of human reasoning about them. It is, in other words, logic itself which attracts Charles Sanders Peirce to Duns Scotus.

Edward C. Moore cites four "basic doctrines" that Peirce takes from Duns Scotus, quoting Peirce's own statements:

1. ... the scholastic doctrine of realism ... the opinion that there are real generals (CP 5. 453).

2. ... the doctrine that existence is not a form to be conceived, but a compulsive force to be experienced (Nation 73: 96, 1901).

3. The realist will ... maintain a doctrine of immediate perception (CP 8. 16).

4. ... the Scotist ... is habituated to thinking of three modes of being (Nation, 79: 15, 1904). (401)

It is the last doctrine, that states the theory most important to the historical connections which I wish to use because it refers to the idea of Thirdness, whereby the human mind makes distinctions and connections between "real" existents and universals. This work of the mind Scotus calls a "formal" distinction, a distinction made in the mind "which [has] a basis in fact, but which [is] still not a real distinction" (Moore 404). For this reason, C. R. S. Harris names Scotus "an empiricist in contrast to the older Augustinian school" because he teaches that all knowledge begins with the senses and that "there are no innate ideas or principles implanted in the mind anterior to experience" (16). The senses inform us of actual existents, but it is the mind, Scotus tells us, which transforms the individual thing into a general concept or universal so that, stored in the memory, that universal concept may be applied to other existents and future knowledge; the mind abstracts the quality or essence of the thing to apply that independent quality to other experiences:

> [T]he senses are not a cause but merely an occasion of the intellect's knowledge, for the intellect cannot have any knowledge of the terms of a proposition unless it has taken them from the senses. But once it has them, the intellect by its own power can form propositions with these terms. (108)

About the reality of the thing, Harris notes that for Scotus it is "held fast in the domain of 'intentional' apprehension by means of language"--the word, which signifies the "species . . . not in [the word's] subjective capacity as psychological idea or mere state of consciousness, but in its objective capacity as representing the real external object" (34). Thus, the word acts as a sign or symbol for the thing it signifies <u>as it exists in the mind</u> mediated by the intelligible species.

From Aristotle, Scotus defines the two modes of learning accomplished by the mind; the first (induction) comes from a limited number of samples or experiences, inferring thereby that "whatever occurs in a great many instances by a cause that is not free, is the natural effect of that cause" (109). In the second mental operation (deduction), the mind examines the experience "by division" to discover the cause or the principle involved. This, Scotus says, is the "lowest degree of scientific knowledge:"

> [S]imple intelligence can know by way of definition all that it knows in a confused manner by the simple expedient of discovering the definition of the thing known by way of division. This definitive knowledge seems to be the most perfect kind of knowledge that pertains to simple intelligence. From this most perfect knowledge of the terms, however, the intellect can understand the principle most perfectly; and from the principle, the conclusion. (121)

Scotus argues, further, that man can begin with things in the material world, form syllogisms to arrive at causes of mutable species until he finally arrives at the Immutable Cause, the Divine Mind,

> for the essence of God is represented to the intellect as something immutable by means of something that is radically changeable. . . . For something can be represented as infinite through what is finite. (117)

This logical or analogical deduction may be accomplished because two principles apply: first, the human mind as a "higher form," what Harris calls the "immateriality of the intellect" (261), is capable of participating in the logic of the universe; and second, "all intelligibles have an intelligible being in virtue of the divine intellect" (Scotus 123). The mind works from the data it receives via the senses, from the "secondary objects of the divine intellect,"

Scotus explains, and arrives at truths about God, the Eternal Light (123). Here, then, according to Scotus, lies the "twofold causality": the Uncreated Light "produces objects in intelligible being and . . . the secondary objects produced actually move the intellect" (125). The effect is this:

> Once these intelligibles are grasped and formulated in a proposition they cause the conformity of what is grasped [viz. the proposition] to themselves [as terms]. For even though God freely co-operates with the intellect when it combines or does not combine these terms, still once the terms have been formed into a proposition, the conformity of the latter with the terms seems to follow as a necessary consequence. . . . (125-26)

One other point should be made concerning Scotus' theory of mind. He contends, after Augustine, that no "special illumination" is required for the human intellect to perform its logical work from immediate perception to "eternal reason." It is true, Scotus concedes, that some minds are more adept at abstracting or more sensitive to the essential purpose behind nature and that some Christians cannot know God by reasoning, but must simply accept the conclusions of difficult truths they are taught about God. Nevertheless, "every intellect can be moved by some object to know that something is true by virtue of [God] (130). To illustrate, Scotus cites two examples:

> [T]o know that a triangle has three [angles equal to two right angles], in so far as this is a kind of participation of God and that it has such an order in the universe that it expresses more perfectly as it were the perfection of God,--this is a nobler way of knowing a triangle has three [angles, etc.] than to know this truth from the notion of the triangle itself. Similarly, to know that one should live temperately in order to attain the supreme happiness, which consists in attaining the essence of God in Himself, is a more perfect way of knowing this practical truth than to be aware of it through some principle in the class of mores. . . . (130)

The attractions Charles Peirce felt toward Duns Scotus are apparent in the scientific exactness of the scholastic philosopher, in the empirical structure of the system, and in the metaphysical conclusions to objective propositions. But the tradition of knowing metaphysical truth by material content does not begin with Duns Scotus. One must move back to Paul the Apostle to find the origin of this "logical" religion.

NOTES

[1] Joseph Esposito cites evidence from manuscripts dated 1860 which suggests that Peirce had begun searching for precedents in Plato and others to lend support to his developing theory of three, rather than two, equal modes of being (46-47). The traditional two having been established from ancient times, Peirce had to demonstrate the necessity, and the equality, of a third--i.e., its role in mediating between the other two entities.

[2] In "The Law of Mind," a paper published in The Monist, 1892, Peirce explains synechism as it applies to mental phenomena. It is because of the law of continuity, "that ideas tend to spread continuously and to affect certain others which stand to them in a peculiar relation of affectibility" (CP 6. 104). Considering an idea as a single event in an individual consciousness occurring in an instant of time, Peirce concludes that "the present [thought] is connected with the past by a series of real infinitesimal steps" (CP 6. 109). In other words, Peirce says we are conscious of a thought for only a fleeting moment, but that passing idea calls forth another (its object), which in turn calls up another in continuous procession. It is this linear progression of thought from past to future that, in part, marks our concept of the "flow" of time itself, a unidirectional movement which makes all temporal events directly affectible by past events and not affectible by, but affecting, future events. In this manner, ideas spread out, lose intensity and particularity, but increase in generality and regularity, acquire habits, become laws, and thus allow prediction and deliberate action based on belief.

[3] Joseph Esposito remarks on Peirce's effort to reconcile his two lifelong causes, science and religion:

> If, then, the theory of categories is correct in all
> its wide implications, the God-hypothesis cannot
> be neglected. . . . The God-hypothesis is "the
> natural precipitate of meditation upon the origin
> of the Three Universes" (CP 6. 487), and
> something like it is found in all scientific
> explanation (230).

In his argument for the reality of God, it is not science on which Peirce ultimately rests his case, Esposito explains, but the strength of the Idea itself-- the possibility of God, the plausibility of God. To be sure, both arguments are interrelated throughout Peirce's work, from first to last; and while it is instinct that urges belief in God, it is, as Esposito says, "an instinct elevated in the light of reason" (230).

[4] In a contribution to a publication entitled Syllabus of Certain Topics of Logic, published in 1903, Pierce explains his sign system as three "trichotomies." On the simplest level, there are "Qualisign," "Sinsign," and "Legisign." A Qualisign is a quality that produces meaning, thereby assuming the role of sign; a Sinsign is "an actual existent thing or event" acting as a sign by being embodied with certain qualities; and a Legisign is a "law" or convention established by society that acts thereafter as a sign for all users, e.g., the word "the" in the English language (CP 2. 246). Peirce emphasizes the interrelatedness of these signs in this summary statement:

> Every legisign signifies through an instance of its application which may be termed a Replica of it. Thus, the word "the" will usually occur from fifteen to twenty-five times on a page. It is in all these occurrences one and the same word, the same legisign. Each single instance of it is a Replica. The Replica is a Sinsign. Thus, even Legisign requires Sinsign (CP 2. 246).

The second trichotomy of signs is more familiar: the Icon, the Index, and the Symbol. An Icon embodies the character and the qualities of its object, not in perfect likeness in every case, as in a photograph which is an icon of the thing pictured, but sometimes by analogy, as in algebraic formulas. The resemblance may, therefore, be conventional (assigned) qualities, but by definition an icon must be associated with its object and recognizable as possessing qualities of its object (CP 2. 279-81). The second sign in the second trichotomy of signs is the Index, a demonstrative sign which denotes its object by cause-effect (e.g., as thunder suggests rain) or other logical representation. An index in Peirce's system always denotes a single thing or unit and "depends upon association by contiguity" (CP 2. 274):

> A low barometer with a moist air is an index of rain; that is we suppose that the forces of nature established a probable connection between the low barometer with moist air and coming rain. (CP 2. 286)

The last sign in the second trichotomy of signs is the Symbol, by far the most common and useful to man because this is language and language substitutes, i.e., conventional signs, like rituals, that represent objects by a rule or "habit" or general agreement within a language community. The spoken word "man," for example, is a succession of sounds which creates a replica of a man or men in the mind because it "prescribes the qualities of its replicas" (CP 1. 191). It is evident, then, by its regularity that a symbol acts as a law by which communication may be conducted, by which new symbols may be created, and by which increasingly complex knowledge may take place. As in the first trichotomy, the second set also has a close interrelatedness; i.e., a symbol may be part icon or part index. Peirce cites an example of a man naming an object for a child, creating a new symbol from a known symbol this way: the man points toward a balloon, and the pointing finger becomes an indexical sign of the balloon; but when he adds, in response to the inquiry of the child, "It is like a great big soap bubble," he is creating a symbol for the child from another symbol that the child already knows (CP 2. 293). The descriptive nature of the symbol is crucial in Peirce's system. A symbol cannot, of itself, identify a new thing; it can only tell about or describe and call to mind something already associated by earlier known symbols. Thus, in figures of speech (as the simile "It is like a giant soap bubble"), the generative power of the symbol is most easily demonstrated, but actually works in all speech when one symbol calls to mind an image along with associated images that expand interminably, creating greater and greater complexity.

To demonstrate the assertive or declarative nature of signs, Peirce explains the symbol "love" in the assertion "James loves Jane." The two names act as an index of the two individuals so designated--i.e., James is a specific man and Jane is a specific woman--and "loves" is the symbol that calls to mind any lover and his beloved. That is to say, a symbol is a declarative statement, an assertion in the formula A is B:

> Thus the sentence "Every man loves a woman" is equivalent to "whatever is a man loves something that is a woman." Here "whatever" is a universal selective index, "is a man" is a symbol, "something that" is a particular selective index, and "is a woman" is a symbol. (CP 2. 296)

In the third trichotomy of signs, there are the Rheme, the Dicisign, and the Argument. The best way to explain this set of signs is in terms of logic. In a syllogism there must be a general term that is given a universal quality or predicate (major premise) which, in turn, yields a logical minor premise and conclusion. In this sequential process the Rheme is the general term in the proposition; the Dicisign is the proposition or premise itself; and the

Argument is the sign that follows logically and thus becomes the law derived from the premises, a law which "urges" toward the truth (CP 2. 253). The "truth" Peirce sought, of course, was metaphysical, which lay outside the purview of empirical phenomena; but what he believed in, as certainly as he believed in empirical facts, were cosmic signs that suggest by their being, by their beauty, by their orderliness that there is a Mind, an Organizer, a Creator behind all things man knows experientially and that logic and reason will finally reveal the truth of the metaphysical just as they reveal the truth of the physical:

> So the poet in our days--and the true poet is the true prophet--personifies everything, not rhetorically, but in his own feeling. He tells us that he feels an affinity for nature, and loves the stone or the drop of water. But the time is coming when there shall be no more poetry, for that which was poetically divined shall be scientifically known. . . . Physics will have made us familiar with the body of all things, and the unity of the body of all; natural history will have shown us the soul of all things in their infinite and amiable idiosyncracies. Philosophy will have taught us that it is this all that constitutes the church. Ah! what a heavenly harmony will be that when all the sciences, one as viol, another as flute, another as trumpet, shall peal forth in that majestic symphony of which the noble organ of astronomy forever sounds the theme. (WP 6. 114) ["The Place of Our Age in the History of Civilization" Oration delivered before Cambridge High School Association, Nov. 12, 1863.]

[5] Peirce distinguishes between the consciousness and the mind. Larry Holmes discusses the distinctions in an essay entitled "Prolegomena to Peirce's Philosophy of Mind" [359-81]. Peirce identifies consciousness as "feeling": "to be conscious is nothing else than to feel" (CP 1. 318), and "what is immediately in consciousness is what consciousness is made of" (CP 7. 540 n8). Using an image of a pool, Peirce calls consciousness a "bottomless lake in which ideas are suspended at different depths" (CP 7. 553). The mind, on the other hand, is "a chemical genus of extreme complexity and instability" (CP 6. 101), a "focus of all the faculties" (CP 7. 343). The function of mind is pure logic: "The entire phenomenal manifestation of the mind is a sign

resulting from inference . . . , a sign developing according to the laws of inference" (CP 5. 313). And in Holmes' view, the pool analogy applied to consciousness applies to mind as well, "the instinctive mind corresponding in a fashion to what is far under surface" (364). Finally, Peirce distinguishes between consciousness and mind by asserting that "feeling [consciousness] is nothing but the inward aspect of things, while mind . . . is essentially an external phenomenon" (CP 7. 364) and that "consciousness is a special, and not a universal, accompaniment of mind" (CP 7. 366).

[6] Murray Murphey cites an unpublished manuscript of Peirce to illustrate the stages of self-development. Peirce calls this "two kinds of self-knowledge":

> . . . two selves, if you please, one known immediately and the other mediately. The mediate knowledge of self is not the inner world . . . is not something presented to us but is a mere product of active thought (qtd. Murphey 89).

Again citing Peirce, Murphey adds that the "inner world" or the "world of feelings" is the "world of memory for it is clear that we can remember nothing except what is within" (89), but this involves time, indeed, it is time, Peirce insists, and therefore linear--moving from past to future--continually creating itself.

[7] Murray Murphey explains this concept in religious terms. If ignorance and error were eliminated, "individuality would cease to exist, but identity would not" (175) because the individual's identity is "a consistency of what he does and thinks," as Peirce says, and this consistency is in the form of language (intellectual in nature) that expresses the character of a person in a cumulative manner:

> [T]o "express" in this sense is to embody an abstraction. The identity of a man lies then in the abstraction he expresses in his life--that is, in his conforming his thought and action to the idea in the divine mind. Thus in so far as ignorance and error are eliminated, men are identified with each other and the divine, and since it is the sole aim of inquiry to eliminate ignorance and error,

so it is the sole aim of inquiry to merge the
individual with the community (175).

[8] In an 1877 article ("Fixation of Belief"), Peirce presents as part of his system of scientific evolution, a doubt-belief theory whereby doubt, as "an uneasy and dissatisfied state from which we struggle to free ourselves," compels an individual to attempt "to pass into the state of belief" (CP 5. 372). The irritation of doubt initiates an inquiry which ultimately leads to belief of what we think to be true; thus, with doubt relieved, one enters a state of rest or habit: "When doubt ceases, mental action on the subject comes to an end" (CP 5. 375). By the turn of the century, however, Peirce has questions regarding this theory because it proposes an evolution governed more by a negative action of mechanical necessity than by a positive action toward universal brotherhood. What he comes up with to solve his deterministic dilemma is what Murphey calls "the evolution of rationality" or "concrete reasonableness" (363), that is, the rule of order which appeals aesthetically to the human mind so that the individual is drawn emotionally as well as logically to an ordered universe. It is critical for Peirce's philosophy of love that evolution become a moral process, and so he links the process to God, not in pantheistic fashion because he considers man and God as separate beings, but, nevertheless, in a natural, instinctive manner so that man enjoys direct "communication" with God.

[9] Jay P. Tellotte has cited Percy's indebtedness to Charles S. Peirce in three areas: in the triadic theory of man, in the theory of abduction (for arriving at hypotheses), and in the pragmatic methods of science ("Walker Percy: A Pragmatic Approach" 217-30). In particular, Tellotte notes Peirce's influence on Percy's view of man as seeker and restless interrogator, his "incessant questioning activity which Peirce mapped out" (224).

CHAPTER 3

THE CHRISTIAN SEMIOTIC OF CHARLES SANDERS PEIRCE

Peirce's Doctrine of Signs

It will serve my purpose of establishing links between the Peircean and the Pauline semiotic systems to review in summary Peirce's theory of signs and to reinforce its metaphysical implications as explained by Josiah Royce.

Peirce, the originator of modern semiotics, defines "semiotic" as the "quasi-necessary, or formal, doctrine of signs" (CP 2. 227):

> By describing the doctrine as "quasi-necessary," or formal, I mean that we observe the characters of such signs as we know, and from such an observation, by a process which I will not object to naming Abstraction, we are led to statements . . . as to what must be the characters of all signs used by a "scientific" intelligence, that is to say, by an intelligence capable of learning by experience (CP 2. 227).

Semiosis is, in other words, the process of human reason and logic, the only manner of knowing anything at all. A sign, then, is "something which stands to somebody for something in some respect or capacity. It addresses somebody, that is, creates in the mind of that person an equivalent sign . . ." (CP 2. 227). Here, again stated in Peircean terms, is the triadic theory of the mental process. The significance of this concept, of course, is that man, unique among all creatures in the universe, can "read" and thereby learn from all forms of sign "language," whether that language is written in the atom, the cloud formation, the rainbow or in the language of Shakespeare, Milton, or Apostle Paul. Man apprehends the signs via his senses, primarily hearing and seeing, then considers the data, recalls, associates, contrasts--in other words, forms relationships--and finally comprehends and knows, albeit incorrectly at times, the meaning contained in the signs, for it has been ascertained that, in the theory under consideration, the sign acts as a cognitive vehicle for ideas or meanings of objects and experience.

Theologian Josiah Royce, contemporary popularizer of Peircean thought, has interpreted Peirce's doctrine of signs in its metaphysical implications and explains the theory in The Problem of Christianity:

> . . . [A]ccording to Peirce, just as percepts have, for their appropriate objects, individual Things; and just as concepts [meanings] possess, for their sole objects, Universals--so interpreta-tions have, as the objects which they interpret, Signs. In its most abstract definition, therefore, a Sign, according to Peirce, is something that determines an interpretation. A sign may also be called an expression of mind; and, in our ordinary social intercourse, it actually is such an expression. Or again, one may say that a sign is, in its essence, either a mind or a quasi-mind--an object that fulfills the function of a mind (345).

Further, according to this theory, a sign calls for another sign, that is, a new expression, a new interpretation on the part of the receiver; this in turn calls for another interpretation, ad infinitum. Royce is here simply illustrating Peirce's Thirds or mediating links between Universals (Firsts) and Individuals (Seconds), links which transfer meaning to comprehending minds. Peirce's semiotic tacitly calls for Royce's metaphysical theory about the "world of interpretation": "The universe consist[s] of real Signs and of their interpretation" (345). In a fuller statement, Royce explains his metaphysical doctrine of signs this way:

> [T]he very being of the universe consists in a process whereby the world is interpreted,--not indeed in its wholeness, at any one moment of time, but in and through an infinite series of acts of interpretation. This infinite series constitutes the temporal order of the world with all its complexities. The temporal order is an order of purposes and deeds, simply because it is of the essence of every rational deed to be an effort to interpret a past life to a future life; while every act of interpretation aims to introduce unity into life, by mediating between mutually contrasting or estranged ideas, minds, and purposes. If we consider the temporal world in its wholeness, it constitutes in itself an infinitely complex Sign. This sign is, as a whole, interpreted to an experience which itself includes a synoptic survey of the whole of time. (346)

Thus, all experience constitutes a "realm of Signs" that, Royce contends, acts as "sign-posts" directing knowledge and behavior, "preceded by an infinite series of facts whose meaning [they summarize], and leading to an infinite series of coming events, into whose meaning [they are] yet to enter" (347).

A. Theory of Interpretation

In this manner, Royce develops his theory of "community of interpretation" or "world of interpretation":

> Now our doctrine of the world of interpretation extends to all reality the presuppositions which we use in all our dealings with past and future time. Our memories are signs of the past; our expectations are signs of the future. Past and future are real in so far as these signs have their real interpretation. Our metaphysical thesis generalizes the rules which constantly guide our daily interpretations of life. All contrasts of ideas, all varieties of experience, all the problems which finite experience possesses, are signs. (348)

Thus, man lives by a tacit philosophy that he deduces from his experiences, his observations, his learning--a philosophy that Royce calls "Voluntarism." This is simply the interpretation of experience according to a person's metaphysical interests, for, Royce argues, it is one's metaphysical interests that direct his will, that define his attitude toward the universe, that make "articulate and practical [his] ideals and [his] resolutions" (349). Moreover, Royce holds, there exists an "Absolute Voluntarism," which asserts that,

> while every metaphysical theory is the expression of an attitude of the will, there is one, and but one, general and decisive attitude of the will which is the right attitude, when we stand in the presence of the universe, and when we undertake to choose how we propose to bear ourselves towards the world. (349)

There is, in other words, a system of moral absolutes in the universe, which, if man learns to read universal signs correctly, will direct his thought, knowledge, and will toward that perfect behavior established by the Universal Mind:

> The creative activity of the will is therefore no mere play with figments. It has the reality of a realm of deeds. And every deed has a value that extends throughout the world of the will. Each act is to be judged in light of the principle: "Inasmuch as ye have done it unto the least of these." (349-50)

Following this line of argument (i.e., man's behavior based upon his metaphysical view of life), Royce finds three distinct attitudes toward the "realm of actual or of possible deeds" (351). There is, on the most elemental level, "The affirmation of the Will to Live," a phrase for which Royce credits Schopenhauer (351) and which identifies a person who "essentially desires to be himself, whoever he may be, and to win his aims, whatever the special aims be to which he commits himself" (351). There is, Royce notes, "a natural solipsism of the individual will" in this kind of individual, an independence, a selfishness, a desperate seeking after its own objective. He illustrates by example:

> I perceive my inner life, or, at all events, my own facts of perception. By analogy I extend the world thus primarily known to me. Other men are, in this way, hypothetical extensions of myself. For the rest, I believe in them because, unless I take due account of them, they snub or thwart my own will to live. My ideas are my own, and it is the essence of my life as this individual that I want my own ideas to "work." Upon this affirmation of my will to live depends all the truth that I shall ever come to know. (353)

The second "attitude of will," Royce calls "the denial of the will to live," citing Schopenhauer and Bergson as his sources, but rejecting the theory of sufficiency for salvation in this mode. This mode of existence is best identified with ascetics and mystics, individuals who practice total self-denial, which, Royce contends, is a form of vanity and hence produces a "vexation of spirit" (355).

B. Doctrine of Loyalty

The third attitude of will represents Royce's own philosophical position, his theory of Christianity: "the attitude of Loyalty" (356). This is the attitude, Royce says, that most nearly represents the Pauline doctrine of salvation, "divine in its origin" but manifested in the will and purpose of life:

> It is a positive devotion of the Self to its cause,--a devotion as vigorous, as self-asserting, as articulate, as strenuous, as Paul's life and counsels always remained. The apostle himself was no resigned person. His sacrifices for his cause were constant, and were eloquently portrayed in his own burning words. They included the giving of whatever he possessed. But they never included the negation of the will, the plucking out of the root of all desire, in which Gotama Buddha found salvation. Paul died at his conversion; but only in order that henceforth the life of the spirit should live in him and through him. (356)

What Royce describes here is his interpretation of Paul's Attitude of Will, the answer to the question of meaning and purpose in life and the identification of certain absolutes that man seeks but never fully knows. It is the search itself that gradually clarifies experience for each man and for the community of man because the search is an active and ongoing interpretation of experience using past interpreta-tions (history) as a sign addressing present experience for current belief and action, which in turn address future belief and action. This is, of course, Peirce's synechistic theory of evolution by which everything moves toward an ultimate resolution in harmony and love. In Pauline terms this means the ultimate brotherhood of all men in the Kingdom of God. And to individuals this means, first, the recognition of the Universal Church as the Body of Christ, in which all believers exist and move and have their being. Royce explains it this way:

> The essential message of Christianity has been the word that the sense of life, the very being of the time process itself, consists in the progressive realization of the Universal Community in and through the longings, the vicissitudes, the tragedies, and the triumphs of the process of the temporal world. Now this message has been historically expressed

> through the symbols, through the traditions, and through the
> concrete life of whatever human communities have most fully
> embodied the essential spirit of Christianity. . . .
>
> On earth, as we have seen, the universal community is
> nowhere visibly realized. But in the whole world, the divine
> life is expressed in the form of a community. Herewith, in
> teaching us this general but immensely practical truth, the
> "kindly light" seems also to show us not, in its temporal
> details, "the distant scene," but the "step" which we most
> need to see "amid the encircling gloom." (387)

But because the process is cumulative (and linear), no single event "can exhaust the meaning of the process of the spirit" [of the Body of Christ]; thus, Royce asserts, "the true church never yet has become visible to men" (367). Ultimately, however, in due course of interpretation (of history and experience), there will be resolution; "for every wrong there will somewhere appear the corresponding remedy; and for every tragedy and distraction of individual existence the universal community will find the way . . . to provide the corresponding unity, the appropriate triumph" (388). More significantly, Royce adds,

> We are saved through and in the community. There is the
> victory which overcomes the world. There is the
> interpretation which reconciles. There is the doctrine which
> we teach. . . . (388)
>
> The apologists for Christian tradition generally fail to express
> such a doctrine, because they misread symbols which
> tradition has so richly furnished. The assailants of
> Christianity are generally ignorant of the meaning of the
> ideal of the universal and beloved community. (388)

What this doctrine of signs means to the individual is the awareness of the need for community, the need, not merely social, to be a part of a larger "self" that will offer interpretation of human experience as well as, ultimately, interpretation of spiritual truth: the probability, according to deductive reading of historical symbols, of Christ, and of the claims of Christ regarding

God as Father and men as brothers within the Kingdom of God. It is the realization that

> Alone I am lost, and worse than nothing. I need a counsellor, I need my community. Interpret me. Let me join in this interpretation. Let there be community. This alone is life. This alone is salvation. This alone is real. (362)

What ends in this spiritual understanding, however, must begin on the secular, merely social, level, for man cannot know himself or any other thing without an interpretive community; it is only within the larger interpretive community that there can exist the Beloved Community (Body of Christ) from which the individual learns the highest good--charity.

In summary, both Peirce and Royce demonstrate the crucial role of signs to human beings: without signs and the ability to read them, man would be like the beast, simply responding to serve his biological needs; with them man can reason, remember, analyze, compare, contrast, and know the universe in which he lives. And, according to Peirce and Royce, with signs rightly construed, man can reason about the Source of all things and arrive at probable conclusions regarding the moral nature of the universe and thus establish proper behavior for himself.

Peirce's Doctrine of Divine Triad

A. Introduction

Royce names Paul the Apostle as the progenitor of his concept of the Christian Community (the church) as interpreter of God and the Body of Christ:

> My main topic is a form of social religious experience, namely, that form which in ideal, the Apostle Paul viewed as the experience of the Church. (40)

> All experience must be at least individual experience but unless it is also social experience, and unless the whole religious community which is in question unites to share it, this experience is but as sounding brass, and as a tinkling

110

> cymbal. This truth is what Paul saw. This is the rock upon
> which the true and ideal church is built. This is the essence
> of Christianity. (41)

In order to have a closer look at Royce's (and Peirce's) social religious system, which Royce terms Pauline, I shall examine their theology as it views the triad of characters in the play of cosmic (metaphysical) communication: the identity and the nature of God as the Ground of Being and ultimate Source of all signs, the identity and the nature of man as receiver of signs, and the nature of the church as interpreter of Divine Signs and as mediator between God and man. I shall go to Apostle Paul and other scripture writers, as Royce and Peirce do, to cite the authority for their pragmatic faith, to find the support they seek in scripture for their "scientific" religion.

B. God as Sign Giver

In considering the nature of God as the first and primary element of Peirce's cosmic triad, I begin with his essay "A Neglected Argument for the Reality of God" (1908). First, Peirce holds that God is Creator of all things and, as Creator, is revealed in the creation itself; that he communicates with man in the natural language of the universe:

> Let a man drink in such thoughts as come to him in
> contemplating the physico-psychical universe without any
> special purpose of his own. . . . The idea of there being a
> God over it all of course will be often suggested; and the
> more he considers it, the more he will be enwrapt with "Love
> of the idea." (CP 6. 501)

An instinct for God, Peirce argues, introduces the idea to a person considering the natural world, and desire for its truth perpetuates it within his heart. There is, of course, support from Paul in this regard; to the Romans, he explains that "the invisible things of him from the creation of the world are clearly seen, being understood by the things that are made, even his eternal power and Godhead" (Rom. 1: 20). And to the Athenians who, Paul concludes, seek the "unknown god" by instinct, erect shrines in his honor, yet do not know his identity, Paul offers, "Whom therefore ye ignorantly worship, him declare I unto you" (Acts 17: 23)

Further, as Creator, God is, by the law of logic, the Absolute First, that is, the "starting point of the universe" (CP 1. 362), and as "terminus of the universe, God completely revealed; in the Incarnate Christ, He is also Absolute Second" (CP 1. 362). Finally, as the Holy Spirit, reconciling the world to himself, God is the ultimate Third.[1]

In another essay--"The Reality of God"--Peirce identifies God as universal Order or "Super Order," that is, "pure mind" and "creative thought" (CP 6. 490). This idea of God is closely related to Peirce's theory of Evolutionary Love, by which he views the process of cosmological evolution as "Cherishing-Love" and, quoting John, the gospel writer, identifies that Love as God--"We know and have trusted the love which God hath in us. God is love . . . (CP 6. 287)--then adds a qualification:

> [T]he love that God is, is not a love of which hatred is the contrary; otherwise Satan would be a coordinate power, but is a love which embraces hatred as an imperfect state of it . . . yea, even needs hatred and hatefulness as its object. For self-love is no love; so if God's self is love that which he loves must be defect of love. (CP 6. 287)

I have examined Peirce's theory of evolutionary love in another place; so I shall not delineate the three modes of the process here, but I should emphasize Peirce's belief in the control of God as the overriding Mind in the flux of time and space.

Finally, God, the First Person in the metaphysical semiotic of Peirce and Royce, is incarnated in Christ and in the Body of Christ (the church). This doctrine is implicit throughout the theological works of both Peirce and Royce, and I shall have much more to say about this in the examination of the church as interpretive community, but the Peircean doctrine of the interrelatedness of the divine Persons should be noted at this point. The nature of God, the work of God, the very identity of God cannot be known apart from the Incarnate Christ, as he lived and taught, Peirce believes, a part of history, and the Supreme Revelation of God the Father. John records Jesus' conversation concerning his identity with God: "If you had known me, you would have known my Father also; henceforth you know him and have seen him. . . . Believe me that I am in the Father and the Father in me" (John 4: 7, 11). Likewise, Peirce and Royce view the Church, the Body of Christ, as the embodiment of the Spirit of God, in some mysterious way indwelt and transformed by God--the nature of God as love and the identity of God as creator and sustainer of (spiritual) life.

C. Man as Sign Receptor

In Peirce's metaphysical triad, as I have identified the relationship of God, man, and Church, man occupies the receptor's position; he is the "scientific intelligence," the only mind in the universe, capable of knowing God by reasoning from signs and of sharing that understanding with other minds. In fact, Peirce identifies man not only as a sign receiver, but as a sign per se (i.e., his word or language), because, Peirce says, "there is no element whatever of man's consciousness which has not something corresponding to it in the word . . ." (CP 5. 314). He explains the concept this way:

> It is that the word or sign which man uses is the man himself. For, as the fact that every thought is a sign, taken in conjunction with the fact that life is a train of thought, proves that man is a sign. . . . Thus my language is the sum total of myself; for man is the thought. (CP 5. 314)

More important to Peirce's theology, the individual man can be known "only by ignorance and error"; that is, only "so far as he is anything apart from his fellows, and from what he and they are to be, is only a negation" (CP 5. 317). The emphasis here is "what he and they are to be," a phrase suggesting unity, fellowship, and loyalty--all of which are critical to the theology of Charles Peirce.

Josiah Royce explains more closely the social nature of man, especially as it pertains to the metaphysical issue of man-God relationship. Royce notes, first, that there is a general acknowledgment among men of their need for God, and, he argues, that "whatever the truth of religion may be, the office, the task, the need of religion are the most important needs, tasks, and offices of humanity" (60). Further, Christianity has, historically, offered "the most effective expression of religious longing" and "man's most impressive vision of salvation, and his principal glimpse of the home-land of the spirit" (60).

Both Peirce and Royce emphasize the fact that man is a social being, a part of a larger body; this idea is crucial to their religious theories. Royce clarifies the theory:

> As an essentially social being, man lives in communities, and depends upon his communities for all that makes his civilization articulate. His communities, as both Plato and Aristotle already observed, have a sort of organic life of their own, so that we can compare a highly developed community, such as a state, either to the soul of a man or to a living animal. A community is not a mere collection of individuals. It is a live unit, that has organs, as a body of an individual has organs. . . . Not only does a community live, it has a mind of its own,--a mind whose psychology is not the same as the psychology of an individual human being. The social mind displays its psychological traits in its characteristic products,--in languages, in customs, in religions. (80-81)

Moreover, the social unit to which the individual belongs demands a certain cooperation, even obedience, to its customs, laws, and language; in this way, the community holds the individual in a kind of bondage, a dependency, to it. But, Royce says after the Apostle Paul, man is naturally wayward; the very community that demands his obedience and loyalty also trains the individual to selfishness then condemns that trait, leaving man with an insufferable moral burden which, alone, he cannot escape. More pragmatic than the theory of original sin, Royce's idea of the sin of individualism emanates from the community itself, a theory which, Royce contends, he adopts from Paul and restates in "relatively modern terminology" (106).

Conduct, Royce argues, is the result of "training which our hereditary predispositions . . . get when the environment has played upon them in a suitable way, and for a sufficient time" (107). The individual is not necessarily aware of his "formed" behavior; he may not judge for himself the normative quality of his life because

> the higher and more complex types of our consciousness
> about our conduct, our knowledge about what we do, and
> about why we do it,--all this more complex sort of practical
> knowledge of ourselves, is trained by a specific sort of
> environment, namely, by a social environment. (107)

Furthermore, Royce argues, this "education" or awareness regarding human conduct is done by the community in "opposing us, [in] criticising us, or [in] otherwise standing in contrast to us" (107), for it is only in a human (social) environment that man can see and compare and thereby learn rules and standards of behavior. And as long as he replicates those rules and standards, he is a working segment of his society, cooperative and anonymous. But when he violates established norms, either out of ignorance or out of defiance, he becomes an individual, distinct from all other cooperating members:

> In brief, it is our fellows who first startle us out of our
> natural unconsciousness about our own conduct; and who
> then, by an endless series of processes of setting us attractive
> but difficult models, and of socially interfering with our own
> doings, train us to higher and higher grades and to more and
> more complexities of self-consciousness regarding what we
> do and why we do it.   Play and conflict, rivalry and
> emulation, conscious imitation and conscious social contrasts
> between man and man,--these are the sources of each man's
> consciousness about his own conduct. (108-09)

This explanation, Royce says, simply illustrates what Paul talks about in Romans 7, the "law" that serves to enlighten him regarding his behavior: "[I]f it had not been for the law, I should not have known sin. I should not have known what it is to covet if the law had not said, 'You shall not covet'" (Rom. 7: 7b).

In this way, a person knows his self and thereby forms a consciousness of an ideal self and a conscience which urges him toward that ideal. And herein lies Royce's critical concern about man's fallen nature--in the consciousness of conduct:

> [F]rom a purely psychological point of view, my consciousness about my conduct, and consequently my power to form ideals, and my power to form any sort of conscience, are a product of my nature as a social being. And the product arises in this way: contrasts, rivalries, difficult efforts to imitate some fascinating fellow-being, contests with my foes, emulation, social ambition, the desire to attract attention, the desire to find my place in my social order, my interest in what my fellows say and do with reference to me,--such are the more elemental social motives and the social situations which at first make me highly conscious of my own doings. (110)

Man's predicament thus described is chaotic, Royce allows, but it is, nevertheless, the source of man's understanding of good and evil, of the establishment of an ideal self, and of the formation of a conscience--all in an effort "to get harmony into this chaos" (110). What happens in the formative period, of course, is not unity and harmony, but discord and tension: "social tension is . . . the primary state. . . . The moral self, the natural conscience, is bred through situations that involve social tension" (111).

The community, on the other hand, seeks to control these private and personal conflicts by prescribing conduct in the form of customs and laws, by teaching its members how to behave toward one another. But codes--"these forms of customary morality, . . . have to be taught to us as conscious rules of conduct" (112), and this, in turn, produces a "higher level of our general self-consciousness," which, Royce contends, produces "new conflicts between the self and its world" (112):

> The higher the training and more cultivated and elaborate is
> our socially trained conscience--the more highly conscious
> our estimate of our own value becomes, and so, in general,
> the stronger grows our self-will. (112)

Even the passive, compliant individual within the community may suffer from
similar tension between his ideal and his actual behavior. This condition
results in what Royce calls the "moral burden of the individual," the sense of
self-will, self-determination, individualism, that brings with it spiritual enmity
and defiance.

What Royce has illustrated in modern terms of community versus the
individual is the Pauline doctrine of sin as basic to human nature and as
cultivated by the law. Law names the sin, Paul says, and thereby enlightens
man of his moral failures:

> Apart from the law sin lies dead. I was once alive apart
> from the law, but when the commandment came, sin revived
> and I died; the very commandment which promised life
> proved to be death to me. For sin, finding opportunity in
> the commandment, deceived me and by it killed me. (Rom.
> 7: 8-11)

Moreover, as the self is brought into knowledge of the law, it responds, if it
has been well trained socially, with obedience and subjection, but, Paul and
Royce attest, the "inner man" rebels:

> We know that the law is spiritual; but I am carnal, sold
> under sin. I do not understand my own actions. For I do
> not do what I want, but I do the very thing I hate. Now I do
> what I do not want, I agree that the law is good. So that it
> is no longer I that do it, but sin which dwells within me.
> (Rom. 7: 14-17)

Royce summarizes Paul's teaching this way:

> What Paul's psychology, translated into more modern terms,
> teaches is that the moral self-consciousness of every one of
> us gets its cultivation from our social order through a
> process which begins by craftily awakening us, as the serpent
> did Eve, through critical observations, and which then
> fascinates our divided will by giving us the serpent's counsels.
> "Ye shall be as gods." This is the lore of all individualism,

> and the vice of all our worldly social ambitions. The
> resulting diseases of self-consciousness are due to the inmost
> nature of the human race. (118)

This, then, is the view of man in Royce and Peirce's theology, their reading of Paul--man as a dependent member of a social unit that paradoxically forms him and teaches him moral behavior, on the one hand, and fosters independence and individualism on the other, thereby generating internal conflict and a moral burden which he cannot overcome on his own. Like Paul, the individual cries out in frustration and guilt: "Oh, wretched man that I am" (Rom. 7: 24).

Lost, isolated, alienated from himself and others, the individual's only hope of redemption (reconciliation) lies in the realm of the spirit, and that means a new life in Paul's terms, a new loyalty in Royce's terms--simply an affiliation with the Beloved Community which lovingly draws the individual into the fold, mysteriously transforms his nature, and offers him a new perspective on life itself.

D. Church as Sign Interpreter

The church is the third element in Peirce and Royce's metaphysical triad, the "interpreter" of God to the wayward creature, man. Peirce does not delineate this theological concept fully; he leaves details to Royce, but he does establish the nature of the church:

> Man's highest developments are social; and religion, though
> it begins in a seminal individual inspiration, only comes to
> full flower in a great church coextensive with a civilization.
> This is true of every religion, but super-eminently so of the
> religion of love. Its ideal is that the whole world shall be
> united in the bond of a common love of God accomplished
> by every man's loving his neighbor. Without a church, the
> religion of love can have but a rudimentary existence. . . .
> (CP 6. 443)

This statement suggests three qualities of Christianity on which Peirce, Royce, and Paul all concur: that is, first, the social nature of the church; second, the

118

universality of the church; and third, the unifying bond of love. Concerning dogmas and creeds, Peirce expresses vehement opposition; they reflect, he says, "strict party regularity" and omit altogether "the central doctrine of love" (CP 6. 450). Contrary to established dogmatic religion, Peirce maintains, "Truth is the fruit of free inquiry and of such docility toward facts as shall make us willing to acknowledge that we are wrong, and anxious to discover that we have been so" (CP 6. 450). Peirce concludes that

> the raison d'être of a church is to confer upon men a life broader than their narrow personalities, a life rooted in the very truth of being. To do that it must be based upon and refer to a definite and public experience. (CP 6. 451)

I turn now to Josiah Royce, Peirce's student in philosophy, for a closer look at the fully developed concept of the church as interpreter of God and, hence, mediator between God and man. For the man who has been awakened to his self and who has thus set about to fulfill all his desires and ambitions, his potential of selfhood, and who has consequently come into conflict with other selves and with the social system in which he lives, experiencing internal struggle, there is no escape either by his own efforts or by the training of his community. This so-called natural man is fallen man and suffers from the "disease of self-consciousness" (127):

> The curse is rooted in the primal constitution which makes man social, and which adapts him to win his intelligence through social conflicts with his neighbors. Hence the curse belongs to the whole "flesh" of man; for by "flesh" Paul means whatever first expresses itself in our instincts and thus lies at the basis of our training, and so of our natural life. (127)

The doom of the natural man thus enlightened to the self is inexorable unless he finds and joins a "lovable" community and afterward devotes himself in absolute loyalty to it:

> Great loyalty . . . must be awakened by a community sufficiently lovable to win the enduring devotion of one who, like Paul, has first been trained to possess and to keep an

> obstinately critical and independent attitude of spirit. . . .
> (129)

This Beloved Community, which Royce describes, or the church which Paul describes, exists on two levels: on the human level as a union of individuals bound by the ideals and the purpose it espouses (i.e., teachings and ethics of Christ) and on the spiritual level as the invisible Kingdom of God governed by the glorified and resurrected Christ. On the social level

> the Beloved Community must be . . . quite unlike a natural social group, whose life consists of laws and quarrels . . . [but] must be a union of members who first love it. The unity of love must pervade it, before the individual member can find it lovable. (129)

It is, Royce and Paul agree, only by "some miracle of grace" that this "new life" can be initiated, "either in the individuals who are to love communities, or in the communities that are to be worthy of their love" (130). Paul states it this way to the Ephesians: "For by grace are ye saved through faith; and not of yourselves: it is the gift of God" (Eph. 2: 8). On the human level, the Beloved Community partakes in the spiritual nature of God himself in the form of love and loyalty. On the spiritual level, the Beloved Community is the embodiment of Christ, its founder, who "both knew and loved his community before it existed on earth; for his foreknowledge was one with that of the God whose will he came to accomplish" (131):

> On earth he called into this community its first members. He suffered and died that it might have life. Through his death and in his life the community lives. He is now identical with the spirit of this community. [Royce's italics] This, according to Paul, was the divine grace which began the process of salvation for man. In the individual life of each Christian this same process appears as a new act of grace. Its outcome is the new life of loyalty to which the convert is henceforth devoted. (131)

Royce calls this the Realm of Grace, "the realm of the powers and the gifts that save, by thus originating and sustaining and informing the loyal life"

(Problem 133), and its structure is comprised of "at the very least, three essentially necessary constituent members": first, "the ideally lovable community of many individuals in one spiritual bond"; second, the Spirit of Christ, "which is present both as the human individual whose power originated and whose example, whose life and death, have led and still guide the community"; third, love, "the love of the community by all its members, and of the members by the community" (133). To Paul and to Royce, these members are divine with "human correlate and foundation wherever the loyal life exists" (133).

Although it is the church as organic body with a physical existence that the world sees, it is, as has been suggested, the spiritual structure that gives it life and power. The fourth Gospel, John, gives the best account of Paul's conception of the Church as "the body of Christ, and of Christ as the spirit of the Church . . ." linked with the doctrine of "the divine Word made flesh" (Problem 139). Royce notes John's statement of the terms of the transformation of the believer via the new birth that makes him "a dweller in the realm which is at once inaccessibly above his merely natural level as an individual . . . ," yet actualized in "the realm of the united and lovable community" (139):

> The union of the concrete and the ineffable which hereupon resulted,--the union of what touches the human heart and stirs the soul as only the voice of a living individual leader can touch it,--the complete union of this with the greatest and most inspiring of human mysteries,--the mystery of loving membership in a community whose meaning seems divine,--this union became the central interest of Christianity. (140)

What Royce is demonstrating here is the mystery of the incarnation, that the life of a Man, and later a whole body of men, is somehow vitiated by, indeed, indwelled by, the divine Spirit of God. Only thus can the mystery of loyalty be explained. Only by the inspiration of Jesus, who prays for his followers-- "Holy Father, keep them in thy name which thou hast given me, that they may be one, even as we are" (John 17: 11)--can the Holy Community receive its credibility as divine participant. The purpose of the Beloved Community is, therefore, to draw men to God, to interpret God in human terms, and to rescue men from the "doom of self-deceit."

I should mention another facet in this role of the Church as divine interpreter; that is, the rescuer of the spiritual "traitor."[2] Royce describes the traitor at great length: he is a person who has been a part of the Beloved Community, "has had an ideal, and has loved it with all his heart and his soul and his mind and his strength"; it was, at one time, the "cause of his life," his religion, his "way of salvation" (168), but he has since renounced it, turned away in rebellion, and has been deliberately false to it. Subsequently, the traitor becomes lost in his own "hell of the irrevocable" because he knows the moral law of God; yet he has defied the precepts and feels in his heart that all is lost to him, that he can never share in the Kingdom, which he has blatantly dishonored. Indeed, the traitor has sought to destroy the fellowship within the Beloved Community, has done what he can to wreck it; thus, the reconciliation "concerns not only the traitor, but the wounded and shattered community" as well (175); so it becomes the role of the Beloved Community to restore the fallen member with "a triumph of the creative will" (180):

> [T]his triumph over treason can only he accomplished by the community [i.e., Beloved Community], or on behalf of the community, through some steadfastly loyal servant who acts, so to speak, as the incarnation of the very spirit of the community itself. (180)

It requires, in other words, "a deed, or various deeds, for which only just this treason furnishes the opportunity" (Problem 180); it is the felix culpa of the original Fall of the traitor that opens the way for a "creative work" so that "The world, as transformed by this creative deed, is better than it would have been had all else remained the same, but had that deed of treason not been done at all" [Royce's italics] (18O). In this way the loss is transformed into gain, a new life for the traitor, who is brought forth "from the grave":

> The triumph of the spirit of the [Beloved] community over the treason which was its enemy, the rewinning of the value of the traitor's own life, when the new deed is done, involves the old tragedy, but takes up that tragedy into a life that is now more a life of triumph than it would have been if the deed of treason had never been done. (181)

Such is the "genuinely reconciling" work of Christ for the church in the face of treachery within its circle, meeting "the deepest and bitterest estrangements by showing a way of reconciliation" (181):

> [T]here was something so precious about the work of Christ, something so divinely wise . . . about the plan of salvation,-- that, as a result of all this, after Christ's work was done, the world as a whole was a nobler and richer and worthier creation than it would have been if Adam had not sinned. (185)

There is yet another aspect of Royce's theory of the church that should be examined: the concept of the single body with many members. This teaching has to do with the movement of the Church through history, with what Royce calls the memory and the hope, a teaching established in Paul's first letter to the Corinthians. The Corinthian Christians ask certain questions regarding their individu-ality in the Resurrection--"How are the dead raised up? and with what body do they come?" (I Cor. 15: 35)--obviously concerned about their identity in the future Kingdom. To explain what he attests to be Paul's answer to the questions, Royce defines and then explicates his definition of the spiritual Body of Christ: "With reference to the ideal common past and future in question, I say that these selves constitute a community" (252). And further,

> The present variety of the selves who are the members of the spiritual body so defined, is not hereby either annulled or slighted. The motives which determine each of them thus ideally to extend his own life, may vary from self to self in the most manifold fashion. (252)

Such variety within the unity of a single Body is possible only because there lies behind it a history of events which leads to the present moment and extends beyond the present to the foretold conclusion of the present (i.e., physical and temporal) manifestation of the church to the end of this age and the coming of the heavenly Kingdom of God. Paul explains the idea to the Corinthians this way:

> The first man Adam was made a living soul; the last Adam [Christ] was made a quickening spirit. . . . The first man is of the earth, earthy: the second man is the Lord from heaven. As is the earthy, such are they also that are earthy: and as is the heavenly, such are they also that are heavenly. And as we have borne the image of the earthy, we shall also bear the image of the heavenly. . . . Behold, I shew you a mystery; We shall not all sleep, but we shall all be changed, in a moment, in the twinkling of an eye, at the last trump: for the trumpet shall sound, and the dead shall be raised incorruptible, and we shall be changed. (I Cor. 15: 45, 47-49, 51-62)

In the present, therefore, the corporate body may indeed manifest great variety, many members with diverse gifts, and none lost in the "mystery" of the whole. In the end, each body will be raised, individually, incorruptible; yet, Royce paraphrases Paul, "The event of the resurrection is one for all of us, for we shall arise together" (159); then he adds,

> In the expected resurrection, as Paul pictures it, the individual finds his own life, and the community its common triumph over all the world old powers of death. And the hope is referred back to the memory. Was not Christ raised? By this synthesis Paul solves his religious problem, and defines sharply the relation of the individual and the community. (260)

> This life of the spirit is also the life of the community. For the individual is saved, according to Paul, only in and through and with the community and its Lord. (260)

E. Summary

In summary, the Church as the Body of Christ, the brotherhood of the Many-in-the-One, acts as God's interpreter on earth, what Royce calls the Community of Interpretation, for

> if we aim to conceive the divine nature, how better can we conceive it than in the form of the Interpreter, who interprets all to all, and each individual to the world, and the world of spirits to each individual? (318)

And if, through the vicissitudes and variations of the temporal Church or visible Body, the individual Christian maintains his firm belief in "the presence of the redeeming divine spirit in the living [invisible or spiritual] Church," he will be, in spirit, a Pauline Christian, Royce insists, "however he otherwise interprets the person of Christ" (377).

I have examined Peirce and Royce's metaphysical semiotic, based on Paul's theology, a semiotic that establishes logical connections between God, the Creator of the universe (and hence maker of all signs that make up the universe), and man, the only species of created beings in the universe capable of understanding signs mediated by a universal interpretive community.

The system I have thus examined has been viable, Royce maintains, ever since Paul wrote his epistles to various churches and individuals in the first century, a tradition that can be traced in a continuous line through the early church Fathers, beginning with Augustine of Hippo, and continuing through the Reformers--Luther, Calvin, and others--to the American Calvinists through the "secularizers," Ralph Waldo Emerson, Charles Sanders Peirce and his school of pragmatists, and back to the current philosopher and writer Walker Percy.

NOTES

[1] Charles Hartshorne, editor of the first collection of Peirce's works, explains in an essay "Peirce's 'One Contribution'" (455-74) that in Peirce's system, "what distinguishes God is not his ordinal degree of relativity (as between First, Second, and Third) but rather his being relative (in all three degrees) in every context. He is absolutely relative" (464). In Him all things relate, in him all things consist, for by Him all things were made.

[2] The theory of the traitor is particularly important, according to John E. Smith, editor of the 1968 edition of The Problem of Christianity, because it represents, to Royce, modern scientific society, men who have known the Christian ideal but who have rejected it in favor of godless science and inhuman values.

CHAPTER 4
CHRISTIAN SEMIOTIC TRADITION

Introduction

In structuring my account of the historical tradition of Pauline semiotics, I have kept in view the semiotic of Walker Percy, who set my study in motion and who established the criteria which align him with the Christian tradition. In his last essay, "The Delta Factor," which introduces The Message in the Bottle, Percy makes his own intention clear: his first interest is man-- the nature of man, the uniqueness of man, the waywardness of man. Why is it, he questions, that twentieth century man, who has, generally speaking, the greatest advantages ever offered a civilization, feels so alienated and displaced?

> Why does man feel so bad in the very age when, more than in any other age, he has succeeded in satisfying his needs and making over the world for his own use? (MB 3)

> Why has man entered on an orgy of war, murder, torture, and self-destruction unparalleled in history and in the very century when he had hoped to see the dawn of universal peace and brotherhood? (MB 3)

> Why is man the only creature that wages war against its species? (MB 4)

> Why do young people look so sad, the very young, who, seeing how sad their elders are, have sought a new life of joy and freedom with each other and in the green fields and forests, but who instead of finding joy look sadder than their elders? (MB 7)

Percy makes it clear in the rhetorical questions at the beginning of his essay that his interest lies primarily in the puzzling, paradoxical behavior of man and that his ambition is to solve the mystery of man's strange behavior. In his search for the key to the human enigma, Percy has discovered, he believes, if not the key to the puzzle, then at least a way to get to the key to the mystery of man's nature. It is language, he contends, that makes man unique among all living creatures; it is language, he adds, that allows man to name his world, completely, without gaps, and to establish a dominance over it; and, he concludes, it is language that allows man to exercise his will and to perform extraordinary deeds of kindness as well as incredible atrocities. For these reasons, Percy becomes a student of language, an explorer, in a sense, searching for his own kind of Rosetta Stone to help him decipher the mystery of language, and, in turn, the mystery of man.

That Percy's search is a religious one quickly becomes apparent to the perceptive reader, first of all, because of the concern with spiritual disease (dis-ease), a concern that pervades the rhetoric from first to last: the thrust of his discourse, whether fiction or nonfiction, is man's displacement in the world, his alienation from others and from himself. There are also references, albeit discredited ones, to outdated Judeo-Christian explanations about man--his nature and his predicament:

> It was the belief [in the Old Modern Age or Christian Era] that man was created in the image of God with an immortal soul, that he occupied a place in nature somewhere between the beasts and the angels, that he suffered an aboriginal catastrophe, the Fall, in consequence of which he lost his way, and, unlike the beasts, became capable of sin and thereafter became a pilgrim or seeker of his own salvation and that the clue and sign of his salvation was to be found not in science or philosophy but in news of an historical event involving a people, a person, and an institution. (MB 18)

The possibility of the orthodox Christian position is always present in varying degrees of visibility, rarely as straightforward as the statement above and always discredited by an acknowledgment of public rejection:

> What I do suggest is that if one states a kind of consensus view of man in the present age, the conventional wisdom of the great majority of the denizens of the democratic technological society in the late twentieth century, this Judeo-Christian credo is no longer a significant component. (MB 18)

A new philosophy of man is needed, Percy argues, or, as he subtly suggests, a revival of the old orthodox one in order to halt the destructive course of mankind, to redeem the race of man before it succeeds in doing what it seems determined to do--annihilate itself completely.

Having established the need to learn more about man's place in the cosmos and about the state of man's soul (or whether in fact he has or is a soul), Percy shifts his investigation to language as the sign of humanness, incorporating in the field of his study "the mind, the idea, the word, the form which [men] make and by which [they] not only understand the world but construe it, even constitute it" (MB 32-33).

Following the lead of Walker Percy, then, I shall use language as the central focus of this historical account of the Christian tradition, considering language, not merely as manmade speech, but in its original semiotic implications, as communication from God to man--the meaning given the term by the psalmist:

> The heavens declare the glory of God; and the firmament sheweth his handywork.
> Day unto day uttereth speech, and night unto night showeth knowledge.
> There is no speech nor language, where their voice is not heard.
> Their line is gone out through all the earth, and their words to the end of the world. (Ps. 19: 1-3)

This, I believe, is a legitimate alliance for Walker Percy's language theory because of his direct ties to Charles S. Peirce, whose semiotic I have demonstrated to be essentially Pauline dogma.

Beginning with the pre-eminent church Father of the fourth century, Augustine of Hippo, I shall trace the theological development of language via Calvin and Luther to the American theologians, ending finally with Percy himself, exploring, at that point, what Percy's theological language theory has to do with his fiction.

Medieval Language Theory

The logical place to begin an examination of this tradition of language is with Augustine's concept of the Holy Trinity--God the Father, God the Son, and God the Holy Spirit--"Of Whom are all things, through Whom are all things, in Whom are all things" (On Christian Doctrine I. 5). Each is God and together a Unity, but also distinct in the individual offices. It is the office of the Second Person of the Trinity, God the Son, to manifest the Wisdom and Truth of God, the Goodness and Beauty of God, the Love and Grace of God, for it is Christ the Living Word who "became flesh and dwelt among us" (John 1: 14). Augustine compares the Incarnate Word of God to man's "incarnate" word, the word incarnating the idea:

> Just as when we speak, in order that what we have in our minds may enter through the ear into the mind of the hearer, the word which we have in our hearts becomes an outward sound and is called speech; and yet our thought does not lose itself, and takes the form of speech without being modified in its own nature by the change: so the Divine Word, though suffering no change in nature, yet became flesh, that He might dwell among us. (I. 13)

The essence of God is life, that is consciousness and absolute knowledge, and his nature is changeless, eternal, incorruptible; he is, likewise, absolute wisdom, absolute goodness, absolute beauty, absolute power, but in the first Person of the Trinity, God the Father, he is unmanifested spirit, incomprehensible, unutterable. It is only as God the Son that he manifests himself as Living Word, the "eternal self-reproduction" of the Father, represented Truth, co-existent with God, a "speaking of Himself" (De Trinitate XIV. 22). Likewise, God the Word is Creator, Maker, Doer: "All things were made through Him, and without Him was not anything made that was made" (John 1: 3). In this manner the universe itself is the "spoken" Word of God in observable phenomena of creation.

Augustine also speaks in rhetorical terms about man's understanding of revelation via the Word. Like God, man is a trinity, of being, knowledge, and love with faculties of memory, understanding, and will. Similarly, man's self-knowledge is his own "word" or language begotten from the mind:

> Thus, in that realm of eternal truth from which all things temporal were made, we behold with our mind's eye the pattern upon which our being is ordered. . . . Thence we conceive a truthful knowledge of things, which we have within us as a kind of <u>word</u> begotten by inward speech, and remaining with us after its birth. When we speak to others, we apply the service of our voice or of some material sign to the indwelling "word," in order that by means of a perceptible prompting there may take place in the hearer's mind something like what remains in the mind of the speaker. (<u>Trinitate</u> IX. 12)

Man's word, again parallel to God's Word, is begotten out of love, Augustine argues, either love for God or love for self, either charity or covetousness; the word is approved by the mind that produces it and hence reveals the character of the man who speaks, for "no one does anything deliberately that he has not previously spoken in his heart" (IX. 12):

> Every good deed or sin is related to this bringing forth of the word in the saying: "From thy mouth thou shalt be justified, and from thy mouth thou shalt be condemned" (Matt. 12: 37); where "mouth" signifies, not the one we see, but the invisible "mouth" of thought and heart. (IX. 14)

But even with communication via the Word and the word, God's and man's, there remains the mystery of Being, the obscurity of the manifested Word, the great enigmas of Life and Truth and Immortality. None of these, Augustine notes, can be known directly, for man sees through the glass (of language) "darkly" ("as in an enigma"), an "opaque" speech which Augustine calls allegory or similitude:

> There need be no surprise that in the manner of seeing permitted us in life, "through a mirror in an enigma," our struggle to see at all must be a hard one. . . . Both not seeing and seeing are unimaginable. For thought is a kind of vision of the mind, whether in the presence of the objects

> seen by bodily eyes or felt by the other senses, or in their
> absence, when their likenesses are perceived by thought.
> (Trinitate. XIV. 16)

Augustine also explains the matter of representation of the word: there is an unuttered word for every thing or situation that corresponds with or is contained in the incarnate word, so that

> When we speak the truth . . . say what we know, there must
> be born out of the knowledge held in our memory a word
> which corresponds in all respects to the knowledge of which
> it is born. (Trinitate XIV. 19)

Thus, when we articulate that word to ourselves or to others, we express that "inwardly luminous" word by some sign or representation, which becomes an incarnation of the unuttered idea:

> We may compare the manner in which our own word is
> made as it were a bodily utterance as a means of displaying
> itself to men's senses, with that in which the Word of God
> was made flesh, but most assuredly not changed into flesh.
> Our word is made utterance, the divine Word flesh, by an
> assumption of an outward form, and not by a consumption
> of itself and a passing into the other. (Trinitate XIV. 20)

Finally, there is the matter of truth in the word. Thought is a vision of knowledge embedded in the mind and becomes a separate thing (a sign) when expressed; the word is true, Augustine explains, when "the word's content is the same as the content of knowledge . . . the truth that is expected of man, wherein that which is in his knowledge is also in his word . . ." (Trinitate XIV. 20). From the mind comes a true word "when we speak what we know" (XIV. 22):

> But this [interior] word exists before any sound, before any
> imagining of a sound. For in that state the word has the
> closest likeness to the thing known, of which it is offspring
> and image; from the vision which is knowledge arises a
> vision which is thing, having nothing of its own but all from
> that knowledge from which it was born. (XIV. 22)

Signs, Augustine emphasizes, are for man's "use and enjoyment": for enjoyment, to make man happy in knowing a thing for its own sake; for use, "to employ whatever means are at one's disposal to obtain what one desires, if it is a proper object of desire" (On Christian Doctrine I. 4), i.e., knowledge of one's heavenly homeland. Men, he explains in a parable, are like wanderers in a strange country, unhappy in their lostness and determined to return to their fatherland but diverted all the while by "factitious delight" from home, "whose delights would make [them] happy" (Doctrine I. 4):

> Such is a picture of our condition in this life of mortality. We have wandered far from God; and if we wish to return to our Father's home, this world must be used, not enjoyed, so that the invisible things of God may be clearly seen, being understood by the things that are made [Rom. 1: 20]--that is, that by means of what is material and temporary we may lay hold upon that which is spiritual and eternal. (Doctrine I. 4)

Robert L. Entzminger, who has written about the Protestant "attitude" toward language, finds that Augustine is especially valuable to the Reformers because of his concern with language as the primary medium to knowledge of God. It is the man of God, entrusted with and trained in the Word, who, through his preaching, leads others to know God; thus, Augustine concludes, it is imperative that the preacher do two things: one, develop his rhetorical skills and, two, pray frequently and fervently. This "formula" results in what Entzminger refers to as the Protestants' "sanctified rhetoric." Marcia Colish also supports this theory of Augustine's Protestant tendency:

> Augustine projected a redeemed rhetoric as the outcome of a revealed wisdom. On the basis of this theory, a twofold linguistic transformation was in order: the faculty of human speech was to be recast as a Pauline mirror, faithfully mediating God to man in the present life; and the agencies appointed for the translation of man's partial knowledge by faith into his complete knowledge of God by direct vision were to be redefined as modes of verbal expression. (19-20)

Both Luther and Calvin insist on education in languages for the purpose of moral edification; neglect in this area of education, Luther argues, will result in moral decay:

> And let us be sure of this: we will not long preserve the gospel without the languages. The languages are the sheath in which this word of the spirit is contained. . . . If through our neglect we let the languages go (which God forbid!), we shall not only lose the gospel, but the time will come when we shall be unable either to speak or write correct Latin or German. As proof and warning of this, let us take the deplorable and dreadful example of the university and monasteries, in which men have not only unlearned the gospel, but have in addition so corrupted the Latin and German languages that the miserable folk have been fairly turned into beasts, . . . and have well-nigh lost their natural reason to boot. . . .
>
> When our faith is thus held up to ridicule, where does the fault lie? It lies in our ignorance of the languages. . . . (360, 361)

And, Entzminger notes, Calvin also adopts Augustine's concept of language, making the doctrine of God the Son as both creating Word and incarnate Word fundamental to his Institutes (Entzminger 12). To emphasize the verbal character of God's revelation, Calvin translates the Greek term Logos as Sermo ("Speech") "in order to avoid the more limited connotations of Verbum":

> As to the Evangelist calling the Son of God the Speech, the simple reason appears to me to be, first, because he is the eternal Wisdom and Will of God; and, secondly, because he is the lively image of His purpose; for as Speech is said to be among men the image of the mind, so it is not inappropriate to apply this to God, and to say that He reveals himself to us by his speech. (qtd. by Entzminger 12)

Entzminger further notes that in shifting the value of Roman Catholicism's images and sacraments to the word as the primary vehicle for communicating divine truth, Calvin reinforces the value of the human word to transform the Word of God: "for Calvin as for Luther and Augustine, knowledge of God is the result of an interaction between external words and the Living Word within" (12).

In Calvinist-Augustinian epistemology, words convey meaning either as "indicative," that is "pointing to a reality not yet known" or as "commemorative," that is, "evoking a prior experience," Entzminger explains (29); applied to theology this means that

> God reveals himself in Creation and in Scripture as parallel ways of accommodating himself to limited human powers of perception, and these external revelations are in part indicative, leading people to an ever fuller experience of their Creator, (29-30)

and part commemorative, recalling "what we already know" (29-30). Memory is thus engaged in the process of acquiring knowledge about God. Entzminger explains this:

> This faculty is first engaged by the signs functioning commemoratively, evoking and in turn being confirmed by the Interior Teacher in a kind of dialectic between internal and external revelation. Further, subsequent knowledge of God subsumes yet never really transcends prior experience, and so education is cumulative, ever augmenting like Creation itself. (30)

In Protestant theology, therefore, the quest for knowledge of God is always that--a quest, Entzminger explains, because one can never know God fully; thus life itself, in Calvinist terms, is a journey for the purpose of knowing God:

> [T]he dialectic between external and internal revelation, between signs that point to God above and the sense of contingency that leads us finally to attend more fully to the inner Word, is a never-ending process. [And] although human words are inadequate, . . . they perform an indispensable function in bringing people to a knowledge of God, a knowledge whose perpetual imperfection offers the opportunity for the joy of unending discovery. (42)

The process of regeneration in the Calvinist tradition is marked by two stages of ascents. On the first level, "prevenient grace" allows one to choose;

this is God's action, God's election, Calvin calls it, a grace offered freely by God and permitting man to act, to persevere in faith. Entzminger elaborates on this Calvinist doctrine further: ". . . [P]revenient grace can neither be earned nor successfully sought, but once given it frees the recipient to choose whether to cooperate with subsequent grace" (94). The second level, then, is man's act of will, choosing to respond and living out (ethically) the Word given both by scripture and by the inner word.

In exploring the concept of language in Milton's <u>Paradise Lost</u>, Entzminger finds that "The prevailing conviction about language during the time that Milton was defining his purpose . . . was that words [are] troublesome, that they tend to obscure or misrepresent reality for which they stand" (168). The reason for this theory in Protestant theology is the belief that when man fell, so did language. Acknowledging this fact, the Reformers, nevertheless, view redemption itself as dependent on language and argue, as support, that the Pentecost "revival" of language balanced the failure of language and the confusion of tongues and "that the <u>felix culpa</u> is a concept which extends to language" (169):

> Following Luther, Calvin, and ultimately Augustine, Milton found illumination to be achieved through an interplay between the divine Word and the spoken or written words of God's ministers and true poets, who can be adequate to their subject only by exploiting all the resources of language at their command. Thus the Original Sin introduced the qualities of confusion and ambiguity into human speech, and Babel made them permanent features of the language, through the Word these attributes are redeemed, their presence adding a dimension to language that permits it to communicate to fallen intellect the complexity, richness, and variety of God's plan. (169)

American Puritan Semiotic

Crossing the Atlantic in the seventeenth century, the Puritan tradition arrives in America with the first English settlers, who quickly establish Protestant theology and ethics in this country. But the Americans claim an older heritage than European; they call themselves the New English Israelites, a people with a mission for God, an errand in the wilderness like Moses' Israelites on their pilgrimage to promised Canaan. And like the ancient Israelites, the New World pilgrims set about establishing a "city on a hill" that will be a beacon for the world to see. They see it as part of a grand design for America, a scheme of history which, they believe, God has predestined to take place. Such a vision is important because it offers a link with a past, as well as a direction for the future; thus, the Jews of Israel, not the English, become the spiritual ancestors of seventeenth century New England Puritans.

Mason Lowance notes that in education, too, spiritual ties are quickly established; the Bible is used as the text for all teaching, both academic and moral. And in the pulpit the so-called "plain style" of language is prescribed, a rhetorical style originated by sixteenth century anti-scholastic theologian Peter Ramus. Its purpose is to avoid elaborate and abstruse figures such as medieval theologians are fond of using and instead to apply scripture in literal, linear, historical fashion to current events; e.g., demonstrating the fulfillment of Old Testament prophecy in American history. This adaptation of typological or figural language is, as Lowance says, a shift away from the scholastic formula in which a Biblical text is interpreted four ways: (1) a simple explanation of the words, (2) instruction on morals and salvation, (3) an allegorical or metaphorical interpretation, and (4) a mystical interpretation associated with "eschatological figures" (17). Early American theologians reject these Platonic readings of scripture, whereby it is given associative interpretation, the literal text made to represent a spiritual truth:

> [I]t was to be New England that would allow the appropriate conflation of historical and geographical forces to give rise to speculation about a literal and historical fulfillment of those metaphorical and figural revelations provided by the divine author through the scriptural language of Canaan. In America--first in New England and later in the American Revolution--the historical cycles of secular development

> could be fused with the biblical pattern of prophecy and
> fulfillment, so that the paradigm of Armageddon followed by
> a pastoral paradise could be demonstrated not only in
> contemporary events but also in the language of scripture
> revelation. (16)

A type, as used by the early American Puritans, is an Old Testament figure
or event foreshadowing an antitype or fulfillment in subsequent history; e.g.,
old Israel is seen as a type for its New English antitype.

According to their "doctrine of accommodation" or "technologia," the
Puritan theologians are allowed to combine various systems of interpretation,
to teach by reason, by scripture, by nature, and by revelation. Perry Miller
explains this doctrine:

> When God created the world, He formed a plan or scheme
> of it in His mind, of which the universe is the embodiment;
> in His mind the plan is single, but in the universe, it is
> reflected through concrete objects and so seems diverse to
> the eyes of human reason; these apparently diverse and
> temporal segments of the single and timeless divine order
> are the various arts; the principles of them are gathered
> from things by men through the use of their inherent
> capacities. . . . (The New England Mind 229)

In this way a new source of theology is introduced into New England
Calvinism--God's voice in nature.

Jonathan Edwards, eighteenth century New England Calvinist, is called
a transitional figure in the early history of American theology because he
directs his instruction toward a "new sense of things" by preaching a
millennialist message of purification and judgment (Lowance 178-207). But
even more significant, Edwards is the first preacher to fuse scripture and
nature. Prompted by the new physics of Newton, Edwards undertakes an
investigation of the natural world "as though no man had seen it before him"
and records spiritual interpretations of natural events in a collection of notes
entitled Images and Shadows of Divine Things (18):

> It is very fit and becoming of God, who is infinitely wise, so
> to order things that there should be a voice of His in His

work, instructing those that behold them and painting forth and shewing divine mysteries and things more immediately appertaining to Himself and His spiritual kingdom. The works of God are but a kind of voice or language of God to instruct intelligent beings in things pertaining to Himself. And why should we not think that He would teach and instruct by His works in this way as well as in others, viz., by representing divine things by His works and so painting them forth, especially since we know that God hath so much delighted in this way of instruction. (61)

This means a shifting of focus away from scripture as the last and ultimate Word of God to a position equating nature and Word and God.

Another important influence on the developing mind of Edwards is his study of Locke's empiricism. According to Miller, Edwards becomes convinced that "the relation of mind to object, of truth to embodiment, is intimate, vital, indissoluble . . ." and that "the facts of experience [are] the 'shadows,' the very 'images' of divinity" ("Introduction" Images, 19):

The act of nature joined together man and nature, whom scholastic psychology had sundered. As Edwards read the new sensationalism, far from setting up a dualism of subject and object, it fused them in the moment of perception. The thing could then appear as a concept and the concept as thing. . . . In this way of thinking the image was no longer a detachable adornment on the surface of truth; it was truth. ("Introduction," Images, 20)

For Edwards, then, the material universe is a projection of God, an emanation of the Divine Mind: nature,

. . . the infinitely exact and perfectly stable ideas in God's mind together with His stable will . . . shall gradually be communicated to us and to other minds according to certain fixed and exact methods of laws. . . . ("The Mind" 32)

Edwards rejects the Puritans' plain style (the old typology) in favor of his own "pure style," whereby he employs "images and types" from the book of nature to allegorize or spiritualize in Platonic fashion the natural world as a reflection of spiritual truths (Lowance 255-56).

> It is apparent and allowed that there is a great and remarkable analogy in God's works. There is a wonderful resemblance in the effects which God produces, and consentaneity in His manner of working in one thing and another throughout all nature. It is very observable in the visible world; therefore it is allowed that God does purposely make and order one thing to be in agreeableness and harmony with another. And if so, why should not we suppose that He makes the inferior in imitation of the superior, the material of the spiritual, on purpose to have a resemblance and shadow of them? We see that even in the material world, God makes one part of it strangely to agree with another, and why is it not reasonable to suppose He makes the whole as the shadow of the spiritual world? (Images, 44)

With Edwards the trend toward pantheism and Emersonian transcendentalism is established; in a demonstrable way, Edwards contends, nature does not merely reflect God; it is the speech of God, the voice of God, the manifestation of God--it is God.

Influence of Coleridge on American Calvinism

During the eighteenth century, scientific theories of Locke and Newton contribute to a more reasoned faith, ideas that are reinforced during the early nineteenth century by new intellectual currents from England and Germany. Coleridge, in particular, becomes a major influence in America. The Reverend James Marsh, President of the University of Vermont, edited and published Coleridge's Aids to Reflection in 1829 and in the "Preliminary Essay" recommends the work because it "proves the doctrines of the Christian Faith to be rational, and exhibits philosophical grounds for the possibility of a truly spiritual religion" (xx). Specifically, Marsh finds in Coleridge's Aids a unifying scheme whereby "all appearance of contradiction between the several manifestations of the one Divine Word" are explained in a single ground of being, a Divine Mind, which man knows intuitively because man himself is linked to this Mind by his own mind or reason:

> So far as we compare our thoughts, the objects of our knowledge and faith, and by reflection refer them to their

> common measure in the universal laws of reason, so far the
> instinct of reason impels us to reject whatever is
> contradictory and absurd, and to bring unity and consistency
> into all our views of truth. (xix)

Further, Marsh finds in Coleridge a defense against the encroaching
reductionist doctrines of John Locke that make the law of cause and effect,
or action and reaction, the sole law of life--both man and brute--thereby
taking away man's free will and rational judgment:

> [In Locke's system] The liberty of the moral being is under
> the same condition with the liberty of the brute. Both are
> free to follow and fulfil the law of their nature, and both are
> alike bound by that law, as by an adamantine chain. The
> very conditions of the law preclude the possibility of a power
> to act otherwise than according to their nature. They
> preclude the very idea of a free-will, and render the feeling
> of moral responsibility not an enigma merely, not a mystery,
> but a self-contradiction and an absurdity. (xxxii)

To counter the new scientific view of man, Marsh finds in Coleridge's Aids an
elevation of man, of man's reason and humanity, for Coleridge teaches that
man holds the clues, the very truth of all Truth within himself:

> The first principles, the ultimate grounds, of [philosophy,
> morals, and religion], so far as they are possible objects of
> knowledge for us, must be sought and found in the laws of
> our own being, or they are not found at all. The knowledge
> of these terminates in the knowledge of ourselves, of our
> rational and personal being, of our proper and distinctive
> humanity, and of that Divine Being, in whose image we are
> created. . . . It is by self-inspection, by reflecting upon the
> mysterious grounds of our own being, that we can alone
> arrive at any rational knowledge of the central and absolute
> ground of all being. (x-xi)

Finally, Marsh notes that the foremost object of Coleridge's work is "to
direct the reader's attention to the science of words," a crucial element in
theology, because words are the "wheels of the intellect," the only vehicle of
thought, and agent of reason, conscience, and will: "Hence the necessity of
associating the study of words with the study of morals and religion" (x).

In the work, Coleridge states as his purpose to "aid [readers] in disciplining their minds to habits of reflection," particularly in matters of "prudence, morality, and religion," but emphasizing finally the "one knowledge which it is every man's interest and duty to acquire, namely, self-knowledge":

> Reflect on your own thought, actions, circumstances, and . . . accustom yourself to reflect on the words you use, hear, or read, their birth, derivation, and history. For if words are not things, they are living powers, by which the things of most importance to mankind are actuated, combined, and humanized. (lx)

All living things belong to the one universal soul, Coleridge tells his reader, a soul, "which by virtue of the enlivening Breath, and the informing Word" indwells both man and beast; but in man there is a living, "self-subsisting" soul with a life in itself" (4). More precisely, man is a "living soul": "not one of human kind, but there is provided for him, . . . a house not built with hands" (5). The soul naturally desires to know God, the "uncreated Spirit" and "Father of spirits," so that "it is never well with the soul, but when it is near unto God, yea, in its union with Him, married to Him" (91). There is, however, a schism between man and God that can be overcome only by an act of will led by reason, which in prior sequence has been prompted by "the All-perfect and Supreme Reason" (102).

> It is the glory of the Gospel charter and the Christian constitution, that its author and head is the Spirit of truth, essential Reason as well as absolute and incomprehensible Will. Like a just monarch, he refers even his own causes to the judgment of his high courts.--He has his Kings Bench in the reason, his Court of Equity in the conscience. . . . He has likewise his Court of Common Pleas in the Understanding, his Court of Exchequer in the prudence. The laws are his laws. And though by signs and miracles he has mercifully condescended to interline here and there with his own hand the great statute-book, which he had dictated to his amanuensis, Nature; yet has he been graciously pleased to forbid our receiving as the king's mandates aught that is and countersigned by the reason. (105)

In Coleridge's metaphysics, then, reason is the "power of the universe," the "fountain of ideas" and the "light of conscience." When an individual subjects his own will to this universal Will and is guided by it, he is said to be "regenerated" and capable of a "quickening inter-communion with the Divine Spirit" (157):

> In this at once most comprehensive and most appropriate acceptation of the word, reason is pre-eminently spiritual, and a spirit, even our spirit, through an effluence of the same grade by which we are privileged to say Our Father! (157)

Understanding, on the other hand, lies at the mercy of the senses, a lower faculty by which man reflects and generalizes; it is the "mind of the flesh" (175):

> [T]he imperfect human understanding can be effectually exerted only in subordination to, and in a dependent alliance with, the means and ordnances supplied by the All-perfect and Supreme Reason; but that under these conditions it is not only an admissible, but a necessary, instrument of bettering both ourselves and others. (102)

Thus, according to Coleridge, the human mind has intuitive access to the Universal Mind via the highest human faculty, reason, which actually partakes in Divine Mind. This is, in fact, the source of all ideas. An idea originates in a "Prothesis," which is an "ineffable name to which no image can be attached" because it is pure identity, the "absolute Real" and exists without "counterpoint or opposition" as an absolute. On the human level, the Prothesis "communicates its name to the Thesis," a substantive which expresses being, and is counterposed by antithesis which expresses act. The thesis is the "subjectively Real," the antithesis is the "objectively Real," and Idea is the "indifference" of the two (163). In The Statesman's Manual, he adds further that

> ... the first man, on whom the Light of an Idea dawned, did in that same moment receive the spirit and the credentials of a Lawgiver: and as long as man shall exist, so long will

> the possession of that antecedent knowledge which exists
> only in the power of an Idea, be the one lawful qualification
> of all Dominion in the world of the senses. (56)

The first step in disciplining the mind, Coleridge teaches, is to learn words, that is, to trace them to their origin, for such a study teaches one how to communicate more effectively, how to image the "unimageable," how to abstract ideas from things. Furthermore, Coleridge links nouns or names of things with the numen or "invisible power and presence, the nomen substantivum of all real objects, and the ground of their reality independently of the affections of sense" (Aids 169):

> [I]t is words, names, or, if image, yet images used as words
> or names, that are the only and exclusive subjects of
> understanding. In no instance do we understand a thing in
> itself, but only the name to which it is referred. (Aids 169)

To be understandable, therefore, "all truth must be fixed as an object of reflection and made expressible in language" (Aids 169).

Finally, in speaking of nature, Coleridge defines it as the antithesis of spirit or, more precisely, as the state by which "we comprehend all things that are representable in the forms of time and space, and subjected to the relations of cause and effect" (Aids 185). The different effects or forms of nature do not exist independently, he says, but originate in "something antecedent"; nature is "that which is always becoming" (185):

> It follows, therefore, that whatever originates its own acts, or
> in any sense contains in itself the cause of its own state, must
> be spiritual, and consequently super-natural. . . . (185)

Influence of Emerson on American Calvinism

In Coleridge, then, the Platonic analogue of the physical universe as representative of the spiritual receives new impetus among American clergy. This is true especially of Emerson, who articulates his philosophy in Nature (1836). Like Coleridge, Emerson believes in man's innate affinity with God or Over-Soul; Man <u>is</u> (not has) a soul, and that soul is "part or particle" of the Infinite:

> That Unity, the Over-Soul, within which every man's particular being is contained and made one with all other; that common heart, . . . within man is the soul of the whole; the wise silence; the universal beauty, to which every part and particle is equally related, the eternal One. (<u>Essays</u> 1. 268)

It is a mysterious, inexplicable link, to be sure, like "a stream whose source is hidden" ("The Over-Soul"), yet a link with an acknowledged higher Will that pervades both animate and inanimate nature: "A leaf, a sunbeam, a landscape, the ocean, make an analogous impression on the mind: (<u>Nature</u> 23).

    Emerson's unifying force in the cosmos bears as many names as faces; called formally Over-Soul or God, it is also Truth, Goodness, Beauty, the Whole, the One, the All, and is, in theory, the Supreme Cause or Law in which all things have being. Within this unitary system there operates a Divine Law of compensation which may be observed in the "inevitable dualism [that] bisects nature, so that each thing is a half, and suggests another thing to make it whole" (<u>Essays</u> 97):

> Polarity, or action and reaction, we meet in every part of nature; in darkness and light; in heat and cold; in the ebb and flow of waters, in male and female. . . . The value of the universe contrives to throw itself into every point. If the good is there, so is the evil; if the affinity, so is the repulsion. . . . (<u>Essays</u> 196)

So it is in man himself; the same law pertains: for every defect there is an excess, for every evil there is a good, for every pain, a compensating pleasure; "the joy that is the sweetest/Lurks in stings or in remorse" ("The Sphinx"):

> What we call retribution is the universal necessity by which the whole appears wherever a part appears. . . . Every act rewards itself, or, in other words, integrates itself, in a two-fold manner; first, in the thing, or in real nature, and

> secondly, in the circumstance, or in apparent nature. (Essays
> I. 103)

The law also holds true in reciprocal human behavior: "Love, and you shall be loved. All love is mathematically just, as much as the two sides of an algebraic equation" (Essays I. 103).

Related to this law of cause and effect is the concept of variety and flux within the One. Man himself illustrates this, so that "Divinity is behind our failures and follies also" (Essays 2. 67):

> Our love of the real draws us to permanence, but health of
> body consists in circulation, and sanity of mind in variety or
> facility of association ("Experience" 228).

> The consciousness in each man is a sliding scale, which
> identifies him now with the First Cause, and now with the
> flesh of his body; life above life, in infinite degrees. (Essays
> 2. 72)

In Emerson's philosophy, this apparent dualism is, however, only that, only appearance, for the overriding law is not division but Unity:

> The soul is not a compensation, but a life. The soul is.
> Under all this running sea of circumstance, whose waters
> ebb and flow with perfect balance, lies the aboriginal abyss
> of real Being. Essence, or God, is not a relation, or a part,
> but the whole. (Essays I. 120-21)

This is the "vast affirmative" in which truth, goodness, beauty--all virtues--are the influx; vice is simply the absence of the affirmative Spirit, the negation of good.

There are, in Emerson's theology, three ways man may gain access to the Divine Mind. He may retreat into the recesses of his own soul and there commune intuitively with the Over-Soul:

> We distinguish the announcements of the soul, its
> manifestations of its own nature, by the term Revelation.
> These are always attended by the emotion of the sublime.
> For this communication is an influx of the Divine Mind into
> our mind .... ("Over-Soul" 178)

> Ineffable is the union of man and God in every act of the
> soul. . . . [Man] must greatly listen to himself. (Essays I.
> 292)

The second means of access to the Over-Soul is through nature, which reflects

ultimate Beauty, hence Goodness and Truth, all synonyms:

> Stars awaken a certain reverence, because though always
> present, they are inaccessible; but all natural objects make a
> kindred impression, when the mind is open to their
> influence. (Nature 1)

Finally, man has access to divine teaching via the "incarnation of the spirit"

in other human beings, "with persons who answer to the thoughts in my own

mind, or express a certain obedience to the great instincts by which I live"

(Essays I. 277):

> I see its presence to them. I am certified of a common
> nature; and these other souls, these separate selves, draw me
> as nothing else can. . . . Persons are supplementary to the
> primary teaching of the soul. . . . In all conversation
> between two persons, tacit reference is made, as to a third
> party, to a common nature. That third party or common
> nature is not social; it is impersonal; is God. (Essays I. 277)

With this social doctrine in Emerson's system, one begins to see the link

between Emerson and Peircean theology. And, as a matter of fact, there are

a number of such links. In Emerson's theory the processes of the cosmos may

be explained in mathematical terms, a geometrical law repeating itself through

the universe in self-perpetuating motion. In Emerson it is the circle

(representing God): in Peirce it is a triangle or triad, but the concept of

mathematical repetition is similar:

> The key to every man is his thought. Sturdy and defying
> though he looks, he has a helm which he obeys, which is the
> idea after which all his facts are classified. He can only be
> reformed by showing him a new idea which commands his
> own. The life of a man is a self-evolving circle. (Essays I.
> 202)

> Every ultimate fact is only the first of a new series. Every
> general law only a particular fact of some more general law
> presently to disclose itself. . . . (Essays I. 303)

The design propagates in all areas; it applies also to moral laws and "extinguishes each in light of a better" (Essays I. 314):

> Yet this incessant movement and progression which all
> things partake could never become sensible to us but by
> contrast to some principle of fixture or stability in the soul.
> Whilst the eternal generation of circles proceeds, the eternal
> generator abides. (Essays I. 318)

There is yet a third principle at least suggested by Emerson and later developed by Peirce, the concept of the mediating mind, the "interpretant" that gives meaning by linking qualities to phenomenon:

> How can we speak of the action of the mind under any
> divisions, as of its knowledge, of its ethics, of its works, . . .
> since it melts will into perception, knowledge into act? . . .
> Its vision is not like the vision of the eyes but is union with
> the things known. (Essays I. 325)

Likewise, the Emersonian theory of mind anticipates the Peircean progression--instinct, opinion, and knowledge--though Emerson values instinct far more than the later pragmatist. But in both, the mind marries thought with nature and produces truth in the world.

This suggests, finally, the Emersonian theory of language, how words come to be and how thought is communicated. Emerson teaches that language originated as poetry, at first symbolizing nature itself but over time becoming dissociated from its forms thereby losing its poetic qualities. The connection can be traced, however, and it is nature that acts as the ground of meaning, a "vehicle of thought." Words, Emerson says, are signs of nature:

> The use of natural history is to give us aid in super-natural
> history: the use of the outer creation, to give us language
> for the beings and changes of the inward creation. (Nature
> 25)

But more important is the link between natural facts and spiritual facts, so that things and events in nature become, like language, symbols of spiritual truth:

> An enraged man is a lion, a cunning man is a fox, a firm man is a rock, a learned man is a torch. A lamb is innocence; a snake is subtle spite. . . . Who looks at a river in a meditative hour, and is not reminded of the flux of all things? Throw a stone into a stream, and the circles that propagate themselves are the beautiful type of all influence . . . . (Nature 26)

Thus it is that even in language Emerson blends the visible with the invisible universe so that words become emblems of the spirit. Likewise, in communication the speaker or artist "detaches" the idea and "magnifies" it with "a power to fix the momentary eminency of an object" (Essays I. 354). To be communicable a thing must become a "picture" or sensible object painted to the senses:

> When the spiritual energy is directed on some outward thing, then is it a thought. The relation between it and you first makes you, the value of you, apparent to me. (Essays I. 335)

Peircean Adaptation of American Calvinism

When Charles Sanders Peirce comes into the sphere of Emerson, he seeks to shift that idealism toward science, to open philosophy to logical and scientific investigation--Objective Idealism, he calls it. And while he maintains the Emersonian interest in man, Peirce changes the focus from soul and meditation to mind and reason, a logical interpretation of the self. The link with God, therefore, becomes more tenuous, the mystery, in a sense, even greater because the old certainties are no longer certain. In Peirce's philosophy God is deduced, not described, a Law toward which all things move.

The place to begin in the Emerson-to-Peirce lineage, then, is with the self rather than with God because it is only external experience (sensation) transformed by the mind to conception, thought, and logic that God can be posited at all. This is, at least, the way Peirce wants God to be "proved": in the field of consciousness, which is all we can know of the soul or self, there is only the thought or idea that has been excited by "the perfectly unthought manifold of sensation" (WP I. 85) of external phenomena. Phenomenon is the only source of consciousness; man has no power of introspection or of intuition, Peirce believes; every cognition is caused by previous ones:

> At any moment we are in possession of certain information, that is, of cognitions which have been logically derived by induction and hypothesis from previous cognitions which are less general, less distinct, and of which we have a less lively consciousness. These in their turn have been derived from others still less general, less distinct, less vivid; and so on back to the ideal first [emphasis mine], which is quite singular, and quite out of consciousness. This ideal first is the particular thing-in-itself. It does not exist as such. That is, there is no thing which is in-itself in the sense of not being relative to the mind. (WP II. 238-39)

The end of Peirce's argument may lead one back to God as the "Ideal First," but not in the manner Peirce wants; there is still the primal truth that man must intuit and interpret without pure reason. Thus, it must commence in instinct and faith, much as Emerson's philosophy does.

Nor does the attempt at objectivity diminish the importance of God in Peirce's philosophy. From first to last he continues to reason about God, about the place of God in human life and history, and about the "final days" of human history. In the 1863 address that has been cited, for example, Peirce sketches six stages of Christianity and concludes that "all civilization is the work of Christianity," for, he adds, "Christianity is not a doctrine, or possible law; it is an actual law--a kingdom" (WP I. 107). Even before the rise of Christianity, the Jews held the form, the "grammar" of it, and pagans had an instinctive knowledge of God:

> . . . [B]efore a man can hear the voice of God or even comprehend an example of religion he must have a notion

> of what religion is, and that implies that he must previously
> have had an inward revelation of religion. In compliance
> with this condition, both heathen and Jews, before the birth
> of Christ, had attained to the idea of an intimate union of
> humanity with Deity, such that they should be brought into
> an ordinated harmony, in which that creature should be so
> completely in unison with the creator that all his motions
> should be brought under law, as much as inanimate natures
> are. . . . (WP I. 110)

Subsequent to this "inward revelation," there follows the "objective revelation"
and culminates in the "phenomenon of perfection . . . in human form" (WP
I. 110).

It is Peirce's belief that the skepticism and materialism of the
nineteenth century, i.e., scientific investigation, will result in "a far greater
faith than ever before" (WP I. 114):

> For then man will see God's wisdom and mercy, not only in
> every event in his own life, but in that of the gorilla, the lion,
> the fish, the polyp, the tree, the crystal, the grain of dust, the
> atom. He will see that each of these has an inward existence
> of its own, for which God loves it, and that He has given to
> it a nature of endless perfectibility. (WP I. 114)

It is noteworthy that Peirce descends the evolutionary scale when he
lists the elements of creation as recipients of God's love, for it will be, Peirce
holds, in just such as evolutionary movement that God will ultimately bring
about perfect harmony and unity in the universe. I have mentioned his paper
entitled "Evolutionary Love," dated 1893, in which he contends that love is the
fundamental agent of evolution in the universe, emanating from the
"cherishing-love" of the Creator, who is called Love and who "embraces hatred
as an imperfect stage" of love, so that some form of this impulse may be
viewed in all acts, in all elements of creation. The movement of love is
circular, at once "projecting creations into independency and drawing them
into harmony" (CP 6. 288). It is the "simple formula we call the Golden
Rule":

> ... the formula of an evolutionary philosophy, which teaches
> that growth comes only from love ... from an ardent
> impulse to fulfill another's highest impulse. (CP 6. 289)

> Love recognizing germs of loveliness in the hateful, gradually
> warms it into life, and makes it lovely. (CP 6. 289)

This agapastic theory of evolution is the highest impulse, but it is not the only form of evolutionary love; there is evolution by fortuitous chance, called tychasm, as well as evolution by mechanical necessity, called anancasm. Peirce contends that each form of evolution is a type of agapasm: in the first, tychasm, evolution results in spontaneous attraction, itself a harmony, "quite after the Christian scheme" (CP 6. 304). Likewise, the second, anancasm, is "a tending on the whole to a foreordained perfection, . . . an intrinsic affinity for good" (CP 6. 305). Thus, both lower or degenerate forms of Darwinian evolution show elements of agapasm, which is a "positive sympathy among the created offspring from continuity of mind" (CP 6. 304).

Like Emerson, Peirce confronts an apparent incongruity in his scheme of the Whole, a great Sphinx-like mystery:

> The fate of the man-child;
> The meaning of man;
> Known fruit of the unknown;
> Daedalian plan;
> Out of the sleeping a waking,
> Out of waking sleep;
> Like death overtaking;
> Deep underneath deep?
>
> (Emerson, "The Sphinx")

And again like Emerson, Peirce takes up the challenge of the Sphinx:

> Thou art the unanswered question:
> Couldst see thy proper eye,
> Alway it asketh, asketh;
> And each answer a lie.
> So take thy quest through nature,
>
> It through thousand natures ply. . . .
>
> (Emerson, "The Sphinx")

I have traced the links and the transformation occurring in American Protestantism, first the transition in Jonathan Edwards from a scriptural orthodoxy to a cosmic religious semiotic that employs not only scripture but nature as well, then the secularizing process of Marsh and Emerson, who affirm the individual's spiritual capabilities and rights, indeed his duty, to know God, through his own participation in the Spirit of God, through a study and imitation of nature and through a spiritual union (or communion) with other people; and finally Charles Peirce, who continues the secularizing process of religion by drawing it within the purview of science, "objectifying" the search for God, that is, making God, the Ideal First, the Ground of all knowledge, and demonstrating logically that God is Love and that Love is the governing law of the universe, in both animate beings and inanimate objects-- all things governed by this principle. I have examined Peirce's theological semiotic as it is developed by Josiah Royce, focusing in that investigation on the Beloved Community or Body of Christ as interpreter of God and as mediator between God and man.[1]

It is with this metaphysical semiotic system that Walker Percy casts his lot, desiring like Charles Peirce to merge his scientific training with his metaphysical inclination. What results, of course, is not a theology or a new science, but a postmodern, coy rendition of a very old world view based on Pauline Christianity.

NOTES

¹ I should note Walker Percy's attraction to George Mead's behaviorist theories at this point, for a number of reasons. First, Mead was a close associate of Charles Peirce, part of the original Peircean school. Second, Mead was himself a theologian under the tutelage of Josiah Royce, and, finally, Mead became the eminent behaviorist out of Peircean pragmatism. Thus, there are a number of connections that must have attracted Walker Percy to this behavioral scientist even though Percy has ostensibly rejected behaviorism.

In his 1958 essay "Symbol, Consciousness, and Intersubjectivity" more than a decade before he tapped into Peirce's system with his 1972 essay "Toward a Triadic Theory of Meaning," Percy cites Mead's behavioral theory. This suggests at least an acquaintance with his mentor, Charles Peirce, long before he adopts the idea of thirdness.

In <u>Mind, Self, and Society</u>, George Mead argues for a physiological structure of mental acts and for the sociological matrix of communication. The mind, Mead believes, is closely related to--one might even say synonymous with--the central nervous system, which is "programmed" by a social milieu from birth, and which stores away an indefinite number of responses to overt stimuli. Thus, "the process of intelligent conduct is essentially a process of selection from among various alternatives, . . . largely a matter of selectivity" (99). Further, Mead argues, the mind is a "Lockean blank" at birth and begins immediately to store up experience so that responses simply call up past experience to apply appropriate action:

> The traces of past experiences are continually playing in upon our perceived world. Now, to get hold of that in the organism which answers to [any] stage of conduct, to our remembering, to our intelligently responding to the present in terms of the past, we set up a parallelism between what is going on in the central nervous system and immediate experience. Our memory is dependent upon the condition of certain tracts in our head, and these conditions have to be picked out to get control of processes of that sort. (113-24)

Patterns of response are etched into "paths" within the central nervous system ready for instant connections with responses; it is the "immediate mechanism through which our organism operates in bringing the past to bear on the present" (116), an "organizing" of experience into accessible data.

But it is the response itself that controls the "content" or the sensation of the stimulus (e.g., a sound makes one jump, a light causes one to look toward it): what we are going to do determines our immediate response to the object. In other words, higher (human) organisms exercise more control over behavior than non-human animals only because of "delayed response" capability (reflective conduct) whereby the organism interposes between the stimulus and the response "a process of selecting one or another of a whole set of possible responses and combinations of responses to the given stimulus (117-18):

> The various attitudes expressible through the central nervous system can be organized into different types of subsequent acts; and the delayed reaction or responses thus made possible by the central nervous system are the distinctive features of mentally controlled or intelligent behavior. (118)

An animal follows blind impulse or instinct in non-reflective behavior; a man pursues a chosen course because he pictures a certain situation and "directs his conduct with reference to it" (119). Thus, the future may be said to be present in all forms of reflective behavior.

This "programming" or internalization of "external conversations of gestures" with others is the "essence of thinking," Mead believes; in this way, the mind has access to numerous "significant symbols," (i.e., symbols that have the same meaning for everyone in a social community).

Meaning, as Mead explains it, is the result of the threefold relationship of "gesture of first organism, of gesture to the second organism, and of gesture to subsequent phases of the given social act" (76). In other words, meaning may be known only in terms of overt act or response:

> The nature of meaning is intimately associated with the social process as it thus appears, that meaning involves this threefold relation among phases of the social act as the context in which it arises and develops; this relation of gesture of one organism to the adjustive response of another

> organism (also implicated in the given act), and
> to the completion of the given act--a relation such
> that the second organism responds to the gesture
> of the first as indicating or referring to the
> completion of the given act. (76-77)

It is something "objectively there," not "a psychical addition" to a stimulus and not an "idea" (76). Meaning exists entirely within the field of experience: the response to a gesture is the meaning of it. Thus, meaning itself results from communication since only a response aroused mutually in two communicating organisms may properly be described as "meaning":

> There are two characters which belong to that
> which we term "meanings," one is participation
> and the other is communicability. Meaning can
> arise only in so far as some phase of the act
> which the individual is arousing in the other can
> be aroused in himself. There is always to this
> extent participation, and the result of this
> participa-tion is communicability, i.e., the
> individual can indicate to himself what he
> indicates to others. (81)

But there is yet another requirement in Mead's theory of meaning, and that is the Peircean element of Firstness or universality. Before there can be a particularity in any experience, there must first be established (by experience) a distinguishable "class" or universal to which a particularity belongs:

> Recognition always implies a something that can
> be discovered in an indefinite number of objects.
> One can only sense a color once, in so far as
> "color" means an immediate relationship of the
> light waves to the retina of a normal nervous
> system. That experience happens and is gone,
> and cannot be repeated. But something is
> recognized, there is a universal character given in
> the experience itself which is at least capable of
> an indefinite number of repetitions. . . . (84)

According to Mead, then, meaning originates in the communication process. And the communication process itself originates in a social milieu, a "universe of discourse" made up of individuals "participating in a common social process of experience and behavior" (89); that is, a system of understood meanings.

Human communication, in Mead's system, is necessary for the identity of the "self," a kind of game or play which takes place in two stages. At first, of course, the child has no self, no individuality; he simply reflects a range of attitudes of other individuals toward himself and toward each other within his social environment:

> The child is one thing at one time and another at another, and what he is at one moment does not determine what is he at another. . . . You cannot count on the child; you cannot assume that all the things he does are going to determine what he will [later] do at any moment. The child has no definite character, no definite personality. (159)

At the second stage the individual self begins to learn and to organize particular individual attitudes as well as "corporate" attitudes of his social group, a "generalized other." He does this by playing roles so that he participates in society in an "acceptable" manner, giving responses which he has observed: "He becomes a something which can function in the organized whole, and thus tends to determine himself in his relationship with the group to which he belongs" (160).

But not only does the individual learn others' roles and others' attitudes, he also objectifies himself, sees himself as a "me," the "organized set of attitudes of others" which he assumes. The individual knows himself objectively as a self only by the attitudes and the patterns of behavior that have been incorporated into his central nervous system and which constitute his conduct. In a close analogy, the "me" is a data bank that responds to stimuli from a memory of observed or experienced responses:

> The attitudes of others which one assumes as affecting his own conduct constitute the "me," and that is something that is there. . . . When one sits down to think anything out, he has certain data that are there. . . . He sees himself from the point of view of one individual or another in the group. These individuals, related all together, give him a certain self. (176)

The "me" is the observable part of the self, the being of action, but there is yet another element of the self--the spontaneous action, the unreflective self or "I." This part of the self is unpredictable and impulsive, like a movement into the future, something one cannot anticipate:

> The "I" gives the sense of freedom, of initiative. The situation is there for us to act in a self-conscious fashion. We are aware of ourselves, and of what the situation is, but exactly how we will act never gets into experience until after the action takes place. (177-78)

In combination, the "I" and the "me" constitute a social self which assumes an identity by participating in a community of selves.

Mead's explanation of language progresses in circular fashion, from social necessity to "self" training back to social interaction. "Unconscious conversation of gestures" is used prior to vocal gestures (language), that is, communication by hand, body, or facial movements. According to Mead, this is the process from which language arose, and he illustrates with a description of the behavior of dogs "approaching each other in hostile attitude," carrying on in a "language of gestures": "They walk around each other, growling and snapping, and waiting for the opportunity to attack" (14). Human language, "conversation of (vocal) gestures," evolves when gestures become "signs":

> . . . [T]hat is, when they come to carry, for the individuals making them and the individuals responding to them, definite meanings or significations in terms of subsequent behavior of the individuals making them; so that, by serving as prior indications, to the individuals responding to them, they make possible the mutual adjustment of the various individual components of the social act to one another. . . . (69n)

Thus, an individual is born into and "created" by a social environment. There is no "self," by Mead's definition, until a person becomes integrated into the community, that is, educated by it and programmed with acceptable responses. In this process, the single most important element, the primary mode of educating and programming, is language, the mechanism by which a person learns behavior and the mechanism by which he communicates that behavior to other selves, a system of "significant" symbols understood by all members of the social group. The individual uses language "to pick out and organize," that is, to identify, to name, and to store experience in memory (13). In this way, then, language facilitates the individual's integration into his social milieu.

In Mead's system, language can generate a response only when that response is shared by both speaker and listener, and it generates a chain of responses when "it becomes a stimulus to a later stage of action which is to take place from the point of view of this particular response (72). Thus, in the total social process, language is simply a part of a cooperative process, "that part which does lead to an adjustment to the response of the other so that the whole activity can go on" (74):

> Language as such is simply a process by means of which the individual who is engaged in co-operative activity can get the attitude of others involved in the same activity. Through gestures, that is, through the part of his act which calls out the response of others, he can arouse in himself the attitude of the others. Language as a set of significant symbols is simply the set of gestures which the organism employs in calling out the response of others. Those gestures primarily are nothing but parts of the act which do naturally stimulate others engaged in the co-operative process to carry out their parts. (335)

Although Mead rejects Peirce's triadic semiotics (or mediation) in favor of (dyadic) behaviorism, he is influenced by Peirce in other areas. His use of pragmatic principles in his communication theory--content and meaning determined by response--reflects Peirce's own definition:

> Consider what effects, that might conceivably have practical bearings, we conceive the object of our conception to have. Then, our conception of these effects is the whole of our conception of the object. (CP 5. 402)

Likewise, Mead's theory of response as generating response in a chainlike network suggests the influence of Peirce's synechism or continuity of thought. And, of course, the major influence of Peirce on Mead lies in the latter's theory of the social matrix of language. In Mead, as in Peirce, there can be no language, no thought, no communication without an other. In Peircean terms it may be simply the other self (internalized conversation), but the universalized other must be there. In Mead the public voice is more prominent, more important to the meaning of an object or action, more important to the identity of an individual, but in both cases

> man is not whole as long as he is single, . . . he is essentially a possible member of society. Especially, one man's experience is nothing, if it stands alone. If he sees what others cannot, we call it hallucination. It is not "my" experience, but "our" experience that has to be thought of; and this "us" has indefinite possibilities. (CP 5. 402N)

Walker Percy cites George H. Mead in various essays, most prominently in "Symbol, Consciousness, and Intersubjectivity" (1958), in which he compares the behaviorist's view of human consciousness with phenomenologist-transcendentalist Edmund Husserl's theory. Both, Percy concludes, are wrong in the result: Mead's view of man as responding creature, not qualitatively different from lower responding animals, and Husserl's view of man as a solipsist locked in his own mind, unable or unwilling to allow for other selves. But, in Percy's view of the matter, behaviorist Mead offers the better bargain for two reasons: first, Mead supports the theory of intersubjectivity (social matrix) of human consciousness, and second, his scientific system is "self-corrective"; that is, "it can be broadened without losing the posture from which Mead theorized, that an observer confronting data which he can make some sense of and of which he can speak to other observers" (MB 267).

CHAPTER 5

WALKER PERCY'S SEMIOTIC AT WORK: "THE MESSAGE IN
THE BOTTLE" AS A GLOSS ON THE MOVIEGOER

I have demonstrated Percy's ties to a long line of Protestant theorists
via his nonfiction, beginning with his debt to Charles Sanders Peirce (the idea
of Thirdness) and culminating in the theology of Apostle Paul. I have also
shown that Percy, like Peirce and the other Christian realists, seeks to link
science and religion through the work of the sign. From the earliest published
essay in 1954, "Symbol As Need," Percy has attempted to educate, if not edify,
his readers concerning the seriousness of the study of man's use of language--
its link with man's essential nature and its metaphysical possibilities. It can,
in fact, be demonstrated that not only in his non-fiction, but also in his fiction,
Percy has repeated the same themes and messages; from the first to the
present, he has been concerned with the mystery of man's nature and with the
possibility that language may solve the mystery. More specifically, he attempts
to demonstrate the role of language in the orthodox Christian belief that
fallen man (man in a post-Christian technological society) stands in desperate
need of God and that if man will read the signs (e.g., Percy's novels), he will
recognize his need and choose to believe.

Soon after his conversion to Catholicism in 1947, Percy began writing
fiction, two novels, neither of which was published: The Charterhouse and
The Gramercy Winner. Abandoning fiction then, he wrote scientific and
philosophical essays, short studies in linguistics, psychology, and metaphysics
that were published between 1954 and 1959. Then in 1959 he returned to
fiction: first with a short allegory, "The Message in the Bottle," published in
1959, then with a novel, The Moviegoer in 1961, Percy initiated his career in
fiction which, since that time, has dominated public awareness and critical
recognition of his work.

I have marked the beginning of Percy's fiction with "The Message in the Bottle," and I have cited also his second work of fiction published shortly after, a pairing which I make intentionally, for it is my belief that Percy intends the short allegory to be a gloss on the novel, much as he uses a later essay--"Notes for a Novel About the End of the World" as a gloss on the subsequent novel, Love in the Ruins.

"The Message in the Bottle" describes the predicament of a castaway, a man shipwrecked on an island with no recollection of his home, though he knows he does not "belong" on the island. Nevertheless, the castaway is an enterprising young man; he sets about making a place for himself--"gets a job, builds a house, takes a wife, raises a family, goes to night school, and enjoys the local acts of cinema, music, and literature" (MB 119). Being an alert fellow and realizing his predicament (i.e., exiled and alienated), the castaway begins searching the beach for bottles containing messages, hoping to find news from "across the seas" that will inform him about his home and his identity. The trouble he encounters is not the dearth of messages--indeed, they wash ashore by the thousands; the problem is that the messages come in a confusion of tongues, so to speak, some in the language of science, art, and philosophy, which do not address the needs of a lost man, and others in the language of the layman and which do answer the needs of man involved in human concerns. The first category of message, the castaway calls "knowledge sub specie aeternitatis" because it is "knowledge which can be arrived at anywhere by anyone at any time" (MB 125). The second category, he classifies as "news" because it "has a bearing on his predicament" (MB 130), is "highly significant to the islander" (MB 123). But the man finds that he must further classify the sentences addressed to his situation, the "news" messages, so that "not only are there two kinds of sentences in the bottle but . . . there are two kinds of postures from which one reads the messages [objective and subjective], two kinds of verifying procedures by which one acts upon them [the scale of significance], and two kinds of responses to the sentences [belief or unbelief]" (MB 125).

To make certain that the reader does not miss the message, Percy explains it carefully at the end; the castaway is lost man in search of "home," that is, his source of being in God:

> Our subject is not only an organism and a culture member; he is also a castaway. That is to say, he is not in the world as a swallow is in the world, as an organism which is what it is, never more or less. Our islander may choose his mode of being. . . . But however he chooses to exist, he is in the last analysis a castaway, a stranger who is in the world but who is not at home in the world. (MB 142)

And the news the castaway seeks, the news from "across the seas," is the Christian message; it is news of the Absolute Paradox (Christ) and it offers lost man a way out of his predicament:

> Once it is granted that Christianity is the Absolute Paradox, then, . . . the message in the bottle is all that is needed. It is enough to read "this little advertisement, this nota bene on a page of universal history--'We have believed in such and such a year God appeared among us in the humble figure of a servant, that he lived and taught in our community, and finally died." (MB 148)

Similarly, the plot of The Moviegoer opens as John Bickerson (Binx) Bolling, self-avowed castaway, receives a "news" message from his Aunt Emily, at least he understands it to be news pertaining to his predicament because it reminds him of other such messages and events which send an "eschatological prickle" down his neck like a dog's hackles when it senses danger. One such metaphysical marker is the death of his brother Scotty that occurred when Binx was eight, but which he now recalls with a tingling down his spine. Another is the death of his father; indeed, all the memories and stories of his father give Binx the same eerie chill. But the most significant clue to his condition is the memory of his own brush with death in Korea eight years earlier when he "came to himself" lying under a chindolea bush with a shell in his shoulder:

> My shoulder didn't hurt but it was pressed hard against the ground as if somebody sat on me. Six inches from my nose a dung beetle was scratching around under the leaves. (Mg 16)

These messages from "across the seas," as it were, prompt Binx to begin a search for God: "There awoke in me an immense curiosity. I was onto something. I vowed that if I ever got out of this fix, I would pursue the search" (Mg 16):

> The search is what anyone would undertake if he were not sunk in the everydayness of his own life. This morning, for example, I felt as if I had come to myself on a strange island. And what does a castaway do? Why, he pokes around the neighborhood and he doesn't miss a trick.
>
> To become aware of the possibility of the search is to be onto something. (Mg 18)

For eight years subsequent to his battlefield experience, Binx anesthetizes himself by assuming the consumer's role in the faceless middle-class suburb of New Orleans--Gentilly. He calls the life he lives the "Little Way" because it protects him from the ultimate issues of life, questions about the purpose and meaning of life, about the origin and end of life, about the possibility of God and immortality: "It is a pleasure to carry out the duties of a citizen and to receive in return a receipt or a neat styrene card with one's right to exist. . ." (Mg 13). But now as he approaches his thirtieth birthday, which falls this year on Ash Wednesday, Binx recalls his brush with death and determines to resume his search. The Moviegoer is an account of Binx's initial efforts at his so-called "horizontal" search (for God).

The story proper takes place the week prior to Ash Wednesday, the last week of Mardi Gras festivities, and the epilogue perhaps a year later. As the story opens Binx is summoned by his Aunt Emily, who "at sixty-five [is] still the young prince" of the family and Binx's guardian after his father's death, a role she has not relinquished with ease. The purpose of this conference, however, is not about his own future, but about Kate, Emily's stepdaughter. Mercer, the household servant, has found a carton of bottles, whiskey bottles Emily thinks, in Kate's room, and during the last week, she has found two empty sodium pentobarbital bottles in the incinerator. Kate, a shy girl of twenty-five, has a history of mental depression, and now Emily requests Binx's help in getting her out of her room and away from the house: "I want you to do whatever it was you did before you walked out on us. . . . Fight with her, joke with her--the child doesn't laugh" (Mg 30). Kate also has a history of rebellious "swings of dialectic"; her father's girl in childhood, charmed by her stepmother's intelligence during adolescence, she has now swung back, her "dialectic of hatred" aimed at Emily as she "rediscovers" her father. Concerned not about her parental preferences ("It is . . . all the same to me which parent she presently likes or dislikes") but about "the meagerness of her resources" ("Where will her dialectic carry her now?"), Binx complies with his aunt's request to help Kate and invites her to accompany him on a business trip to Chicago. It is on the journey that the two discover their likenesses, their spiritual and psychological compatibility: "You're nuttier than I am," Kate informs Binx, "One look at you and I have to laugh. Do you think that is sufficient ground for marriage?" (Mg 153).

In the end the two do marry, the search now a real possibility for Binx and for Kate through him. Reading the clues from the dead past (Scott, his father, and his own brush with death), from the dead living (people around him playing with forms of life), from the wonder of the world around ("never a moment without wonder"), and from the movies that are "onto" the search (but blow it in the end), Binx finds the object of his search in his crippled stepbrother Lonnie's faith in the face of death, faith that he will see God and be whole again.[1]

Critic Anselm Atkins examines the novel from the perspective of Percy's Kierkegaardian essay "The Man on the Train" and the Christian essay "The Message in the Bottle" and finds no particular object of the search: "The object of the search, for Percy as for Binx, is not a cut and dried thing. It is not known prior to being found. It is a treasure hidden in a field, and one searches for . . . the field" (95). Binx is at once "Marcel's homo viator and Augustine's peregrinus, whose true home is a distant unknown land--not Hollywood" (95). And Atkins concludes, "only . . . if we see Binx as the beachcomber of "The Message in the Bottle" will we be able to assess this peculiar 'moviegoer' correctly" (95).

I agree with Atkins that the character of Binx is informed by "The Message in the Bottle," but, I contend, in a much more complex way. Specifically, "The Message in the Bottle" informs The Moviegoer in three ways: first, the allegory establishes the "predicament" of Binx, the protagonist, and the metaphysical nature of his situation: a castaway and an exile from God. Second, "The Message in the Bottle" establishes the nature of the news and the clues that the castaway (Binx) receives in his search; and, finally, the allegory establishes the character types in the novel: castaway-seeker, philosopher-scientist, and apostle.

First of all, "The Message in the Bottle" establishes the situation or, what Percy calls, the predicament of the protagonist. Like the man in the allegory, Binx Bolling calls himself a castaway, attempting on the social level to find a place for himself in an alien city, to carve out a niche and to "stick" himself into the world in the most comfortable and conventional fashion. For four years he has lived in Gentilly, a middle-class suburb of New Orleans, a peaceful, albeit uneventful, existence, he admits, compared to the displacement he suffered in the Quarter and to the rage and depression he felt at his Aunt Emily and Uncle Jules' gracious home in the Garden District. But even in his life in Gentilly he is an exile and practices "the worst kind of self-deception" (Mg 22). To "certify" his existence, Binx performs all the duties of a citizen, carries around "a neat styrene card" as proof, subscribes to Consumer Reports, and as a result, owns "a first-class television set, an all but silent air conditioner and a long lasting deodorant" (Mg 13). His employment as a stock broker is equally unassuming and disappointing to the family, which has produced professional men up to the present generation. In Binx's mind, however, his life in Gentilly is not unpleasant; indeed, "there is much to be said for giving up such grand ambitions and living the most ordinary life imaginable; a life without the old longings; selling stocks and bonds and mutual funds; quitting work at five o'clock like everyone else; having a girl and perhaps one day settling down and raising a flock of Marcias and Sandras and Lindas of my own. . . . It is not a bad life at all" (Mg 15).

Again like the castaway in "The Message in the Bottle," Binx must deal with his predicament on the metaphysical level. That the island is not his "home," the castaway in the allegory knows, though he has no precise memory about his real home; and so too does Binx know, instinctively if not objectively, that he does not belong, somehow. He knows, for one thing, that his own life is a sham because the good times are not good to him at all, but leave him aching with malaise; everything is upside down: "What are generally considered to be the best times are for me the worst times, and that worst of times [war] was one of the best" (Mg 16). At times Binx suffers from restless insomnia, lying awake, "watchful as a sentry, ears tuned to the slightest noise" (Mg 71), and other times from disturbing dreams:

> Three o'clock and suddenly awake amid the smell of dreams
> and of the years come back and peopled and blown away
> again like smoke. A young man am I, twenty-nine, but I am

> as full of dreams as an ancient. At night the years come
> back and perch around my bed like ghosts. (Mg 117)

But not only does Binx find spiritual "dis-ease" in his own life, he also sees it in other people:

> It happens when I speak to people. In the middle of a
> sentence it will come over me: yes, beyond a doubt this is
> death. . . . At such times it seems that the conversation is
> spoken by automatons who have no choice in what they say.
> (Mg 83)

Nell and Eddie Lovell are examples. Binx runs into Eddie on Canal Street, and the two talk briefly about inanities, Eddie's lips moving "muscularly, molding words into pleasing shapes, marshalling arguments, and during the slight pauses are held poised, attractively in a Charles Boyer pout . . ." (Mg 22). There is "no mystery here," Binx concludes, Eddie is "as cogent as a bird dog quartering a field" (Mg 22). Later, Nell, too, demonstrates "that plaintive lost eagerness American college women get at a certain age" (Mg 84). Binx shifts uncomfortably as he attempts to "escape death" and wonders: "Why does she talk as if she were dead? Another forty years to go and dead, dead, dead" (Mg 84).

Binx finds this disease of spirit manifested in yet another way; in his own life, as well as in others', there is a preoccupation with promiscuous sex:

> What a sickness it is . . . , this latter-day post-Christian sex.
> To be pagan it would be one thing; to be Christian it would
> be another thing, fornication forbidden and not even to be
> thought of in the new life. . . . But to be neither pagan nor
> Christian but this: oh this is a sickness . . . , prized, first last
> and always by the cult of the naughty nice. . . . (Mg 165)

Even the homes, whole residential areas, suffer from this "noxious despair," as Binx names it:

> I try to fathom the mystery of this suburb at dawn. Why do
> these splendid houses look so defeated at this hour of the
> day? . . . [T]hese new homes look haunted. Even the

> churches out here look haunted. What spirit takes
> possession of them? (Mg 72)

Binx's conclusion about the condition of man is summed up in a sarcastic tone and his band of bitter irony when he describes modern society as

> the great shithouse of scientific humanism where needs are satisfied, everyone becomes an anyone, a warm and creative person, and prospers like a dung beetle, and one hundred percent of people are humanists and ninety-eight percent believe in God, and men are dead, dead, dead; and the malaise has settled like a fall-out . . . . (Mg 180)

But Binx, like the islander in "The Message . . . ," is sensitive to signs in his own life and in the world around him, clues which tip him off to the possibility of God and which prompt him to initiate a search. There is, in fact, a certain physical reaction accompanying the metaphysical signs; Binx feels a strange prickling down his neck "like a dog's." This occurred first, he recalls, when he was eight years old; his brother Scotty had just died, and Aunt Emily had announced the news, adding, "Now it's all up to you. It's going to be difficult for you but I know you're going to act like a soldier" (Mg 11). Other deaths also tip him off to the possibility of the search: his father, pictured prominently in Aunt Emily's home, holds a special place in Binx's mind, and when any reference is made to him, Binx feels the familiar "dreadful-but-not-unpleasant eschatological prickling" down his neck (Mg 46): "Any doings of my father, even his signature, is in the nature of a clue in my search" (Mg 61).

Binx also finds clues to the search in nature: the "little carcass out of the garbage can, a specimen which has been used and discarded"--it is what is "left over" that acts as a metaphysical sign; and the "mystery of . . . summer afternoons," motes of dust in the sunlight, rising and falling in the heavy air; the wonder of the "smoky blue valleys"--"not five minutes will I be distracted from the wonder" (Mg 39). Then there are the Jews, a special kind of sign. Binx is unsure why, but when he approaches a Jew, "the Geiger counter in my head starts rattling away like a machine gun; and as I go past with the utmost circumspection and with every sense alert--the Geiger counter subsides" (Mg 74). He knows that he shares one thing in common with the Jews he meets; both are "exiles," but what Binx does not know, and what Percy does not tell the reader forthrightly is that both the Jews and Binx are seekers after God--the Jews seek knowledge of God's promised Messiah and Binx seeks a knowledge of God's existence:

> [W]hen a man awakes to the possibility of a search and when such a man passes a Jew in the street for the first time, he is like Robinson Crusoe seeing the footprint on the beach. (Mg 75)

The image suggests that the Jews have news to offer the seeker and that if the seeker is prudent, he will follow the Jews (their history and law) to find the Source of all truth.

Finally, the incident that plays the most significant role in Binx's search, the initial impetus for the search, is his war experience. It is true in all Percy's theological fiction; pain, trauma, disaster--catastrophe of some kind occurs before a man "comes to himself" and realizes the possibility of God and the necessity of a search for Him. In "The Message . . . ," the castaway has been shipwrecked; in The Moviegoer Binx has suffered a wound while fighting in the Orient. It is what Binx calls his horizontal search, not for scientific knowledge, but for metaphysical answers to the ultimate questions about the origin, the meaning, the purpose, and the end of life. It is, Binx argues, "what anyone would undertake if he were not sunk in the everydayness of his own life" (Mg 18). Alert to the clues of his own and all men's predicament, Binx becomes a seeker of truth--"news," Percy calls it in his allegory--news from "across the seas" to enlighten him to the mystery of life and the mystery of death.

News must come in the form of signs, that is, communication, and primarily language. Thus, Binx, the exile in The Moviegoer, becomes the reader and the interpreter of news messages, so that he, like the castaway in "The Message . . . ," must first abstract the meaning and intention of a statement then classify it in five ways. He must first determine the character of the message, whether it is "knowledge sub specie aeternitatis" (objective statements) or whether it is news relevant to his predicament. He must next determine his own posture toward the message, that is, whether he reads it objectively as a scientist would, dispassionately, or whether he reads it subjectively for an answer to his spiritual dilemma. Third, he must rank the news on a "scale of significance"; that is, in the castaway's situation whether the news answers a critical (e.g., spiritual need) or some less significant need. Next, he must establish "canons of acceptance"; that is, credible news statements delivered by reputable newsbearers offering relevant explanations to his predicament. And, finally, Binx, the seeker, must make a choice regarding the news: whether he will respond and act on the news, place his faith in the veracity of the word and thenceforth live his life according to the news.

The primary concern in "The Message . . ." is not apologetic, Percy insists, not a "teaching," but "news as a category of communication." It is news, however, about Christ who offers hope for the man in despair through a faith in Christ's death, his resurrection, and his Body of witnesses. But the Good News does not come supernaturally or even Providentially, Percy insists; the pilgrim must "come to himself," become aware of the possibility of a search, then initiate the search for God. Moreover, the Good News is brought by human newsbearers, that is, prophets who are called by God and who preach or teach the Word in the language of men. The wayfarer accepts the message as truth when it is brought by a dedicated and devout minister with a message from God:

> How then may we recognize the divine authority of the apostle? What, in other words, are the credentials of the newsbearer? The credential of the apostle is simply the gravity of his message: "I am called by God; do with me what you will, scourge me, persecute me, but my last words are my first; I am called by God and I make you eternally responsible for what you do against me. (MB 147)

This, then, is the task set forth for the castaway in "The Message in the Bottle," and, as I have suggested, the same role designed for Binx Bolling in The Moviegoer.

It is apparent from the opening paragraph that the novel is concerned with language generally and with messages (i.e., news), specifically: Binx receives a message from his Aunt Emily that says one thing but intends another. He knows how to interpret it because he has received other such messages from her. Moreover, it is a request for one of her "talks," a word about a word, in this sense, and "can mean only one thing":

> This morning I got a note from my aunt asking me to come for lunch. I know what this means. Since I go there every Sunday for dinner and today is Wednesday, it can mean only one thing: she wants to have one of her serious talks. It will be extremely grave, either a piece of bad news about her stepdaughter Kate or else a serious talk about me, about the future and what I ought to do. It is enough to scare the wits out of anyone, yet I confess I do not find the prospect altogether unpleasant. (Mg 11)

Binx is keenly alert to messages from other people; he has learned to interpret not only the words themselves, but the freight they carry, that is, the "spirit" of the word, what is suggested or intended as well as what is said.

Using the discourse of the four major characters--Binx, Kate, Aunt Emily, and Lonnie--I shall first establish the category of communication of the language of each, according to those identified by Percy in "The Message . . ."

172

(castaway/seeker, scientist, and apostle or newsbearer); then using Binx as the receiver and interpreter of the discourse of the others, I shall examine the effect of the others on the castaway/seeker.

Binx is, of course, the primary figure, the castaway that Percy describes in "The Message . . . ," and like the castaway in "The Message . . .," Binx "comes to himself," that is, becomes aware of himself as a misfit, an alien, on a "strange island," a new awareness that compels him to begin a search for some metaphysical answers to his dilemma. It is significant that Binx begins his search for the metaphysical where he lives--in the neighborhood itself--not in theological circles. Percy also considers this significant in the allegory:

> A castaway, everyone would agree, would do well to pay attention to knowledge and news, knowledge of the nature of the world and news of events that are relevant to his life on the island. Such news, the news relevant to his survival as an organism, his life as a father and husband, as a member of a culture, as an economic man, and so on--we can well call island news. (MB 143)

As a castaway/seeker, then, Binx notices everything around him; everything becomes a sign, either of death--most people he meets fall into this category, just as the magnificent homes do--or of potential (i.e., metaphysical) life--the natural universe (the North Carolina mountains, the dust motes in the New Orleans lab), the deaths of close family members (Scotty and his father), and the innocent goodness and death of Lonnie, his half-brother.

Binx understands instinctively that he is not at home in the world; this, according to Percy's commentary in the allegory, is the first requirement for reading metaphysical messages or searching for metaphysical answers:

> Our subject is not only an organism and a culture member; he is also a castaway. That is to say, he is not in the world as a swallow is in the world, as an organism which is what it is, never more or less. Our islander may choose his mode of being. . . . But however he chooses to exist, he is in the last analysis a castaway, a stranger who is in the world but who is not at home in the world. (MB 142)

Binx knows, for example, that he does not think like his aunt; as noble and as high minded as she is--behaving with a "natural piety and grace," living and dying by her "lights," and defying the high gods, "whoever they may be"--Binx sits silently during each conversation with her, unable to answer her probing questions or to satisfy her demand of him to live up to the family's noblesse oblige:

> I did my best for you, son. I gave you all I had. More than anything I wanted to pass on to you the one heritage of the men of our family, a certain quality of spirit, a gaiety, a sense of duty, a nobility worn lightly, a sweetness, a gentleness with women--the only good things the South ever had and the only things that really matter in this life. (Mg 178)

Binx responds to this discourse, and others like it by Aunt Emily, with monosyllables or silence; he cannot argue because he has no argument for the way he feels about his life, about others' lives, and about the world around him. From all these, he reads messages of death and life, not, as Aunt Emily reads signs, as relative to a way of life, i.e., as "common" and therefore ignoble and cheapening or as "class" and therefore noble and uplifting. The two do not speak the same language; as a castaway and a seeker, Binx does not operate, intellectually, on the same level--his language is metaphysical, hers is philosophical. There is a difference; Binx knows this and so does not participate in her discourse. Percy makes the application: "[I]n his heart of hearts there is not a moment of his life when the castaway does not know that life on the island, being 'at home' on the island, is something of a charade" (MB 143).

The role of Binx in the novel is, clearly, the lost man in search of God. Percy makes this clear, and so does Binx in his interpretations of other characters' discourse, in his interpretation of social conditions, in his interpretation of natural signs, and often in his own subjective discourse and in imaginary conversation with movie stars whom he admires and imitates.

He would like to behave as "Rory" does in a wonderful gesture of self-control when he gives his bed to "Debbie" and lies staring at the ceiling from the couch in the living room, or--and here Binx interprets his own role--

> do what a hero in a novel would do: he too is a seeker and a pilgrim of sorts and he is just in from Guanajarto or Sambuco where he has found the Real Right Thing or from the East where he apprenticed himself to a wise man and became proficient in the seventh path to the seventh happiness. Yet he does not disdain this world either . . . . (Mg 159)

An examination of Kate's language places her in a parallel role with Binx; though dependent and fledgling in her journey, she, nevertheless, speaks the language of a castaway and a seeker. She has been "onto" the search ever since she experienced a tragic auto accident in which her fiance, Lyell Lovell, was killed. Like Binx's brush with death, hers has awakened her to a strange condition; it is for her, not a tragedy, but "the happiest moment of my life" (Mg 52). She speaks of this to Binx:

> Have you noticed that only in times of illness or disaster or death are people real? I remember at the time of the wreck--people were so kind and helpful and solid. Everyone pretended that our lives until that moment had been every bit as real as the moment itself and that the future must be real too, when the truth was that our reality had been purchased only by Lyell's death. In another hour or so we had all faded out again and gone our dim ways. (Mg 69)

Again like Binx, Kate rejects stepmother Emily's philosophy of life, though in a more aggressive manner; "The knives have started flying," she confides to Binx, speaking of her quarrels with Emily, even attempts, it seems, to provoke the older woman to "kick her out":

> "They think they're helping me, but they aren't," comes the low voice in my ear. "How much better it would be if they weren't so damned understanding--if they kicked me out of the house. (Mg 57)

Not succeeding in that, Kate disappears for long periods of time, swallows a number of nembutal tablets that put her out half a day, and in general rebels against the conventions of the elite Bolling/Cutrer heritage. The turning point in Kate's life comes when she discovers, at a session with her psychiatrist, her individuality, her "error" or divergence from other human beings. She has tried, she says, to live up to Doctor Mink's book, to have her symptoms identified, named, and applied to psychopathic illness, but she has failed and realizes suddenly that she does not have to fit the categories in the "book":

> Poor Merle. You see there is nothing he can say. He can't tell me the secret even if he asked me: what comes to mind? I sat up and rubbed my eyes and then it dawned on me. It was so simple. My God, can a person live twenty-five years, a life of crucifixion, through a misunderstanding? . . . I had discovered that a person does not have to be this or be that or be anything, not even oneself. (Mg 94)

It is here, in language of a metaphysician, that Kate announces her discovery of her freedom from the world's conventions, and it is here that Binx first speaks of marriage, recognizing her movement toward a spiritual search and her need for assistance and support. At this point, she is still turned inward in her egocentricity, unable to see the reason for a metaphysical search, even teases Binx about his "death house optimism":

> You remind me of a prisoner in the death house who takes a wry pleasure in doing things like registering to vote. Come to think of it, all your gaiety and good spirits have the same death house quality. No thanks. I've had enough of your death house pranks. (Mg 154)

It is during their microcosmic journey on a train from New Orleans to Chicago that Kate and Binx examine their new relationship and discover themselves and each other, the roles each is to play in their subsequent "dark journey" together. First, Kate confides to Binx that she is "religious"; she means by that that she must depend on rules and laws and directions--to be told what to believe and what to do:

> Don't you see? What I want is to believe in someone completely and then do what he wants me to do. If God

> were to tell me: Kate, here is what I want you to do; you
> get off this train right now and go over there to that corner
> by the Southern Life and Accident Insurance Company and
> stand there the rest of your life and speak kindly to people--
> you think I would not do it? You think I would not be the
> happiest girl in Jackson, Mississippi? I would. (Mg 157)

The religion she means is not the religion of Binx; indeed, she argues that he is not religious at all, that like God, he stands above all laws and conventions, independent and sure:

> You can do it because you are not religious. God is not
> religious. You are the unmoved mover. You don't need
> God or anyone else--no credit to you, unless it is a credit to
> be the most self-centered person alive. I don't know
> whether I love you, but I believe in you and I will do what
> you tell me. Now if I marry you, will you tell me: Kate, this
> morning do such and such, and if we have to go to a party,
> will you tell me: Kate, stand right there and have three
> drinks and talk to so and so? (Mg 157)

Kate has found her proper mate in Binx; she believes wholeheartedly in him: "The only time I'm not frightened is when I'm with you" (Mg 185)

Toward Kate, Binx assumes the posture of mentor and protector. He recognizes the same inclination for the metaphysical that he himself feels: her despair shaken to awareness by her confrontation with death, her recognition of the sham and hypocrisy of society, and finally her realization of her need for God. Binx takes charge with adult-role authority, instructs her carefully as a father would a child: "You can ride the streetcar down St. Charles. It is nice sitting by an open window. . . . I'll call Mr. Klostermann and he'll hand you an envelope. Here's what you do . . ." (Mg 190). This is part of Binx's new philosophy: to "listen to people, see how they stick themselves into the world, hand them along aways in their dark journey . . ." (Mg 184).

In Percy's categories of communicators, Binx's Aunt Emily is the objective-minded individual that Percy names "scientist." The term is generic and refers to any person who places himself outside the world or, as Percy says, "over against the world" to name it, define it, and know it. This includes not only the scientist, but the philosopher, the artist, the poet; it is the "posture of objectivity" (MB 128):

> If the reader has discovered the secret of science, art, and philosophizing, and so has entered the great company of Thales, Lao-tses, Aquinas, Newton, Keats, Whitehead, he will know what it is to stand outside and over against the world as one who sees and thinks and knows and tells. He tells and hears others tell how it is there in the world and what it is to live in the world. (MB 128)

The messages the scientist gets, the only sentences he understands, are knowledge sub species aeternitatis; he does not accept "news" messages at all in his posture as scientist. In The Moviegoer the strong-willed matriarch, Emily Cutrer, is an aristocratic Stoic philosopher with a firm grip on her own opinions, values, and duties and would like very much to ascribe her opinions, values, and duties to her nephew, Binx, and her stepdaughter, Kate. First, she comments on the disintegration of culture: "The world I knew has come crashing down round my ears. The things we hold dear are reviled and spat upon" (Mg 48). Then she pleads with Binx to accept the old verities of truth, honor, duty; though she cannot define the purpose or the end of life, she lives by her "lights," never flinching, never wavering:

> . . . [Y]ou have too good a mind to throw away. I don't quite know what we're doing on this insignificant cinder spinning away in a dark corner of the universe. That is a secret which the high gods have not confided in me. Yet one thing I believe and I believe it with every fiber of my being. A man must live by his lights and do what little he can and do it as best he can. In this world goodness is destined to be defeated. But a man must go down fighting. That is the victory. To do anything less is to be less than a man. (Mg 48-49)

In a metaphysical analysis, Emily Cutrer is obviously a negative quality; she believes only in the material world. There may be another, but because it cannot be perceived, it is not relevant to her life. She is like Percy's scientist who abstracts himself from his own predicament "in order to achieve objectivity" (MB 130). To Emily it is man's world, and the man who performs the noblest (with "natural piety and grace") is the hero; she derogates the "common man" who "prizes mediocrity for mediocrity's sake" (Mg 176). Indeed, the whole nation, she argues, has become a "sinkhole of history," the "moral fiber is rotten," the whole system corrupt.

The effect on Binx of the two tirades of Aunt Emily may be likened to a cannon and a pop-gun. She fires all her ammunition in quick succession with hardly a pause, while Binx sits politely listening, absorbing, but unable to answer except in nods and monosyllablic agreement. In fact, he envies his Aunt's certainties, his being shaky at best. At one point, in a halting voice, he begins to tell her about his search, but stops himself because it suddenly "seems absurd" (Mg 49). And in the final encounter when she rails against him for taking Kate to Chicago without telling anyone, he simply sits in silence, patient, respectful, but noncommittal and undefensive. He understands where she comes from, understands her "unfallen," "unrepentant" posture and knows that his own stance as a seeker would make no sense to her. So he remains silent.

In Percy's categories of communicators as I have identified them, there are three: the scientist, the news seeker, and the news bearer. I have identified Emily Cutrer as the scientist-philosopher who stands apart from the world, names it and knows it; and I have identified Binx and Kate as news seekers who stand in a "predicament" of exile and alienation. But there is a third category of communicator, the newsbearer who brings the Good News of Christ. In The Moviegoer this is Lonnie Smith, Binx's half-brother. Lonnie is confined to a wheelchair, physically deformed and ill most of the time, but his spirit is angelic, his manner exemplary; he is Percy's authentic newsbearer: his message comes from the "sphere of transcendence," his behavior is sacrificial, and he brings news about the "unique Person-Event-Thing in time" (Mg 141). At the time Binx begins his metaphysical search, Lonnie is fourteen, a deformed child and an invalid who suffers from frequent and serious illnesses, but who takes pleasure in offering his sufferings "in reparation for men's indifference to the pierced heart of Jesus Christ" (Mg 112). Devout in his faith and knowledgeable about his Catholic doctrine, Lonnie practices abstinence during Lent even with a serious illness; he has, he says, "an habitual disposition" which he must conquer. Not only his behavior, but Lonnie's speech as well possesses a peculiar advantage; his words remain meaningful, not "worn out" as words are when they are lightly and carelessly used. When he asks Binx "straight out," "Do you love me?," there is a quality of seriousness that compels a serious answer: "Yes, I love you" (Mg 137). The boy discusses his faith freely with Binx, unlike the rest of the family who are embarrassed at the mention of God. Even Lonnie's blue eyes "engage . . . in lively converse, looking, looking away, and looking again" (Mg 132); it is a pleasant time for both Lonnie and Binx, even though Binx plays it as a game, using Lonnie's rules. Nevertheless, Lonnie basks in the joy of the quiet moments and ends their talk with a plea: "I am still offering my communion for you" (Mg 133). The effect of Lonnie's faith on Binx may be inferred by the devotion of the boy to the older brother and by the reciprocated love of the older for the younger brother. Binx, as interpreter of the language, reads into the meaning of Lonnie's words, the serenity of soul, his peace about death, his joy in his faith; and in the end, as he leaves the bedside of the dying boy, Binx offers the same peace and hope to the younger children when Donice asks whether Lonnie will have a wheelchair "When Our Lord raises us up on the Last Day" or whether he "will be like us" (Mg 190). Binx does not hesitate, does not waver, but in seriousness, answers Donice: "He'll be like you" (Mg 190).

A number of conclusions may be drawn about Binx (Jack Bickerson) Bolling, the interpreter of Percy's "message," and about the message per se. First, as a seeker, he is instinctively aware of his own and others' spiritual condition; he can read the signs in the eyes, in the manner, as well as in the words. He also senses the impending doom, the eschatological end or Last Days of Creation: "Whenever I feel myself sinking toward a deep sleep, something always recalls me: 'Not so fast now. Suppose you should go to sleep and it should happen'" (Mg 71). Finally, Binx is cognizant of the teachings of Apostle Paul; he can discuss theological issues with Lonnie, albeit by Lonnie's "rules," can hold his own in a theological argument with Lonnie about fasting; he knows the correct terms, and he has the right answers:

> [Binx:] "Are you still worried about [envying brother Duval]? You accused yourself and received absolution, didn't you?"
>
> [Lonnie:] "Yes."
>
> [Binx:] "Then don't be scrupulous."
>
> [Lonnie:] "I'm not scrupulous."
>
> [Binx:] "Then what's the trouble?"
>
> [Lonnie"] "I'm glad he's dead."
>
> [Binx:] "Why shouldn't you be? He sees God face to face and you don't." (Mg 131)

Binx, in short, is the hero with a death house optimism because he has found the Real Right Thing.

Like Walker Percy, the novelist-prophet, the Apostle Paul is concerned about the nature and the condition of man; to the Romans, he warns, "All have sinned and fall short of the glory of God" (Rom. 3: 23); "None is righteous, no, not one; no one understands, no one seeks for God. All have turned aside, together they have gone wrong; (Rom. 3: 10-12). Furthermore, is death" (Rom. 8: 6). But he adds quickly in each instance the possibility for overcoming sin and its penalty, death:

> Since all have sinned and fall short of the glory of God, they are justified by his grace as a gift, through the redemption which is in Christ Jesus, whom God put forward as an expiation by his blood to be received by faith. (Rom. 3: 23-25)

And again:

> For the wages of sin is death, but the free gift of god is eternal life in Christ Jesus our Lord. (Rom. 6: 23)

Finally,

> To set the mind on the flesh is death, but to set the mind on the Spirit is life and peace. (Rom. 8: 6)

This is the concern and the message in Percy's allegory "The Message in the Bottle" and in The Moviegoer; even though his method must, of necessity, be allegorical and fictional, he would edify and persuade his readers that this world is not all there is, that this life is not the end, and that factual science is not infallible or supreme. He has, of course, repeated his message in fiction half a dozen times already in novels and has interpreted his message freely in interviews and essays so that his meaning will not be missed. That is the purpose of the earliest short fictional account of the gospel message, "The Message in the Bottle," I contend, an interpretation of The Moviegoer, which quickly followed. The characters are all represented in the allegory, labelled by their attitude toward the Logos (God), whether He exists or not; labelled also by their attitude toward language itself, whether factual only or metaphysical as well, labelled again by their attitude toward the world, whether it is home or alien; and labelled finally by their attitude toward themselves and other humans, whether self-sufficient and unfallen or fallen and undone. The major characters--Binx, Kate, Emily, and Lonnie--illustrate the categories of communicators in the world, and each demonstrates Percy's allegorical interpretation of both the word and the Word: man's language as both a means of learning facts and a way of knowing God. Binx--wayfarer, pilgrim, and castaway--is the seeker of the Good News, clues and messages to tell him who he is, where he comes from, and why he is here. Kate, likewise, joins Binx in the search and begins, with Binx, the search for the metaphysical answers. Emily Cutrer fits Percy's philosopher-scientist category, the objective thinker who knows only knowledge sub specie aeternitatis, that is, "knowledge which can be arrived by anyone at anytime" (MB 125). And finally, Lonnie represents the messenger of God, who brings the Good News that Paul speaks of--the Redemption offered by God's grace.

NOTES

[1] The largest group of critics of The Moviegoer is the existentialist writers, those who, beginning with Martin Luschei's definitive study in 1972 (The Sovereign Wayfarer: Walker Percy's Diagnosis of the Malaise), find that a close reading of Soren Kierkegaard is the most helpful source in interpreting Percy's novel. Critics in this group include Janet Hobbs ("Binx Bolling and the Stages of Life's Way"), Edward Lawrey ("Literature as Philosophy: The Moviegoer"), Jerome Thale ("Alienation on the American Plan"), and Jac Tharpe (Walker Percy). John F. Zeugner ("Walker Percy and Gabriel Marcel: The Castaway and the Wayfarer") substitutes Marcel for Kierkegaard and emphasizes the idea of intersubjectivity instead of states of life: "Percy has been obsessed with intersubjectivity," a concept "which the corpus of Percy's work suggests is the ground of being, the basis of consciousness, the way out of alienation, and the path of salvation" (22).

Lewis A. Lawson gives the best reading regarding moviegoing per se ("The Allegory of the Cave and The Moviegoer"). It is a modern Gnosticism, Lawson says, and should be read as a "Withdrawal-and-Return" after the theory of Toynbee, the idea that "a civilization grows when there is a great leader who, defeated or frustrated in his project, withdraws psychologically (and often physically), communes with himself, then returns, to gain victory over the conditions that had originally stopped him" (13). Toynbee lists examples, among which he names Plato's "Allegory of the Cave" as withdrawal-and-return movement of Plato's philosopher-king and adds a footnote suggesting that "the situation of an audience in a cinematograph theatre with its eyes glued to the screen on which a lantern at their backs projects the lights and shadows of a moving film" is a more apt example than anything Plato could have imagined in his day. It is from Toynbee that Binx "takes his self-image" as moviegoer, Lawson says, launches a "vertical" search only after reading Toynbee's A Study of History, and emerges from the "Cave" to see the world in ultimate generalization (like a good Cartesian scientist) as an outsider looking on. But this is also the ultimate despair, Lawson points out, because the self is "left over," unaccounted for in the big picture of the scientist. As a wanderer, then, Binx arrives at the possibility of a "horizontal" search, observing people "in the cave, that is, at home in a purely material world" and others "who have come out of the cave, that is, at home in a totally abstract world," and finally admits "that faith is something answered" (17-18). Half-brother Lonnie, also a moviegoer, is "one of Plato's viewers of the Sun," Lawson notes, but qualifies that interpretation by associating Lonnie with Augustine:

> Augustine confesses that he had been a Platonist,
> that he had believed in the Truth represented in
> the Simile of the Cave. He too had been . . . a
> theater-goer, had been one who satisfied his
> desire for the flesh. But, in time, he had gained
> the faith to believe in Christ, had come to see the
> Light of the World not as a Transcendent Form,
> but the Logos, the Incarnation. (18)

It is thus easy to understand, as Lawson notes, why Percy's original title was The Confessions of a Moviegoer.

Susan Kissel ("Walker Percy's 'Conversions'") reads in this novel and all the other Percy fiction an awakening by protagonists to false values and an acceptance and affirmation of a whole new way of life, a final reversal in religious conversion. Sara Henisey ("Intersubjectivity in Symbolization"), on the other hand, concludes that Binx "does not rule out the possibility of God, but he gives up the old search as a foolish notion" (214).

Thomas LeClair ("The Eschatological Vision of Walker Percy") finds a twofold vision in Percy's treatment of death: death as an existential condition (immanent eschatology) and death as an event in the "economy of salvation" (transcendent eschatology).

A number of writers assume a Southerner's position, that a writer who grows up in the South must, whether he intends to or not, write about the South--southern tradition, southern aesthetics, southern philosophy--and thus they interpret The Moviegoer as the reflection of that tradition. Michel T. Blouin ("The Novels of Walker Percy: An Attempt at Synthesis") for example, holds that "the young white southerner of today remains essentially a figure of irony and pathos in so far as he is fixed by the historical past in a posture of defense and reaction" (19) and confronts essential questions--"How to live and how to die?" and "What do bravery and courtesy mean?"--without traditional support for answering them "correctly" (19). Lewis Lawson ("Walker Percy's Southern Stoic") reads Aunt Emily Cutrer as the ghost of Walker Percy's foster father, William Alexander Percy, and Anneke Leenhouts ("Letting Go of the Old South: An Introduction to Walker Percy") finds the "demise of the old aristocratic South" in Walker Percy's fiction, but "not in a devastating way" (50); the alternatives mediate the loss. Richard Pindell ("Basking in the Eye") links Percy aesthetically with William Faulkner in Percy's use of irony and paradox, creating "the chaos we must endure . . . [keeping] green the ground for renewal" (229). And, finally, Max Webb ("Binx Bolling's New Orleans: Moviegoing, Southern Writing and Father Abraham") sees the paradox of Binx in a dual journey--a physical as well as a spiritual journey--likened in this way to patriarch Abraham.

CONCLUSION

I have placed Walker Percy in the American Calvinist tradition, following the scientific and theological influence of Charles Sanders Peirce, whom Percy names as his semiotic mentor. I have demonstrated the crucial role of Peirce's triadic theory in Percy's system: in establishing the transcendent nature of man and in reviving the medieval concept of logos as language which man can read and thereby know, not just himself, his fellows, and the cosmos, but God as well. Language, Walker Percy argues from first to last, is the key to the mystery of man--his nature and his origin. According to this theological system--or Percy's adaptation of it--the only hope for man in a post-Christian, scientifically controlled world lies in the Beloved Community or Body of Christ (the church), which alone can teach man the meaning of, what Percy calls, defunct words like "faith," "salvation," "baptism." In Calvinistic terms, it is only through this Beloved Community that man can be restored to the covenant relationship with God, the Creator and Father of mankind.

I have specified the Calvinistic strand of Protestantism, and I have traced it in American history and philosophy from the New England colonists through Jonathan Edwards to Emerson and Charles Peirce to Walker Percy. I have singled out this tradition as the dominant Protestant line in this country, but I should, perhaps, mark the significant differences between this tradition and the other major one: Lutheranism, which is itself divided into two strands--the first, pietism, is an introspective faith based on belief in a divine "inner light"; and the second is a faith grounded in scripture.

Pietism originated in Germany with Philipp Jakob Spener in the seventeenth century and was brought to this country from Europe by Germantown settlers in Pennsylvania and by Quakers via England. This sect is best known for its heart religion, a subjectivism based on the doctrine of the priesthood of the believer. It teaches that the inner person receives an illumination from God and that the enlightenment then transforms the heart and the life of the individual. Dale Brown quotes Spener in this regard:

> One should therefore emphasize that the divine means of Word and sacrament are concerned with the inner man. Hence it is not enough that we hear the Word with our outward ear, but we must let it penetrate to our heart, so that we may hear the Holy Spirit speak there, that is, vibrant emotion and comfort feel the sealing of the Spirit and the power of the Word. Nor is it enough to be baptized, but the inner man, where we have put on Christ in baptism, must also keep Christ on and bear witness to him in our outward life. Nor is it enough to have received the Lord's Supper externally, but the inner man must truly be fed with that blessed food. Nor is it enough to pray outwardly with our mouth, but true prayer, and the best prayer, occurs in the inner man. (108, qtd. from Spener's <u>Pia Desideria</u>)

The heart, Spener teaches, is the locus of the soul, man's center of being, and the place of God's dwelling. This psychological base for religious experience generates an intensity of emotion and a purity of behavior that, to Spener and other pietists, testify to a saving faith.

The Germantown settlement in Pennsylvania, founded by Spener's disciple Heinrich Muhlenberg, began, perhaps, the most famous American strand of pietism; but Quakerism, a pietistic movement from England was also an important Protestant movement in this country. John Woolman, eighteenth century American Quaker, gives an account of his religion in his <u>Journal,</u> the testimony of "the power of the Spirit to shape a life in harmony with the absolute demands of the Sermon on the Mount" (vii). As in earlier Spenerian writing, the message speaks of a "sensitiveness to the promptings of the divine Light within" (vii). Marked by close introspection, Woolman's life, as recorded in his <u>Journal,</u> speaks of intense psychological conflict, periods of self-recrimination and sadness, followed by "heavenly visitation":

> I sought deserts and lonely places, and there with tears did confess my sins to God and humbly craved his help. And I may say with reverence, he was near to me in my troubles,

> and in those times of humiliation opened my ear to
> discipline. (7)

And he testifies that early in life he became convinced "that true religion [consists] in an inward life, wherein the heart doth love and reverence God the Creator, and learns to exercise true justice and goodness, not only to all men, but also toward the brute creatures; that, as the mind was moved by an inward principle to love God as an invisible, incomprehensible Being, so by the same principle, it was moved to love him in all his manifestations in the visible world" (8). In this manner, John Woolman demon-strates one brand of Protestantism that contrasts sharply with the Percy-Peircean empirical tradition of Christianity.

The second strand of Lutheranism, a faith based on the Text, i.e., Holy Scripture that acts as God's instructions to man, was developed by John Bunyan and John Milton, two literary figures who hold that the written word, both the Word of God and the word of God's spokesmen, is fundamental in knowing God's manner of dealing with man, his expectations for man, his laws and judgments. Milton wrote Paradise Lost "To justify the ways of God to men," and Bunyan did the same in The Pilgrim's Progress.

In the latter work, for example, the writer has Christian lecture Ignorance about the necessity of scripture in achieving salvation: "Except the Word of God beareth witness in this matter, other testimony is of no value" (215). Although Ignorance is, he avows, a "good liver" who fasts, prays, pays tithes, and gives alms; though he is "always full of good motions" (i.e., desires God and heaven); and though his heart testifies to his goodness and his "hopes of heaven, all is vanity, Christian warns, unless it "agrees with what the Word saith to him" (217). And thus it happens: having no "certificate of admission," Ignorance is bound in chains, carried through the air, and cast into hell, "even from the gates of heaven" (243).

188

And in his autobiography, <u>Grace Abounding to the Chief of Sinners</u>, Bunyan testifies to the spiritual edification of scripture; when he suffers remorse from "my many blasphemies" and "saying in my mind, What ground have I to think that I, who have been so vile and abominable, should ever inherit eternal life," a scripture comes to mind: "What shall we say to these things? If God be for us, who can be against us? (Rom. 8: 31)" (36). When he is haunted by doubt planted by other men's false teachings, he turns to the "holy Word," and when temptations come, he retreats to scripture, there to restore faith and stability:

> The Lord made use of two things to confirm me in [his teachings], the one was the errors of the Quakers, and the other was the guilt of sin; for as the Quakers did oppose his Truth, so God did confirm me in it, by leading me into the Scripture that did wonderfully maintain it. (39)

Thus, against many "vile and abominable" assertions, Bunyan is "driven to a more narrow search of Scriptures, and [is] through their light and testimony, not only enlightened, but greatly confirmed and comforted in the truth" (39). Bunyan retreats to scripture on each experience of doubt or struggle or pain, "to see if I could find that saying" (<u>Grace Abounding</u> 21) or to clarify some doctrine, "to give place to the Word, which with power, did over and over make this joyful sound within my Soul" (29):

> The Scriptures now also were wonderful things unto me; I saw that the truth and verity of them were the keys of the Kingdom of Heaven; those that the Scriptures favor they must inherit bliss; but those that they oppose and condemn, must perish for evermore. O this word, <u>For the Scripture cannot be broken</u>, would rend the caul of my heart. . . . (76)

In a similar manner, John Milton defers to scripture as the ground of faith and states his position explicitly in the introduction to "The Christian Doctrine":

> [H]aving taken the grounds of my faith from divine revelation alone, and having neglected nothing which depended on my own industry, I thought fit to scrutinize and

> ascertain for myself the several points of my religious belief,
> by the most careful perusal and meditation of the Holy
> Scriptures themselves. (900)

In compiling his doctrinal position, Milton remains close, as he testifies, to Biblical statements, believing that only in "constant diligence" and "an unwearied search after truth . . . by the rule of Scripture" lies truth (901). It is not reason, Milton repeats, but "evidence of Scripture" that must ultimately prevail in man's search for doctrinal fidelity, and because he believes this, he, like Bunyan, "fills [his] pages even to redundance with quotations from Scripture": "For my own part, I adhere to the Holy Scriptures alone" (901). And he takes it as his duty "to justify the ways of God to man" by engraving the words and thoughts of scripture in the minds of his readers.

In America, this same Bunyanesque fidelity to the text may be traced in rhetorical methods of writers and critics, beginning with Nathaniel Hawthorne and Herman Melville, two major writers concerned, not with organized religion or public dogma like the Calvinists and not with the God-enlightened heart of the Pietists, but with a respect for the text, for the printed page.

Even more than Calvinism, this text-based "religion" has become secularized, has, in fact, lost its ties with the Bible, but has maintained the veneration for the printed word. It can be seen in Hawthorne's allegorical prose used to expose the flaws of New England Calvinism as he does in The Scarlet Letter, to track the progress of Christian Pilgrim in "The Celestial Railroad," and to condemn the hypocrisy of Quaker pietists in "The Gentle Boy." This same Bunyanesque style of writing may be found in Herman Melville's exploration of the central mystery of the universe, the power of evil and the conflict between the forces of good and the forces of evil. He adapts other texts, other styles, speaks in multiple voices, so that in reading Moby Dick, for example, or "Billy Budd," one finds assimilations of Shakespeare and other texts, other styles, speaks in multiple voices, so that in reading <u>Moby Dick</u>, for example, or "Billy Budd," one finds assimilations of Shakespeare and the Gospels, dramatic and allegorical rhetoric grounded in other texts. Poe, too, establishes an alliance with this school of thought. In "The Philosophy of Composition" he speaks of creating a "single effect" whereby the text is focused tightly, singlemindedly toward the dénouement, and he describes the "sole legitimate province" of a literary work as beauty, that is, "the intense elevation of the <u>soul</u>--not of intellect, or heart." Words become, with Poe, the ultimate concern, so that the success of "The Raven," for example, rides on the choice of a single word to be used for a refrain.

Today, this close attention to the text is found in modern criticism--with critics who find a world created by the text, who read the text by word relationships, by contrast and adumbration, by connotation and ambiguity, who draw upon echo texts that mingle with new ones and complicate the whole by the mixture. William Empson explains this textual analysis in <u>Seven Types of Ambiguity</u>:

> [A] word may have several distinct meanings; several meanings connected with one another; several meanings which need one another to complete their meaning; or several meanings which unite together so that the word means one relation or one process. (5)

Supporting this theory of the word is the "notion of the way . . . a word is regarded as a member of the language" (6):

> For one may know what has been put into the pot, and recognize the objects in the stew, but the juice in which they are sustained must be regarded with a peculiar respect because they are in there too, somehow, and one does not know how they are combined or held in suspension. (6)

All the tricks of language that one finds both puzzling and appealing may be traced to John Bunyan's reverence for the Holy Word.

With Walker Percy language means something different, of course, a vehicle to deliver messages for man, the interpreter, messages ultimately designed by the God of the universe.

Abadi-Nagy, Zoltan. "A Talk with Walker Percy." Southern Literary Journal 61 (Fall 1973): 3-19. rpt. Conversations With Walker Percy. Eds. Lewis A. Lawson and Victor Kramer. Jackson: University Press of Mississippi, 1985.

Allen, William Rodney. Walker Percy: A Southern Wayfarer. Jackson: University of Mississippi Press, 1986.

Aquinas, Thomas. Summa Theologica I-II. Trans. Fathers of English Dominican Province. Chicago: Encyclopedia Britannica, Inc., 1952.

Archer, Emily. "Naming in the Neighborhood of Being: O'Connor and Percy on Language." Studies in the Literary Imagination 20.2 (Fall 1987): 97-108.

Arrington, Robert L. "The Mystery of Language." Sewanee Review 84 (1976): 127-30.

Atkins, A. "Walker Percy and Wednesday Afternoons." Humanist 43 (1983): 33-34.

Atkins, Anselm. "Walker Percy and the Post-Christian Search." Centennial Review 12 (Winter 1968): 73-95.

Augustine. The Confessions. Trans. Edward Bouverie Pusey. Chicago: Encyclopedia Britannica, Inc., 1952.

---. De Trinitate. Trans. Rev. Arthur West Haddan. A Select Library of the Nicene and Post-Nicene Fathers. Ed. Philip Schaff. Grand Rapids: Wm. B. Eerdmans, 1988.

---. On Christian Doctrine. Trans. J. F. Shaw. A Select Library of the Nicene and Post-Nicene Fathers II. Grand Rapids: Wm. B. Eerdmans, 1988.

Baker, Lewis. The Percys of Mississippi. Baton Rouge: LSU Press, 1983.

Bender, Todd K. Gerard Manley Hopkins: A Classical Background and Critical Reception of His Work. Baltimore: Johns Hopkins, 1966.

Bercovitch, Sacvan. The Puritan Origins of the American Self. New Haven: Yale Univ. Press, 1976.

Bernstein, Richard J. "Peirce's Theory of Perception." Studies in the Philosophy of Charles Sanders Peirce, Second Series. Eds. Edward C. Moore and Richard S. Robin. Amherst: Univ. of Mass. Press, 1964: 165-89.

Berrigan, J. R. "An Explosion of Utopias." Moreana 38 (1973): 21-26.

Betts, Doris. "The Christ-Haunted Psyche of the Southern Writer." Books and Religion 13 (March 1985): 1, 14-15.

Bigger, Charles P. "Logos and Epiphany: Walker Percy's Theology of Language." Southern Review 13 (January 1977): 196-206.

---. "Walker Percy and the Resonance of the Word." Walker Percy: Art and Ethics. Ed. Jac Tharpe. Jackson: Univ. of Mississippi Press, 1980.

Bischoff, Joan. "Walker Percy." American Novelists Since World War II. Ed. Jeffrey Helterman and Richard Layman. Detroit: Gale, 1978: 309-97.

Bloom, Harold, ed. Walker Percy. New York: Chelsea, 1986.

Blouin, Michael T. "The Novels of Walker Percy: An Attempt at Synthesis." Xavier Univ. Studies 6 (February 1967): 29-42.

Boler, John F. Charles Peirce and Scholastic Realism: A Study of Charles Peirce's Relation to John Duns Scotus. Seattle: Univ. of Washington, 1968.

---. "Habits of Thought." Studies in the Philosophy of Charles Sanders Peirce, Second Series. Eds. Edward C. Moore and Richard S. Robin. Amherst: Univ. of Massachusetts Press, 1964: 165-89.

Bonner, Thomas, Jr., and Michael P. Dean. "Light in New Orleans: Change in the Writings of Mark Twain, Lafcadio Hearn, William Faulkner, and Walker Percy." University of Mississippi Studies in English 10 (1992): 213-26.

Boyd, G. N., and L. A. Boyd. Religion in Contemporary Fiction: Criticism from 1945 to the Present. San Antonio, Texas: Trinity Univ. Press, 1973.

Bradbury, John M. "Absurd Insurrection: The Barth-Percy Affair." South Atlantic Quarterly 68 (1969): 319-29.

Bradley, Jared W. "Walker Percy and the Search for Wisdom." Louisiana Studies 12 (1973): 579-90.

Bretall, Robert. A Kierkegaard Anthology. Princeton: Princeton Univ. Press, 1947.

Brinkmeyer, Robert H., Jr. "Percy's Bludgeon: Message and Narrative Strategy." Southern Quarterly, 18.3 (1980): 80-90.

---. Three Catholic Writers of the Modern South: Allen Tate, Caroline Gordon, Walker Percy. Jackson: Univ. Press of Mississippi, 1985.

Brooks, Cleanth. "The Southernness of Walker Percy." South Carolina Review 13.2 (1981): 34-38.

---. "Walker Percy and Modern Gnosticism." Southern Review n.s. 13 (1977): 677-87.

Brooks, Cleanth. "Walker Percy, 1916-1990" New Criterion. 9.1 (1990): 82-85.

Broughton, Panthea Reid, ed. The Art of Walker Percy: Stratagems for Being. Baton Rouge: LSU Press, 1979.

---. "A Bottle Unopened, a Message Unread." Christian Scholar's Review 6.2-3 (1976): 272-73.

---. "Walker Percy and the Myth of the Innocent Eye." Literary Romanticism in America. Ed. William L. Andrews. Baton Rouge: LSU Press, 1981.

Brown, Ashley. "An Interview with Walker Percy." Shenandoah 18 (Spring 1967): 3-10. Rpt. Conversations With Walker Percy. Eds. Lewis and Kramer. Jackson: Univ. Press of Mississippi, 1985.

Brown, Dale. Understanding Pietism. Grand Rapids: Wm. B. Eerdmans, 1978.

Buchler, Justus, ed. Philosophical Writings of Peirce. New York: Dover Publications, 1955.

Buckley, William F., Jr. "The Southern Imagination: An Interview with Eudora Welty and Walker Percy." Mississippi Quarterly, 26 (Fall, 1973): 493-516.

Buber, Martin. "Distance and Relation." William Alanson White Memorial Lectures, 4th series. Psychiatry, 20 (1957).

Buckmaster, Henrietta. Paul: A Man Who Changed the World. New York: McGraw-Hill, 1965.

Bunting, Charles T. "An Afternoon with Walker Percy." Notes on Mississippi Writers, 4 (1971): 43-61. Rpt. Conversations With Walker Percy. Eds. Lewis and Kramer. Jackson: Univ. Press of Miss., 1985.

Bunyan, John. Grace Abounding to the Chief of Sinners. Ed. Roger Sharrock. London: Clarendon Press, 1962.

---. The Pilgrim's Progress. New York: D. Appleton-Century, 1934.

Burke, Kenneth. The Rhetoric of Religion: Studies in Logology. Boston: Beacon Press, 1961.

Byrd, Scott. "Mysteries and Movies: Walker Percy's College Articles and The Moviegoer." Mississippi Quarterly 25 (Spring 1972): 165-81.

Carafiol, Peter C., ed. Selected Works of James Marsh, VI. New York: Scholar's Facsimiles and Reprints, 1976.

Carr, John. "Rotation and Repetition: Walker Percy." Kite-flying and Other Irrational Acts. Baton Rouge: LSU Press 1972.

Cash, W. J. The Mind of the South. New York: Vintage, 1941.

Cassirer, Ernst. The Philosophy of Symbolic Forms. New Haven: Yale Univ. Press, 1955.

---. Substance and Function. New York: Dover, 1953.

Cheney, Brainard. "To Restore a Fragmented Image." Sewanee Review 69 (1961): 691-700.

Chesnick, Eugene. "Novel's Ending and World's End: The Fiction of Walker Percy." The Hollins Critic 10.5 (Oct. 1973): 1-11.

Chomsky, Noam. Aspects in the Theory of Syntax. Cambridge, Mass.: MIT Press, 1965.

---. Language and Mind. New York: Harcourt Brace, 1968.

---. "Review of B. F. Skinner's Verbal Behavior." Language 35 (1959): 26-58.

Churchill, John. "Walker Percy, Wittgenstein's Tractatus and the Lost Self." Soundings: An Interdisciplinary Journal 67.3 (1984): 267-82.

Ciuba, Gary M. Walker Percy: Books of Revelations. Athens: University of Georgia Press, 1991.

Coleridge, Samuel Taylor. Aids to Reflection. New York: Swords, Stanford and Co., 1839.

---. The Statesman's Manual. Burlington: Chauncey Goodrich, 1832.

Coles, Robert. That Red Wheelbarrow: Selected Literary Essays. Iowa City: Univ. of Iowa Press, 1988.

---. "Shadowing Binx." Literature and Medicine 4 (1985): 151-60.

---. Walker Percy: An American Search. Boston: Little, Brown, 1979.

Colish, Marcia. The Mirror of Language: A Study in Medieval Theory of Knowledge. New Haven: Yale Univ. Press, 1968.

Conkin, Paul K. Puritans and Pragmatists: Eight Eminent American Thinkers. New York: Dodd, Mead, Inc., 1968.

Copleston, F. C. Aquinas. Baltimore: Penguin Books, 1967.

Cotton, James Henry. Royce on the Human Self. New York: Greenwood Press, 1968.

Cousineau, Thomas. "Walker Percy's The Moviegoer." Caliban 24 (1987): 153-65.

Cremeens, Carlton. "Walker, the Man and the Novelist: An Interview." Southern Review, 4 n.s. (1968): 171-290. Rpt. Conversations With Walker Percy. Eds. Lewis and Kramer. Jackson: Univ. of Mississippi Press, 1985.

Crowley, Joseph Donald. Critical Essays on Walker Percy. Boston: G.K. Hall, 1989.

---. and Sue Mitchell Crowley. "Walker Percy's Grail" in King Arthur through the Ages, II, eds. Valerie M. Lagorio and Mildred Leake Day. New York: Garland, 1990

Cuiba, Gary M. "The Moviegoer: Signs of the Divine Eiron." Notes on Contemporary Literature 17.5 (Nov. 1987): 10-13.

---. "Man the Symbol-Monger." The Yale Review, 65 (1975-76): 261-66.

Cunningham, Lawrence. "Catholic Sensibility and Southern Writers," Bulletin of the Center for the Study Southern Culture and Religion 2 (Summer 1978): 7-10.

Davies, W. D. Paul and Rabbinic Judaism: Some Rabbinic Elements in Pauline Theology. London: SPCK, 1955.

De Man, Paul. "The Rhetoric of Temporality." Blindness and Insight: Essays in the Rhetoric of Contemporary Criticism. Minneapolis: Univ. of Minnesota Press, 1983.

Derrida, Jacques. "The Supplement of Copula: Philosophy Before Linguistics." Textual Strategies: Perspectives in Post-Structuralist Criticism. Ed. Josu V. Harari. Ithaca, N.Y.: Cornell Univ. Press, 1981.

Desmond, John F. "From Suicide to Ex-Suicide: Note on the Southern Writer as Hero in the Age of Despair." Southern Literary Journal 25.1 (1992): 89-105.

---. "Walker Percy, Flannery O'Connor and the Holocaust." The Southern Quarterly 28.2 (1990): 35-42.

Dewey, Bradley R. "Walker Percy Talks About Kierkegaard." Journal of Religion 4 (1974): 273-98.

Dewey, John. Experience and Nature. Chicago: Open Court Publishing Co., 1925.

---. How We Think: A Restatement of the Relation of Reflective Thinking in the Educative Process. New York: D.C. Heath, 1933.

---. Human Nature and Conduct: An Introduction to Social Psychology. New York: The Modern Library, 1957.

Doar, Harriet. "Walker Percy: He Likes to Put Protagonist in Situation." The Charlotte Observer 30 Sept. 1962: D6. Rpt. Conversations With Walker Percy. Eds. Lewis and Kramer. Jackson: Univ. Press of Miss., 1985: 4-6.

Dougherty, David C. "Ghosts of the Old South: Walker Percy's Conservative Horrors." West Virginia University Philological Papers 28 (1982): 154-61.

Eco, Umberto. The Aesthetic of Thomas Aquinas. Trans. Hugh Bredin. Cambridge, MA: Harvard Univ. Press, 1988.

Edman, Irwin. The Mind of Paul. New York: Henry Holt, 1935.

Edwards, Jonathan. Images and Shadows of the Divine World. Ed. Perry Miller. New Haven: Yale Univ. Press, 1948.

---. "The Mind." "The Mind" of Jonathan Edwards: A Reconstructed Text. Ed. Leon Howard. Los Angeles: Univ. of California Press, 1963.

Emerson, Ralph Waldo. Essays. First and Second Series. Complete Works Vol. 1. New York: Houghton Mifflin, 1921.

---. Nature, Addresses and Lectures and Letters and Social Aims. Complete Works Vol. 2. New York: Houghton Mifflin, 1921.

Empson, William. <u>Seven Types of Ambiguity</u>. 3rd ed. Norfolk, Conn.: New Directions, 1953.

Entzminger, Robert L. <u>Divine Word and the Redemption of Language</u>. Pittsburgh: Duquesne Univ. Press, 1985.

Esposito, Joseph L. <u>The Development of Peirce's Theory of Categories</u>. Athens, Ohio: Ohio Univ. Press, 1980.

Eubanks, Cecil L. "Walker Percy: Eschatology and the Politics of Grace." <u>Southern Quarterly</u> 18.3 (1980): 121-36.

Filippidis, Barbara. "Vision and the Journey to Selfhood in Walker Percy's <u>The Moviegoer</u>." <u>Renascence</u> 33.1 (1980): 10-23.

Fitzgerald, John. <u>Peirce's Theory of Signs as Foundation for Pragmatism</u>. The Hague: Mouton, 1966.

Freshney, Pamela. "<u>The Moviegoer</u> and <u>Lancelot</u>: The Movies as Literary Symbols." <u>Southern Review</u>, 18 (1982): 718-27.

Frye, Northrop. <u>The Great Code: The Bible and Literature</u>. New York: Harcourt, Brace, Jovanovich, 1982.

Godshalk, William Leigh. "Walker Percy's Christian Vision." <u>Louisiana Studies</u> 13 (1974): 130-41.

Goudge, Thomas A. "Peirce's Evolutionism--After Half a Century." <u>Studies in the Philosophy of Charles Sanders Peirce</u>, Second Series. Eds. Edward C. Moore and Richard S. Robin. Amherst: The Univ. of Mass. Press, 1964: 323-41.

Gray, Richardson. "Novels That Diagnose the Culture's Pathology." <u>Christianity Today</u> 25 (20 Nov. 1981): 78.

Gretlund, Jan Nordby. "Southern Stoicism and Christianity: From William Alexander Percy to Walker Percy" in <u>The United States South: Regionalism and Identity</u>. eds. Valeria Lerda, et al. Rome: Bulzoni, 1991.

---., ed. <u>Walker Percy: Novelist and Philosopher</u>. Jackson: Univ. P. of Mississippi, 1991

Gretlund, Jan Nordby. "Novelists of the Third Phase of the Renaissance: Walker Percy, Madison Jones, and Barry Hannah." Revue Francaise d'Etudes Americaines 10.23 (1985): 13-24.

---. "Walker Percy: A Scandinavian View." South Carolina Review 13.2 (1981): 18-27.

Gulledge, Jo. "The Reentry Option: An Interview with Walker Percy." Southern Review 20 (1984): 93-115. Rpt. Conversations with Walker Percy. Eds. Lewis and Kramer. Jackson: Univ., Press of Mississippi, 1985.

Hardy, John Edward. The Fiction of Walker Percy. Urbana: Univ. of Illinois Press, 1987.

---. "Percy and Place: Some Beginnings and Endings." Southern Quarterly, 18.3 (1980); 5-25.

Harris, C. R. S. Duns Scotus. New York: The Humanities Press, 1959.

Hartshorne, Charles. "Charles Peirce's 'One Contribution to Philosophy' and His Most Serious Mistake." Studies in the Philosophy of Charles Sanders Peirce. Second Series. Eds. Edward C. Moore and Richard S. Robin. Amherst: The Univ. of Mass. Press, 1964: 455-73.

Hawkins, Peter S. The Language of Grace: Flannery O'Connor, Walker Percy and Iris Murdock. Cambridge, MA: Crowley Publications, 1983.

Henisey, Sarah. "Intersubjectivity in Symbolization." Renascence 20 (1968): 208-14.

Hill, Samuel S., Jr. Religion in the Solid South. Nashville: Abington Press, 1972.

Hobbs, Janet. "Binx Bolling and the Stages on Life's Way." The Art of Walker Percy. Ed. Panthea Reid Broughton. Baton Rouge: LSU Press, 1979.

Hobson, Fred. Tell About the South: The Southern Rage to Explain. Baton Rouge: LSU Press, 1983.

Hobson, Linda Whitney. "Percy's South: A Nation in Microcosm." Alabama Society for the Fine Arts 3 (1981): 3-4.

---. Understanding Walker Percy. Columbia: Univ. of South Carolina Press, 1988.

---. Walker Percy: A Comprehensive Bibliography. New Orleans: Faust Pub. Co., 1988.

---. "Walker Percy: Man vs Malaise." Louisiana Life 3.3 (1983): 54-61.

---. "Walker Percy: A Sign of the Apocalypse." Horizon 23 (Aug. 1980): 56-61.

Holley, Joe. "Walker Percy and the Novel of Ultimate Concern." Southwest Review 65 (1980); 225-34.

Howland, Mary Deems. The Gif of the Order: Gabriel Marcel's Concept of Intersubjectivity in Walker Percy's Novels. Pittsburgh: Duquesne Univ. Press, 1990.

James, William. Psychology. New York: Macmillan, 1962.

---. The Will to Believe and Other Essays in Popular Philosophy. New York: Longmans, Green, and Co., 1927.

Johnson, Mark. "The Search for Place in Walker Percy's Novels." Southern Literary Journal 8.1 (Fall 1975): 55-81.

Jones, Eric L. "Percy's Parousia." Southern Quarterly 23.4 (1985): 48-56.

Kasemann, Ernst. Perspectives on Paul. Philadelphia: Fortress Press, 1971.

Kazin, Alfred. "The Pilgrimage of Walker Percy." Harper's Magazine 292 (June 1971): 81-86.

Kennedy, J. Gerald. "The Sundered Self and the Riven World: Love in the Ruins. The Art of Walker Percy: Stratagems for Being. Ed. Panthea Reid Broughton. Baton Rouge: LSU Press, 1979.

Kenner, Hugh. "On Man the Sad Talker." National Review 27.35 (12 Sept. 1975): 1000-02.

Kierkegaard, Soren. <u>Philosophical Fragments</u>. Princeton: Princeton Univ. Press, 1952.

---. "Either/Or." <u>A Kierkegaard Anthology</u>. Ed. Robert Bretall. Princeton: Princeton Univ. Press, 1947.

King, Richard H. "Alienation and the Word." <u>The New Leader</u> 58 (13 (Oct. 1975): 18-19.

Kirby, Martin. "Neither Far Out Nor in Deep." <u>The Carleton Miscellany</u> 16 (1976): 209-14.

Kisor, Henry. "Dr. Percy on Signs and Symbols." <u>The Critic</u>, 39.4 (1980): 2-5.

Kissel, Susan S. "Voices in the Wilderness: The Prophets of O'Connor, Percy, and Powers." <u>Southern Quarterly</u> 18.3 (1980): 91-98.

---. "Walker Percy's Conversions.'" <u>Southern Literary Journal</u> 9 (1977): 124-36.

Ladd, George Eldon. <u>Theology of the New Testament</u>. Grand Rapids: William B. Eerdmans Pub., 1974.

Langer, Susanne. <u>Feeling and Form</u>. New York: Scribner's 1953.

---. <u>Introduction to Symbolic Logic</u>. 3rd ed. New York: Dover, 1953.

---. <u>Philosophy in a New Key</u>. 3rd ed. Cambridge: Harvard Univ. Press, 1957.

Lauder, Robert E. "The Catholic Novel and the 'Insider God.'" <u>Commonweal</u> 101 (1983): 314-31.

---. "Walker Percy: The Existential Wayfarer's Triumph Over Everydayness." <u>American Catholic Philosophical Association Proceedings</u> 56 (1982): 41-49.

Lawry, Edward G. "Literature as Philosophy: <u>The Moviegoer</u>." <u>The Monist</u> 63 (1980): 547-57.

Lawson, Lewis A. "The Allegory of the Cave and <u>The Moviegoer</u>." <u>South Carolina Review</u> 13.2 (1981):" 13-18.

---. "'English Romanticism . . . and 1930 Science' in The Moviegoer." Rocky Mountain Review of Language and Literature 38.1-22 (1984): 70-84.

---. "Kierkegaard and the Modern American Novel." Essays in Memory of Christine Burlson. Ed. Thomas G. Burton. Johnson City, TN: Research Advisory Council, 1969: 111-25.

---. "The Moviegoer and the Stoic Heritage." The Stoic Strain in American Literature. Ed. Duane J. MacMillan. Toronto: Univ. of Toronto Press, 1979: 179-91.

---. "Time and Eternity in The Moviegoer." Southern Humanities Review 16 (1982): 129-41.

---. "Walker Percy: Physician and Novelist." South Atlantic Bulletin 37 (April 1972): 58-63.

---. "Walker Percy as Martian Visitor." Southern Literary Journal 8 (1976): 102-13.

---. "Walker Percy's Indirect Communication." Texas Studies in Literature and Language 11 (1969): 867-900.

---. "Walker Percy's The Moviegoer: The Cinema as Cave." Southern Studies 19.4 (1980): 331-54.

---. "Walker Percy's Southern Stoic." Southern Literary Journal 3.1 (1970): 5-31.

---. "William Alexander Percy, Walker Percy, and the Apocalypse." Modern Age 24 (1980): 396-406.

Lawson, Lewis A. Following Percy: Essays on Walker Percy's Work. Troy, N.Y.: Witston Pub., 1988.

---. "Pilgrim in the City: Walker Percy" in Literary New Orleans: Essays and Meditations ed. Richard S. Kennedy. Baton Rouge: LSU Press, 1992.

Lawson, Lewis A., and Victor A. Kramer, eds. Conversations with Walker Percy. Jackson: Univ. Press of Mississippi, 1985.

LeClair, Thomas. "The Eschatological Vision of Walker Percy." Renascence 26 (Sept. 1976): 115-22.

Leenhouts, Anneke. "Letting Go of the Old South: An Introduction to Walker Percy." Dutch Quarterly Review of Anglo-American Letters 15.1 (1985): 36-51.

Lehan, Richard. A Dangerous Crossing: French Literary Existentialism and the Modern American Novel. Carbondale: Southern Illinois Univ. Press, 1973.

---. "The Way Back: Redemption in the Novels of Walker Percy." The Southern Review 4 n.s. (April 1968): 306-19.

Lisher, Tracy Kenyon. "Walker Percy's Kierkegaard: A Reading of The Moviegoer." The Cresset 41.10 (1978): 10-12.

Lowance, Mason I. The Language of Canaan: Metaphor and Symbol in New England from the Puritans to the Transcendentals. Cambridge, MA: Harvard Univ. Press, 1980.

Luker, Ralph E. "To Be Southern/To Be Catholic: Interpretation of the Thought of Five American Writers." Southern Studies 22.2 (1983): 168-76.

Luschei, Martin. "The Moviegoer as Dissolve." The Art of Walker Percy: Stratagems for Being. Ed. Panthea R. Broughton. Baton Rouge: LSU, 1979: 24-36.

---. The Sovereign Wayfarer: Walker Percy's Diagnosis of the Malaise. Baton Rouge: LSU Press, 1972.

Macchioro, Vittorio. From Orpheus to Paul: A History Orphism. New York: Henry Holt, 1930.

MacMillan, Duane J. "Walker Percy in Canada: A Case for the Saskatchewan Sleeping Bag." Notes on Mississippi Writers 16.1 (1984): 3-12.

Makowsky, Veronica A. "The Message in the Novels: Walker Percy and the Critics." Review 7 (1985): 305-27.

Marcel, Gabriel. Being and Having. Boston: Beacon Press, 1951.

---. The Existential Background of Human Dignity. Cambridge, MA: Harvard Univ. Press, 1963.

---. The Mystery of Being. Chicago: Henry Regnery, 1951.

Maritain, Jacques. Art and Scholasticism. New York: Scribner's 1947.

Marsh, James. Selected Works of James Marsh Vol. I. Ed. Peter C. Carafiol. New York: Scholars' Facsimiles and Reprints, 1976.

Matthews, Donald G. Religion in the Old South. Chicago: Univ. of Chicago Press, 1977.

McFague, Sallie. "The Parabolic in Faulkner, O'Conner, and Percy." Notre Dame English Journal 15 (Spring 1983): 49-66.

McNaspy, C. J. "Why Does Man Feel So Sad?" National Catholic Reporter 11 (29 Aug. 1975): 7.

Mead, George. Mind, Self and Society. Chicago: Univ. of Chicago Press, 1952.

Miller, Perry. Jonathan Edwards. Toronto: William Sloane Associated, 1949.

---. New England Mind. Cambridge, MA: Harvard Univ. Press, 1953.

Milton, John. "The Christian Doctrine." John Milton: Complete Poems and Major Prose. Ed. Merritt Y. Hughes. New York: Odyssey Press, 1957.

Monroe, William. "Performing Persons: A Locus of Connection for Medicine and Literature" in The Body and the Text: Comparative Essays in Literature and Medicine eds. Bruce Clarke and Wendell Aycock. Lubbock: Texas Tech Univ. Press, 1990

Moore, Edward D. "The Influence of Duns Scotus on Peirce." Studies in the Philosophy of Charles Sanders Peirce, Second Series. Eds. Edward C. Moore and Richard S. Robin. Amherst: Univ. of Mass. Press, 1964: 401-13.

Moore, Heather. "Walker Percy's The Moviegoer: A Publishing History" Library Chronicle of the University of Texas 22.4 (1992): 122-43.

Morris, Charles. Sings, Language and Behavior. Englewood Cliffs, N.J.: Prentice-Hall, 1950.

---. Signification and Significance: A Study of the Relations and Values. Cambridge, MA: M.I.T. Press, 1964.

Mukherjee, Srimati. "The Moviegoer of Mimesis and Awareness" Publications of the Arkansas Philological Assoc. 17.2 (1991): 35-43.

Murphey, Murray G. The Development of Peirce's Philosophy. Cambridge, MA: Harvard Univ. Press, 1961.

Murphy, Christina. "'Exalted in This Romantic Place': Narrative Voice and the Structure of Walker Percy's The Moviegoer." Publications of the Mississippi Philological Association (1984): 55-68.

Murray, Albert. South to a Very Old Place. New York: McGraw-Hill, 1971.

Oliver, W. Donald. "The Final Cause and Agapasm in Peirce's Philosophy." Studies in the Philosophy of Charles Sanders Peirce. Second Series. Eds. E. C. Moore and Richard S. Robin. Amherst: Univ. of Mass. Press, 1964: 289-303.

Parker, Frank. "Walker Percy's Theory of Language: A Linguist's Assessment." Delta (Montpellier, France) 13 (Nov. 1981): 145-67.

Pearson, Michael. "Art as Symbolic Action: Walker Percy's Aesthetic." Southern Quarterly 18.3 (1980): 55-64.

---. "The Search for Walker Percy." Southern Literary Journal 19.2 (1987): 108-12.

Peirce, Charles Sanders. Collected Papers of Charles Sanders Peirce. Eds. Charles Hartshorne and Paul Weiss. 8 vol. Cambridge, MA: Belknap Press of Harvard Univ. Press, 1965.

---. Writings of Charles Sanders Peirce: A Chronological Edition. Vol. 1. Eds. Edward C. Moore, et al. Bloomington: Indiana Univ. Press, 1982.

---. Selected Writings: Values in a Universe of Chance. Ed. Philip P. Wiener. New York: Dover Pub., Inc., 1966.

Percy, Walker. "The American War." Commonweal 29 (Mar. 1957): 655-57.

---. "The Coming Crisis in Psychiatry." Part 1. America, 96 (5 Jan. 1957): 391-93; Part 2, 96 (12 Jan. 1957): 415-18.

---. "The Culture Critics." Commonweal (5 June 1959): 247-50.

---. "The Diagnostic Novel: On the Uses of Modern Fiction." Harper's Magazine 292 (June 1986): 39-45.

---. "The Divided Creature." The Wilson Quarterly 13 (Summer 1989): 77-87.

---. "The Failure and the Hope." Katallagete 1 (1965) 16-21.

---. "From Facts to Fiction." Writer 80 (Oct. 1967): 27-28.

---. "Herman Melville." New Criterion 2.3 (1983): 39-42.

---. "Introduction." Lanterns on the Levee by William Alexander Percy. Baton Rouge: LSU Press, 1973.

---. The Last Gentleman. New York: Farrar, Straus, and Giroux, 1966.

---. Lost in the Cosmos: The Last Self-Help Book. New York: Farrar, Straus, and Giroux, 1983.

---. Love in the Ruins. New York: Farrar, Straus, and Giroux, 1971.

---. The Message in the Bottle: How Queer Man Is, How Queer Language Is, and What One Has to Do With the Other. New York: Farrar, Straus, and Giroux, 1975.

---. "Metaphor As Mistake." Sewanee Review 66 (Winter 1958): 79-99. Rpt. in MB: 64-82.

---. The Moviegoer. New York: Alford A. Knopf, 1960.

---. "Naming and Being." The Personalist 41 (Spring 1960): 148-57.

---. "Semiotic and a Theory of Knowledge." Modern Schoolman 34 (1957):
     225-46. Rpt. MB: 243-64.

---. "The State of the Novel: Dying Art or New Science?" Michigan
     Quarterly Review 16 (Fall 1977): 359-73.

---. "Symbol, Consciousness, and Intersubjectivity." Journal of Philosophy 55
     (17 July 1958): 631-41. Rpt. in MB: 265-76.

---. "Toward a Triadic Theory of Meaning." Psychiatry 35 (Feb. 1972): 1-19.
     Rpt. in MB: 159-88.

---. "Symbol As Hermeneutic in Existentialism." Philosophy and
     Phenomelogical Review 16 (June 1956): 522-30. Rpt. MB: 277-87.

---. "Symbol As Need." Thought 29 (Autumn 1954): 381-90. Rpt. MB:
     288-97.

---. "Truth--or Pavlov's Dogs?" America 97 (8 June 1957): 306-07.

---. "Uncle Will and His South." Saturday Review (6 Nov. 1973): 22-25.

---. Signposts in a Strange Land. New York: Farrar, Straus, Giroux, 1991.

Percy, William Alexander. Lanterns on the Levee: Recollections of a
     Planter's Son. Baton Rouge: LSU Press, 1973.

Pindell, Richard. "Basking in the Eye of the Storm: The Esthetics of Loss in
     Walker Percy's The Moviegoer." Boundary 2 (1975): 219-30.

Poteat, William H. "Reflections on Walker Percy's Theory of Language."
     The Art of Walker Percy: Stratagems for Being. Ed. P. R. Broughton.
     Baton Rouge: LSU Press, 1979: 192-218.

Poteat, Patricia Lewis. Walker Percy and the Old Modern Age: Reflections
     on Language, Argument, and the Telling of Stories. Baton Rouge:
     LSU Press, 1985.

Prochaska, Bernadette. Myth of the Fall and Walker Percy's Last Gentleman.
     N.Y.: Peter Lang, 1992.

Quagliano, Anthony. "Existential Modes in The Moviegoer." Research Studies 45 (1977): 214-23.

Rhein, Phillip. "Walker Percy's European Connection." French-American Review 7 (1983): 19-33.

Richard, Claude. "The Exile of Binx Bolling: Walker Percy's Moviegoer." Critical Angles: European Views of Contemporary American Literature. Trans. Carolyn Grim Williams. Carbondale: Southern Illinois Univ. Press, 1986.

---. "L'Exil de Binx Bolling." Delta (Montpellier, France) 13 (Nov. 1981): 27-54.

Royce, Josiah. Fugitive Essays. Freeport, New York: Books for Libraries Press, 1968.

---. Logical Essays. Ed. Daniel S. Robinson. Dubuque, Iowa: W. C. Brown, 1951.

---. The Problem of Christianity. Chicago: Univ. of Chicago Press, 1968.

Rubin, Louis D., Jr. "The South's Writers: A Literature of Time and Change." Southern World 1.2 (1979): 26-27.

--- and C. Hugh Holman. Southern Literary Study: Problems and Possibilities. Chapel Hill: Univ. of North Carolina Press, 1975.

Samway, Patrick. "An Interview with Walker Percy." America 154 (Jan.-June 1986): 121-23.

Savan, David. "Peirce's Infallibilism." Studies in the Philosophy of Charles Sanders Peirce. Second Series. Eds. Edward C. Moore and Richard S. Robin. Amherst: Univ. of Mass. Press, 1964: 190-211.

Scharlemann, Robert P., and Gilbert E. M. Ogutu, eds. God in Language. New York: Paragon House Pub., 1987.

Schweitzer, Albert. The Mysticism of Paul the Apostle. Trans. William Montgomery. New York: Henry Holt, 1931.

Scotus, John Duns. Duns Scotus: Philosophical Writings. Ed. Allen Wolter, O. F. M. New York: Nelson, 1962.

Serebnick, Judith. "First Novelists--Spring 1961." Library Journal 86 (1 Feb. 1961): 597. Rpt. Conversations With Walker Percy. Eds. Lewis and Kramer. Baton Rouge: LSU Press, 1985: 3.

Shepherd, Allen. "Percy's The Moviegoer and Warren's All the King's Men." Notes on Mississippi Writers 4 (Spring 1971): 2-14.

Sheriff, John K. The Fate of Meaning: Charles Peirce, Structuralism and Literature. Princeton: Princeton Univ. Press, 1989.

Simmons, Philip E. "Roward the Postmodern Historical Imagination: Mass Culture in Walker Percy's The Moviegoer and Nicholson Baker's The Messanine" Contemporary Literature 33.4 (1992): 601-24.

Simpson, Lewis P. "Home By Way of California: The Southerner as the Last European." Southern Literature in Transition. Eds. Philip Castille and William Osborne. Memphis: Memphis State Univ. Press, 1983.

---. "The Southern Aesthetic of Memory." Tulane Studies in English 23 (1978): 207-27.

Sims, Barbara B. "Jaybirds as Portents of Hell in Percy and Faulkner." News of Mississippi Writers 9 (1976): 24-27.

Singal, Daniel Joseph. The War Within: From Victorian to Modernist Thought in the South, 1919-1945. Chapel Hill: Univ. of North Carolina Press, 1982.

Sloan, Jacob. "Walker Percy: The Moviegoer." Existentialism in American Literature. Ed. Ruby Chatterji. Atlantic Highlands, N.J.: Humanities, 1983: 147-57.

Smith, Marcus. "Talking About Talking." New Orleans Review 5.1 (1976): 13-18.

Spivey, Ted R. The Journey Beyond Tragedy: A Study of Myth and Modern Fiction. Orlando: Univ. Presses of Florida, 1980: 148-64.

---. "Religion and the Reintegration of Man in Flannery O'Connor and Walker Percy." The Poetry of Community: Essays on Southern Sensibility of History and Literature. Ed. Lewis P. Simpson. Atlanta: Georgia State Univ. Press, 1972: 67-79.

---. "Walker Percy and the Archetypes." The Art of Walker Percy: Stratagems for Being. Baton Rouge: LSU Press, 1979: 273-94.

Stanwood, P. G., and Heather Ross Asals. John Donne and the Theology of Language. Columbia: Univ. of Missouri Press, 1986.

Stelzmann, Rainuff A. "Adam in Extremis: Die Romane Walker Percy." Stimmen de Zeit 191 (1973): 206-10.

---. "Das Schwert Christi: Zwei Versuche Walker Percys." Stimmen der Zeit 195 (1977): 641-43.

Stephenson, Will, and Mimosa Stephenson. "Father Boomer as Boanerges in Walker Percy's The Last Gentleman. Notes on Contemporary Literature. 22.3 (1992): 2-3.

---. "A Keats Allusion in Walker Percy's The Last Gentleman. Notes on Contemporary Literature. 22.3 (1992): 3-4

---. "A Porter-Percy Connection (Or, Katherine Anne in Feliciana)" JASAT 23 OCT. 1992: 32-40.

Stevenson, John W. "Walker Percy: The Novelist as Poet." Southern Review 17 (Jan. 1981): 164-74.

Sullivan, Walter. Death by Melancholy: Essays on Modern Southern Fiction. Baton Rouge: LSU Press, 1972.

---. "Southerners in the City: Flannery O'Connor and Walker Percy." The Comic Imagination in American Literature. Ed. Louis D. Rubin, Jr. New Brunswick: Rutgers Univ. Press, 1973.

---. Walker Percy. Jackson: Mississippi Library Commis-sion, 1977.

Sumner, L. W., John G. Slater, and Fred Wilson, eds. Pragmatism and Purpose: Essays Presented to Thomas A. Goudge. Toronto: Univ. of Toronto Press, 1981.

Sweeny, Mary K. Walker Percy and the Postmodern World. Chicago: Loyola Univ. Press, 1907.

Tanner, Tony. "Afterword: Wonder and Alienation--the Mystic and The Moviegoer." The Reign of Wonder: Naivety and Reality in American Literature. Cambridge, England: Cambridge Univ. Press, 1965.

Taylor, L. Jerome. In Search of Self: Life, Death, and Walker Percy. Cambridge, MA: Cowley Publications, 1986.

---. "Walker Percy and the Self." Commonweal 100 (1974): 233-36.

---. Walker Percy's Heroes: A Kierkegaardian Analysis. New York: Seabury Press, 1983.

---. Walker Percy's Knights of the Hidden Inwardness." Anglican Theological Review 56 (1974): 125-51.

Tellotte, Jay Paul. "Butting Heads with Faulkner's Soldiers." Notes on Contemporary Literature 9.3 (1979): 7-8.

---. "Charles Peirce and Walker Percy: From Semiotic to Narrative." Southern Quarterly 18.3 (1980): 65-79.
---. "A Symbolic Structure for Walker Percy's Fiction." Modern Fiction Studies 26 (1980): 227-40.

---. "Walker Percy's Language of Creation." Southern Quarterly 16 (1978): 105-16.

---. "Walker Percy: A Pragmatic Approach." Southern Studies 18 (1979): 217-30.

Thale, Jerome. "Alienation on the American Plan." Forum 6 (1968): 36-40.

Thale, Mary. "The Moviegoer of the 1950's." Twentieth Century Literature 14 (1968): 84-89.

Tharpe, Jac. Walker Percy. Boston: Twayne Pub., 1983.

---, ed. Walker Percy: Art and Ethics. Jackson: Univ. of Mississippi Press, 1980.

214

Thompson, Manley. "Peirce's Experimental Proof of Scholastic Realism."
    Studies in the Philosophy of Charles Sanders Peirce. Second Series.
    Eds. Edward C. Moore and Richard S. Robin. Amherst: Univ. of
    Mass. Press, 1964: 414-29.

Thorton, W. "Homo Loquens, Homo Symbolificus, Homo Sapiens: Walker
    Percy on Language." The Art of Walker Percy: Stratagems for Being.
    Baton Rogue: LSU Press, 1979: 169-91.

Tolson, Jay. "The Education of Walker Percy." The Wilson Quarterly 8.2
    (1984): 156-66.

Tremonte, Collen M. "Percy in a Groove" Mississippi Quarterly 44.2 (1991):
    225-28.

Van Cleave, Jim. "Versions of Percy." Southern Review 6 (Autumn 1970):
    990-1010.

Vanderwerken, David L. "The Americanness of The Moviegoer. Notes on
    Mississippi Writers 11.1 (1978): 40-52.

Vauthier, Simone, "Le Temps et la Mort dans The Moviegoer." Recherches
    Anglaise et Americaines (RANAM) 4 (1971): 98-115.

---. "Narrative Triangle and Triple Alliance: A Look at The Moviegoer." Les
    Americanistes: New French Criticism on Modern American Fiction.
    Eds. Ira D. and Christiane Johnson. Port Nash, New York: Kennikat,
    1978.

---. "Title as Microtext: The Example of The Moviegoer." The Journal of
    Narrative Technique (1975): 219-29.

Walter, James. "Spinning and Spieling: A Trick and a Kick in Walker Percy's
    The Moviegoer." Southern Review 16.3 (1980): 574-90.

Webb, Max. "Binx Bolling's New Orleans: Moviegoing, Souther Writing, and
    Father Abraham." The Art of Walker Percy: Stratagems for Being.
    Baton Rouge: LSU Press, 1979: 1-23.

Weinberg, Helen. The New Novel in America: The Kafkan Mode
    Contemporary Fiction. Ithaca: Cornell Univ. Press, 1970.

Westarp, Karl Heinz. "Lost in the Cosmos: Place in Walker Percy" The Dolphin 20 (1991): 108-17.

Winslow, William. "Modernity and the Novel: Twain, Faulkner, and Percy." The Gypsy Scholar 8 (1981): 19-40.

Wolter, Allen, O.F.M., ed. Duns Scotus: Philosophical Writings. New York: Nelson, 1962.

Wood, Ralph. "To Be a Namer." Christian Century 92 (3 Dec. 1975) 1115-16.

---. "Walker Percy as Satirist: Christian and Humanist Still in Conflict." Christian Century 97 (19 Nov. 1980): 1122-27.

---. The Comedy of Redemption: Christian Faith and Comic Vision in Four American Authors. Notre Dame, Ind.: Univ. of Notre Dame Press, 1988.

Woolman, John. The Journal of John Woolman and A Plea For the Poor. New York: Corinth Books, 1961.

Yardley, Jonathan. "The New Old Southern Novel." Partisan Review 40 (1973): 286-93.

Young, Thomas Daniel. "Intimations of Nortality: The Moviegoer." The Past in the Present: A Thematic Study of Modern Southern Fiction. Baton Rouge: LSU Press, 1981: 137-66.

---. "A New Breed: Walker Percy's Critics' Attempts to Place Him." Mississippi Quarterly 33 (1980): 489-98.

Zamora, Lois Parkinson. "The Reader at the Movies: Semiotic Systems in Walker Percy's The Moviegoer and Manuel Puig's La Traicion de Rita Hayworth. American Journal Semiotica 3.1 (1984): 50-67..

Zeugner, John. "Walker Percy and Gabriel Marcel: The Castaway and the Wayfarer." Mississippi Quarterly 28 (Winter 1974-75): 21-53.

Zoltan, Abadi-Nagi. "A Talk With Walker Percy." Southern Literary Journal 6 (Fall 1973): 3-19.

Zorach, Cecile Cazort. "Peter Handke as Translator of Walker Percy." <u>South Atlantic Review</u> 57.1 (1992): 67-87.

INDEX